Siberian Survival

To Sergei
from author-migrator

30.01.01

SIBERIAN SURVIVAL

The Nenets and Their Story

Andrei V. Golovnev *and*
Gail Osherenko

CORNELL UNIVERSITY PRESS
Ithaca and London

First published 1999 by Cornell University Press

Printed in the United States of America

Library of Congress Cataloging-in-Publication Data
Golovnev, A. V. (Andrei Vladimirovich)
    Siberian survival : the Nenets and their story / Andrei V. Golovnev and Gail Osherenko.
      p. cm.
    Includes bibliographical references and index.
    ISBN 0-8014-3631-1 (cloth : alk. paper)
      1. Nenets—History. 2. Nenets—Government relations. 3. Nenets—Social life and customs. 4. Reindeer herding—Russia (Federation)-Yamal Peninsula. 5. Yamal Peninsula (Russia)—Politics and government. 6. Yamal Peninsula (Russia)—Social life and customs.
I. Osherenko, Gail. II. Title.
DK34.N4G5 1999
957'.3—dc21   98-48118

Cloth printing
10 9 8 7 6 5 4 3 2 1

Contents

List of Maps

Preface

July 1992—the peak of summer. Clouds of mosquitoes hover around our heads. We take the path to the tent of Ngoet (in Russian, Vladimir) Tadibe on Cape Yaptik-Sale, named for the Yaptik clan who lived here. Nenets and a few Russians live here in the small village of Yaptiksale, in Northwestern Siberia. Nenets villagers are mostly from the clans Niarui, Salinder, Vanuita. Yaptiks listed in the town census books live mostly in the tundra and avoid the village. Walking near the houses we can hear mixed Nenets-Russian chat; in the tundra camps, Nenets is spoken, and Russian sounds occasionally when Russians come to buy fur, reindeer meat, or fish. There, in the tundra, Yaptik kin are masters of the territory that has belonged to their ancestors for many centuries. Several decades ago many Yaptiks were resettled by authorities from this land to the southern tundra or even farther away. That happened after Yaptiks rose up against Soviet power. Old Man Tadibe told us that story yesterday. He himself didn't participate in that "tundra war" because he was on another battlefield—that of World War II. He showed us his medals and recollected the revolt. He also told about intertribal wars between clans of Samoyeds (the old name of Nenets), even about human sacrifices that took place long ago on the northern cape of the Yamal Peninsula. That was his mood.

We didn't know what Tadibe would tell us today. From the distance we recognized him talking with his grandson who lives in the regional center Salekhard, far south (three hours by helicopter). Tadibe's son (the boy's father) is a surgeon in the Salekhard hospital. Tadibe loves his grandson, who is about four or five, and teaches him Nenets. The old man is troubled that the boy can't speak Nenets. As we come closer, we overhear the old man tell his grandson, who is struggling with mosquitoes, "Be calm. Don't kill mosquitoes; otherwise they will eat all your reindeer." That a boy living most of the year in the city could own tundra reindeer was a surprise. But compassion toward mosquitoes was more surprising from a man so familiar with human cruelty.

That was the beginning of our joint research. We hoped to find a clue, a path to understand Nenets culture, to explain their phenomenal capacity to keep their traditions. It is extraordinary that roughly half of the Nenets population living on the Yamal Peninsula continues a nomadic lifestyle dependent on reindeer—for food, clothing, shelter, transportation, even sewing thread. Outside authorities imposed new and often unwanted institutions (rules governing rights, roles, and relationships in society) on Nenets (and other indigenous peoples of Russia). Soviet authorities reorganized economic activity into collectives; they forced people to relocate—many into a sedentary lifestyle in small, poor fishing villages—they redistributed reindeer and pasturelands, they punished wealthy and successful herders, and they attempted to eradicate the animistic belief system by killing or repressing shamans and destroying sanctuaries. By the 1970s, virtually all herders worked within brigades under the authority of state farms. Despite all this, many Nenets herders have retained their material and spiritual culture, their values, beliefs, and behavioral norms. They continue to speak Nenets, although, having been sent to boarding schools, most speak Russian as a second language.

In this book we seek to provide a better understanding of how and why the Nenets and other indigenous peoples (but the Nenets in particular) endured—how they held onto their culture, language, and lifestyle through the conquests and colonizations of the seventeenth, eighteenth, and nineteenth centuries and the subsequent era of Soviet rule. How did the Nenets emerge at the end of the twentieth century with fewer social ills and a greater sense of community self-worth than that which appears to be the case among other arctic indigenous peoples? How is it that the nomadic herding economy continues and that families travel across the tundra together? What accounts for the differences between the Nenets and other indigenous groups of Northwestern Siberia—the Selkup, the Khanty, and the Mansi? Was it merely geography, a combination of remoteness and the vast expanse of tundra into which nomads might disappear? Was it the Nenets' ability as nomads to retreat further from the rapidly growing arctic cities and towns? Is it possible that the Soviet institutions, however intrusive, did not undermine some essential elements of indigenous governance? These questions lie at the heart of our research and this book.

The book is the product of collaboration between a Russian anthropologist and an American lawyer. When we first met in Moscow in 1991 (at a workshop on arctic social science jointly sponsored by the Russian and U.S. Academies of Science), we could barely understand each other. Yet the following summer we found ourselves far north of the Arctic Circle in Yaptiksale. Our team included Ivan Golovnev (then thirteen), who, being a good shot, occasionally supplied our supper and always provided good company, and Lidia V. Kiripova, a Nenets translator and journalist who grew up on the Yamal Peninsula. Although Andrei had conducted ethnographic and ethnoarchaeological research in Northwestern Siberia and particularly on Yamal since the mid-1970s, he had never been to Yaptiksale. Gail, whose primary interest was in new developments in environmental law, hoped to gain an understanding of how impending gas and oil development might affect the native population.

Our approaches, our research questions, and our methodology—not to mention our tolerance for cold, mosquitoes, and vodka—varied greatly. Nevertheless, we met again the following summer in Ekaterinburg, traveled the Ob and Irtysh rivers to Khanty-Mansiisk and Tobol'sk, and developed a research plan.

A few funding sources and a few of our colleagues had faith in our proposed project: The John D. and Catherine T. MacArthur Foundation, the International Research and Exchanges Board (IREX), and the Trust for Mutual Understanding supported us. We had decided to focus particularly on social dimensions central to cultural change, especially leadership and gender. These were subjects almost untouched by research during the Soviet era. The special topic of twentieth-century rebellions, which became essential to understanding the Nenets' responses to Soviet policies, also had not been explored before in Siberian history or anthropology.

When we returned to Yamal in 1994, this time to examine the institutional changes occurring in the years of glasnost, the International Northern Sea Route Programme (INSROP) supported our research. (INSROP is a multidisciplinary research program investigating the possibilities for international commercial navigation through the Northeast Passage and jointly sponsored by the Ship and Ocean Foundation, Japan; the Central Marine Research and Design Institute, Russia; and the Fridtjof Nansen Institute, which hosts the INSROP Secretariat in Lysaker, Norway.)

Three years of studying, writing, translating, and searching for ways to understand our subject and each other followed. The book has been composed and rewritten many times. We are grateful to the reviewers who both encouraged and pushed us to revise. Igor Krupnik, our colleague, shared data, challenged assumptions, and offered helpful advice. Grey Osterud impelled us to radically restructure the book, much to its benefit. Our editor, Roger Haydon, appealed to our patience and persistence. We hope we have met their challenges.

Several colleagues aided in the book's research; first and foremost, two of our colleagues at the Ethnographic Bureau in Tobol'sk. Svetlana Lezova helped in collecting archival and field data on the Northwestern Siberian rebellions for Chapter 4. The book benefited greatly from Elena Perevalova's deep ethnographic and historical research into northern Khanty (taiga dwellers), which assisted in the comparisons with Nenets in Chapter 3. Yuri Pribyl'skii, professor of history, and Natalia Golovneva, senior researcher of historical sciences, both from the Tobol'sk Pedagogical Institute, provided valuable historical data on institutional and educational changes in Northwestern Siberia during the Soviet period. This book could not have come together without the thousand-handed help of Alexei Roginko, a political geographer. Alexei gave us logistical, communication, and computer support in Moscow, and he and his family provided a home away from home for Gail on many occasions. Finally, in 1994, Alexei accompanied us in the field as a collaborator in the research for Chapter 6. Archaeologists William Fitzhugh, Natalia Fedorova, Sven Haakanson, and Vladimir Pitul'ko, who, accompanied by Andrei in archaeological surveys and excavations on the Yamal Peninsula, gave many valuable suggestions about ancient stages of tundra occupation.

We gratefully acknowledge the support of our home bases for this project, the Institute of Arctic Studies within the Dickey Center for International Understanding at Dartmouth College, Hanover, New Hampshire; the Institute of History and Archaeology at the Russian Academy of Sciences (Ural Branch) in Ekaterinburg; and the Ethnographic Bureau (an independent research institute in Tobol'sk). Ivar Bjørklund and Alf Hakon-Hoel of the University of Tromsø and the Ethnographic Museum in Tromsø, Norway, invited us to lecture in the fall of 1996 and provided a quiet working space that allowed us to complete the manuscript for publication. We wish to thank especially the Yamal-Nenets Okrug administration, the Yamalskii Raion administration in Yar-Sale, and local administrations of Yaptiksale, Seyaha, Novyi

Port, Laborovaia, and Aksarka. Thanks are also due to all those who so graciously granted us interviews and provided data and information; this includes Yamalflot (Yamal-fleet, a ship repair company) its director, Alexander Tomilov; and the fine crew of the *Skif* that carried us to settlements in Ob Bay in July 1994.

We also extend our sincere thanks to Jane Miller, for her literary-quality translation of some of Andrei's draft materials (in Chapters 2 and 4) and for preparation of the index; to Sergei Kan, for working side by side with Andrei to edit and refine the leadership materials; to Deborah Robinson, for editorial assistance; to the copy editor, Barbara Sutton; to Nancy Winemiller, manuscript editor at Cornell University Press; and to Oran Young, who supported the project from the outset, then offered useful advice and encouragement. Finally, our thanks go to our families for their understanding and their intellectual and emotional support throughout this long work.

Andrei V. Golovnev
Gail Osherenko

Siberian Survival

"The People" or "the Others"

The ethnic name Nenets means "people." For the Nenets, "others" are all of their neighbors, near and far. In legends, the latter neighbors could be hostile, as were the Evenk and the Nganasan; friendly, as were the Khanty and the Mansi; mysterious, as were the dwarf predecessors Sihirtia; or merely present, as were the Russians borne by the junior wife of the lord of the underworld, *Nga*. It is usual for peoples to define themselves simply as "the people" (as do the Dene, the Inuit, the Inupiat, the Saami, and so on), to regard only their culture as "true" and only their values as "genuine." For the Nenets, this would be "true" if they lived on their own lands and worshiped their own gods forever. But the Nenets were destined by history to mix with others—their conquered or their victors—with whom they kept contacts or waged conflicts.

The ancestors of the Russians at one time also called themselves "the people" (Slavs, from "person"—*slovak-cholovik-chelovek*). Some generations later, however, being already "Russians," they first used the name *Samoyed* to refer to the strange northern people who lived in "Midnight's lands" and used to die every winter, had mouths between their shoulders, or drank human blood.[1] The common Russian etymology of the name *Samoyed*, meaning "self-eater," deepened the Russians' already exotic image of far-northerners. The most probable linguistic origin of *Samoyed*, however, is from the Saami—*saam-edne*, "land of the people."[2]

From the eleventh century to the 1930s, the Nenets (together with the Nganasan and the Enets) were referred to in Russian chronicles and literature as *Samoyad or Samoyedy*. Russian colonizers considered Samoyeds, like other non-Russians, *inorodtsy*—"others."[3]

That was (and in some respects still is) the counter attitude of two peoples who for a long time did not recognize each other as "the people." That was understandable in the eleventh or the thirteenth century, when the two groups were divided by other peoples and lands. But even in the sixteenth century, when the border disappeared and the Samoyed together with all the Siberians were incorporated into Russia, the Nenets remained "others" (*inorodtsy*) in their own land. Their real name, *Nenets*, returned to them four centuries later, after the revolution of 1917. Ironically, at the same time they regained their name, they lost much more important things—their property, many of their leaders, shamans, and a number of their reindeer. The Nenets became even more "others" for the new Soviet authorities than they were for the previous Russian authorities.

For the Nenets themselves, Russians are not exclusively "the children of the Devil" (according to folklore). Russians vary; at one time they ruled the land of the Samoyed; sometimes they conquered each other, one Russian authority changing places with another, so that occasionally the Nenets (as happened in 1917–18) could not tell who were the real representatives of Russian authority. For the Nenets today, Russians are neither "good nor bad"; rather, they are inevitable neighbors. In former times Russians were a "given phenomenon"; now some Nenets (especially the younger Nenets) believe they are able to influence Russians (at least local residents) positively, through their own values.

Is this the beginning of a dialogue between cultures that are at last trying to converse with each other on the basis of mutual respect as "peoples" instead of "others"? In previous centuries, and especially in recent decades, Nenets culture survived mostly in defiance of Russian-Soviet influence, and that "cultural defense" provided amazing results. The Nenets (especially the nomadic part of the population) have preserved their traditions so thoroughly that someone who stumbled upon a nomad camp might mistakenly attribute their ancient way of life to lack of contact with outsiders when it is instead a path of choice.

We cannot venture to predict even the immediate future, particularly in today's tumultuous Russia, but we believe that past and current ideas about cultural change need to be observed as a dialogue between "peoples," from both native and newcomers' perspectives, "from inside" of the indigenous culture and "from outside" of (and toward) it. In telling the story of the Yamal Nenets, we have tried to merge these vantage points using ethnographic (myths, legends, observation, field notes, and so forth) and historical (archival) sources. To bring the story to the present, our research took us to the tents of indigenous leaders and the offices of administrators.

Nenets nomads consider their culture, people, and habitat as "the core of the universe." Their position in the dialogue is mostly defensive, targeted more toward preserving their own values than borrowing those of another people for so-called civil development. The Nenets do not pretend to compete economically or culturally with the Russians, the Americans, or the Japanese. They have no global interests; for them, the tundra and their society is the world.

Contemporary Nenets do not treat Russia as the Evil Empire (as they did at some points in their history). They treat it as "political nature"—one that could be severe, dramatically changeable, or dangerous—but as a "nature" nonetheless, not so different from the real arctic nature. Today's Nenets need to find a convenient way to adapt themselves to social conditions just as they have long adapted themselves to environmental conditions. What core characteristics might allow them to apply the same strengths they have achieved environmentally as reindeer herders to their social sphere? What features of their culture provide the stability to their interior (that is, ethnic) structure in horizontal (primarily gender interactions) and vertical (hierarchical) relationships?

For the Soviet state, Nenets were and are one of the twenty-six (now officially thirty) small-population nations of the Far North. Russian "nationality policy" was never specifically addressed to one nation (except for the temporary acute attention paid to Tatars, Jews, Ukrainians, and Chechens) but to "small," remote nations as a group. Imperial treatment was uniform concerning "all of Siberia," "all of the North," or "all of the peripheries." It would be useless to look for any Russian state structure and policy targeted particularly toward the Nenets.

One and the same policy and practice intruded outside values and norms on each of the Siberian (or northern) peoples, including the Nenets. The foci of imperial policy changed over time. At the start of colonization, Russians sought mostly furs; later they sequentially widened their scope of interest to social, administrative, and broader economic affairs, thus bringing to remote peoples Christianity, trade, administrative organization, a new system of settlement, prisons, military strategy, extractive industry, and so on.

The movement for indigenous cultural survival that is now active in Russia is being led by representatives of the distinct indigenous groups themselves and supported by ethnographers, anthropologists, sociologists, lawyers, and others. This movement has been stimulated and strengthened by an international movement for indigenous rights and recognition. The renewed attention in post-Soviet Russia to shaping institutions to allow for indigenous cultural survival follows a worldwide trend that has spread rapidly across the Arctic. Some of today's most creative and far-reaching models of indigenous self-governance can be found in the circumpolar North—for instance, Greenland's Home Rule, the Saami Parliament, and most recently the Canadian decision to create a new northern territory and government—Nunavut—encompassing a vast area of the eastern Canadian Arctic.[4]

These efforts assume that institutions matter, that the design of governance systems (especially official and customary laws, rules, and norms regarding property, group rights, and leadership) play a role in cultural resilience or disintegration. We sought in part to test this hypothesis, aiming our research at the drivers of cultural endurance and sustainability. It is certainly difficult (maybe impossible) to determine the relative importance of "institutional" change in contrast to other changes, be they ecological, climatic, or economic. We hoped that by examining the culture change depicted in legend, history, and practices, and by tracing institutional changes from both an anthropological and a historical-legal-political perspective, we would reach some conclusions useful to policy makers.

Indigenous communities across the circumpolar North and throughout the world are struggling to maintain their own languages, values, and even their very existence. Many are enduring the serious, painful, and perhaps even terminal ills that result when people lose their sense of identity and place in the world. Suicide, alcohol abuse, accidents, infant mortality, and spousal abuse have appeared in abnormally high rates in many arctic indigenous communities exceeding the already high rates in northern cities (in contrast to more southerly regions). The average life span of an indigenous male in northern Russia is even shorter than the life expectancy of all Russian males, which itself is staggeringly low for an industrialized country in the late twentieth century.[5]

How can any small-scale society whose culture relies on hunting and foraging, pastoral or agricultural activity resist cultural disintegration or even extinction? How much of the ability to resist destructive change is inherent in the culture itself? Are there particular characteristics that make a culture prone to survival or disintegration? Are the apparent differences due to the extent of intrusion by large-scale extractive industries such as mining, oil and gas development, and forestry? Are the nomadic Nenets of Yamal destined to suffer the same loss of language and engage in a similar process of assimilation as the Mansi and the Khanty to the south—peoples who have lived longer alongside Russian merchants and later with Soviet oil drillers? Are nomadic Nenets headed toward a "tragedy of the commons" as individuals enlarge their private herds, a practice that collectively results in overgrazing the available pastureland? How might they respond to the threat of large-scale crises in their herding culture? What role do governance systems play in provoking or avoiding a tragedy of the commons? Can institutions that determine who decides what according to what rules and procedures make a difference in whether extractive industry is a blessing or a curse to indigenous communities?

We began our joint task by integrating all these questions about the relationship between governing institutions and cultural survival into just two: (1) What social dimensions *within* the culture determine its change (sustainability, adaptation, or transformation)? and (2) What social institutions *outside* the culture impel or influence its change? Only after addressing both fundamental research questions could we hope to address the more practical policy question: How can policy makers shape institutions to enhance prospects for cultural resilience? We first prepared our results as analytic, systematic treatment of specific themes—leadership, ownership, gender, and institutional change.[6] In the end, however, we found that the best way to answer these questions was to synthesize historical records, ethnographic data, and interviews with the actors shaping current policy into a single story covering several centuries of Nenets' encounters with outsiders. These we present in their "natural," chronological sequence. The events themselves—what constitutes the Yamal Nenets' story—reveal the most authentic answers to these questions.

The Yamal Nenets and Their Land

The largest among the so-called small peoples of the Russian North, the Nenets (numbering about 35,000) belong to the Samoyed group of the Uralic language family.[7] Their nearest neighbors by territory and relatives by language are Samoyedic-speaking peoples: the Enets and the Nganasan (Taimyr Peninsula dwellers) and the Sel'kup (whose southern group lives on the middle Ob River and whose northern group lives near the Taz and Turukhan rivers). Southern neighbors of the Nenets in Western Siberia are the Ugrians, the Khanty, and the Mansi (peoples belonging to the Ugric group of the Uralic language family), who live in the forest (*taiga*) territory of the middle and lower Ob River. Southern neighbors of the Nenets in the European tundra are the Komi-Zyrians; western neighbors on the Kola Peninsula are the Saami (both belong to the same Uralic language family). Today all area inhabited by

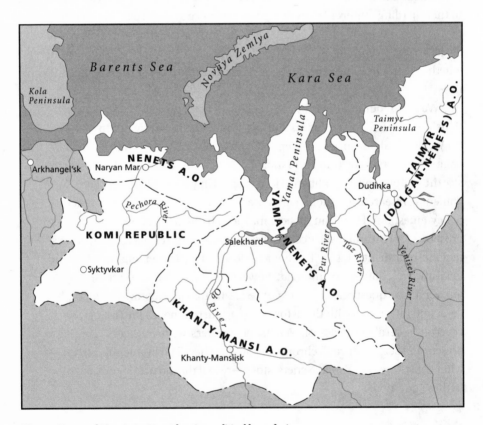

Map I.   Range of Nenets territory showing political boundaries

the Nenets is widely populated by Russians, Ukrainians, and other new outsiders.

More than one-quarter of all Nenets, approximately 9,000, lived on the Yamal Peninsula in 1994. Geographically, the Yamal tundra lies in the middle of Nenets territory, which spans four administrative *okrugs* (regions): the Nenets Autonomous Okrug of the Arkhangel'sk *Oblast* (Province), the Yamal-Nenets and Khanty-Mansiisk Autonomous Okrugs of the Tiumen Oblast, and the Dolgan-Nenets Autonomous Okrug of Krasnoyarsk Krai. Sixty-five percent of Nenets live in the Tiumen Oblast. See Maps 1 and 2.

The Nenets are mostly reindeer-herding nomads. Like the Saami and the Chukchi, they developed large-scale reindeer breeding in the tundra. Fishing and hunting polar fox, waterfowl, and sea mammals are important secondary

Map 2.   Indigenous peoples of the Tiumen Oblast

branches of their traditional economy. Today, large-scale domestic reindeer breeding is the backbone of the Nenets' economy and culture in the Yamal-Nenets Autonomous Okrug. More than 4,500 Nenets (and a few Khanty) lead a nomadic or semi-nomadic life in the Yamal district (Russian singular: *raion*), encompassing most of the Yamal Peninsula. The Nenets live in canvas and reindeer-hide tents and move with their families and herds to designated pastures throughout Yamal and the mainland in a six-season rotational cycle. The traditional economic activities of the native peoples—hunting, fishing, and reindeer herding—all have important seasonal aspects.

Today the indigenous population of Yamal can be divided roughly into nomadic and sedentary. Although administratively each nomad family is listed as belonging to a particular village or settlement, most move with the herds, living in tents on the land. In contrast to many arctic communities, the demography of Yamal's nomadic society is surprising. In 1994 women composed 52 percent of the nomad population. For a Nenets herder, a woman (usually a wife, mother, or sister) makes life on the tundra possible. And the herding life still attracts boys and girls in roughly equal numbers even after they complete boarding school. The sedentary population of Yamal lives permanently either in small villages of 200 to 500 people or in the larger administrative or economic centers. In the villages, natives hold jobs related to the fishing and fish-processing industry or work for one of the cooperatives, the state farms, or for the government. Only tiny minorities of nonnatives live in the small settlements, but they frequently hold the leadership posts and top-paying jobs. Summer tents are a common sight close to or even in the villages, as settled Nenets families expand their cramped quarters with the traditional form of the mobile summer home. A wider ethnic mix of Russians, Nenets, Khanty, and others live in the district center, Yar-Sale, and in towns tied to fish factories or oil and gas development—Panaevsk, Novyi Port, and Mys Kamennyi. Most settled Nenets families have relatives and ties to tundra families and, like their nomadic relatives, define their culture in terms of reindeer herding, not life in the settlements.

Ya-mal—literally the "edge of the land"—juts from the northeast foothills of the Polar Urals to touch the Arctic Ocean at the seventy-third parallel. At the northwestern-most point of the Asian continent, it is the heart of our study area. The Yamal Peninsula lies within the Yamal-Nenets Autonomous Okrug, with its administrative center in Salekhard (earlier called Obdorsk) on the Arctic Circle. The *okrug* in turn lies within the Tiumen Oblast, which continues to exercise considerable influence over its northern *okrugs* despite the fact that the autonomous *okrugs* enjoy equal status with the *oblasts* under the 1993 Constitution of the Russian Federation.[8] The Yamal-Nenets Okrug is composed of five smaller administrative districts: Yamal, Priural, Taz, Nadym, and Pur. The Yamal district, with its administrative center in the town of Yar-Sale, covers most of the peninsula. The southwestern portion of the peninsula falls partly within the Priural district, the administrative center of which is in the settlement of Aksarka.

The Yamal Peninsula lies entirely north of the Arctic Circle (66.33 degrees N). Its length, 750 kilometers (466 miles) is more than 3 times its width, which varies from 140 to 240 kilometers (87 to 149 miles). The Peninsula is located in an area of significant permafrost: the depth of the seasonally melting layer of ground ranges from 0.2 meters in the northern part of Yamal to 2.0 meters in the southern parts. Geomorphologically an elevated portion of the Western-Siberian plain, the peninsula was once covered by water. Consequently, its soils are composed of marine sands and clays. The peninsula has a low, flat shoreline, which is engulfed by tides in some places. Moving from the coastline to the interior, the elevation of the peninsula increases along wide terraces. At its maximum elevation the peninsula is only 70 meters above sea level.[9]

The peninsula's climate is affected by both arctic marine and continental air masses. Summers are short and cold; winters are windy and frigid. The average annual temperature in southern Yamal (near the city of Salekhard, for example) is –6.6 degrees C (20 degrees F), while on the northern edge of the Peninsula it dips to –10.2 degrees C (14 degrees F). Owing to the relative high humidity, coastal districts tend to be very cloudy. The areas of Yamal adjoining the Kara Sea and its gulfs have roughly 80 to 90 days per year of dense fog: on an average of 10 days per year, this fog is so dense as to be very dangerous, with visibility at less than 100 meters. The total amount of annual precipitation fluctuates from 230 to 400 millimeters, falling primarily during the summer in the form of drizzling rain (sometimes mixed with snow). The average annual wind speed is 7 meters per second; during storms it can reach 15 meters per second. Snowstorms on Yamal occur roughly 140 days of the year. Local snowstorms and frequent surface winds under clear skies serve to redistribute the snow cover across the peninsula.[10]

Ice forms in the sea along the coastline of Yamal in the second half of October; ice breakup begins at the end of May or the beginning of June. Surface water, in the form of rivers and lakes, predominates on Yamal. The peninsula's rivers are divided between two drainage systems/basins. The watershed traverses the peninsula from north to south, roughly along the center; therefore the rivers' flow is divided relatively evenly among numerous branches/arteries. The largest rivers are the Yuribei (450 kilometers long), the Mordyyakha (about 300 kilometers long), the Kharasavei (300 kilometers long), and the Seyaha (about 165 kilometers long). These relatively flat rivers with slow currents meander widely in the broad, low valleys.

More than 50,000 lakes dot the peninsula: most are small, with diameters of up to several hundred meters. Two lake systems are particularly important—Yara-to in the south and Nei-to in the north; together they consist of six lakes with a combined area of more than five square kilometers. While many lakes and rivers of Yamal are fished, these two lake clusters are particularly important sources of subsistence. The southern cluster also supports a commercial fishery. In the north of Yamal, lakes and swamps are primarily associated with river valleys and low sea terraces, while in the south they occupy both river valleys and watersheds. The large lakes are ice-free only in the middle of the summer; they freeze again in the second half of October.[11]

The ecology of Yamal varies as one moves from north to south. A gradual transition from arctic tundra in the north to woody-shrub tundra in the south can be traced along the peninsula's length. On most of Yamal, forests are absent. In the peninsula's southern parts, woody vegetation of a northern taiga type intrudes into the tundra landscape along the valleys of the Khadytayakha, the Yadayakhodayakha, and other rivers. The watersheds are lichen- and moss-covered tundra. In the river valleys, sedge[12] swamps prevail. In the summer, the arctic tundra in the north, relatively poor in faunal resources, is intensively used for pasturing domestic reindeer, primarily because of the lack of mosquitoes.

Twenty-six mammal species live on Yamal. Several of these migrate across the peninsula sporadically: lynx (*Lynx lynx*), otter (*Lutra lutra*), brown bear (*Ursus arctos*), fox (*Vulpes vulpes tobolica*), caribou or wild reindeer (*Rangifer tarandus*), wolverine (*Gulo gulo*), and elk (*Alces alces*). Polar bears (*Ursus maritimus maritimus*) are encountered infrequently. Two types of lemmings (*Lemmus sibiricus* and *Dicrostonyx torquatus*) play a crucial role in the peninsula's ecosystem; owing to their abundance and range, many larger species are dependent on them for food. The domestic reindeer and arctic fox (*Alopex lagopus*) are most significant economically and ecologically.[13] Domestic reindeer herds are so large that they affect ecosystem structure and function. Decades of high levels of reindeer grazing and trampling have reduced lichen cover and increased grass cover, thus increasing the scarcity of winter pastureland. The muskrat (*Ondatra zibethica*), white hare (*Lepus timidus begitschevi*), and ermine (*Mustela erminea tobolica*) are also important economic resources.

Seals congregate on the beaches north of Baidarata Bay and on the northern banks of Ob Bay on both the Yamal and Gydan peninsulas.[14] The bearded seal (*Erignathus barbatus*, Latin; *lakhtak*, Russian; *ngarti*, Nenets), hunted on the arctic coastline and at sea, is particularly important for the Nenets as a source of material for making reindeer harnesses.[15]

Bird species found on Yamal number 186, of which 103 species regularly nest on the peninsula. One special characteristic of the bird population is the predominance of water and shorebird species. The most varied concentration of species is found in southern Yamal, where 89 different species, including the rare gyr falcon (*Falco gyrfalco*), nest. Thirty-two species nest in northern Yamal. Several species of waterfowl have economic significance: species *Anser* and *Anas*, *Clangula hyemalis*, *Somateria spectabilis*, the white partridge (*Lagopus mutus*), and others.

The most varied concentration of fish species (twenty-six) is found in Ob Bay. Thirty-two species of fish have been identified in Yamal's lakes and rivers, of which twenty-six are commercially significant. Sigs (*Coregonus*) are the most numerous fish. In northern Yamal, however, the rivers and lakes are home to only eight species of fish.[16] Three fishing plants at Novyi Port (*Novoportovskii*), Puiko (*Puikovskii*), and Aksarka (*Aksarkovskii*) are responsible for industrial fishing on Yamal. The most intensive fishing is done on the eastern shores of Yamal, near Novyi Port and Yaptiksale. The latter is a particularly rich fishing area at the confluence of several rivers and Ob Bay, at the point where the salt water of the Kara Sea mixes with the fresh water of the Ob river estuary.

Beginning in the 1960s, the exploration and exploitation of gas and oil fields on Yamal has gained in importance at both the national (Soviet/Russian) and international levels. In 1964 the Novoportovskoe gas-condensate field was discovered, and between 1964 and 1990 Soviet oil and gas surveying expeditions discovered twenty-one important fields, fifteen gas and gas-condensate fields, and six oil/gas-condensate fields.[17] A railway and road corridor from southern Yamal to bring supplies and services to the gas and oil fields in central and northern Yamal has been under construction since the late 1980s. (See Map 3.) As of 1995, this corridor stretched approximately 210 kilometers north of Labytnangi.

The most prominent industrial impacts in the Yamal-Nenets Auton-

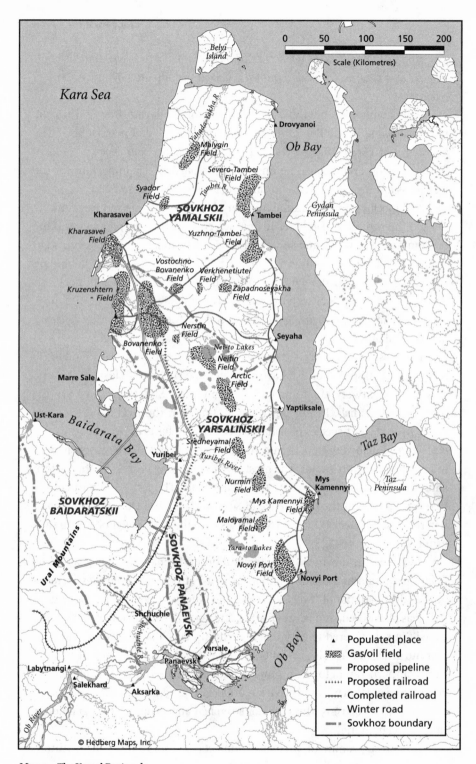

Map 3. The Yamal Peninsula

omous Okrug include loss of pastureland owing to allotment for oil and gas development and related transport; damage to additional areas from industrial activity; contamination of rivers and sea-coast areas by oil, oil products, and other chemical agents; damage to bird, mammal, and fish breeding grounds, habitat, and migratory routes; and destabilization of the permafrost. Potential accidental spills from oil and gas complexes, pipelines, and sea transport pose additional threats. Blowing dust and sand from the numerous sand quarries that have been created (these occur every two to five kilometers along the corridor) have changed the plant community's composition and cover (notably reducing lichens and mosses) in a wide swath around the corridor.[18]

While oil and gas-condensate reserves on Yamal are smaller than gas reserves, they are economically attractive. They present somewhat different, although also problematic, environmental risks. Oil reserves (proven and probable) on Yamal total 375.3 million metric tons (mmt) located in 8 fields, a small part of the larger 4,462.5 mmt located in the *okrug* (133 fields). Options for export of oil from the peninsula include a 400-kilometer hot-oil pipeline bisecting the peninsula from fields in the southeast to connect to a proposed tanker terminal on Baidarata Bay or shipment via tanker through Ob Bay as well as from a terminal on the west coast.[19] The thick ice and shallowness of Ob Bay, particularly in the area of greatest industry interest, Novyi Port, limit the size of tankers that can operate there.[20]

Although extensive exploration, development of infrastructure, and some modest production of oil and gas have occurred on Yamal, full-scale production of the gas fields there cannot take place without substantial investment in either a pipeline or liquid natural gas (LNG) terminal. The development of Norwegian offshore gas fields in recent years combined with other economic factors have pushed the specter of large-scale gas production on Yamal into the next century,[21] thus allowing time for an institutional infrastructure and regulatory framework to be worked out.

Guide to the Yamal Nenets Story

The first chapter of this book contains the story of the biggest cultural change in Nenets history—when, at the beginning of Russian colonization (1600s), the Nenets transformed their economic system from hunting and gathering (reliant on a few reindeer for transportation) to large-scale reindeer herding. Many legends and myths provided information for this book, but the legend retold here, "Five Yaptiks," is pivotal. We return to it in each of the subsequent chapters. Interrupting the chronological story, Chapter 2 introduces the main actors of the story, the nomadic Nenets, as depicted in myths, observations, and our own photographs. Our studies of gender roles and relationships were particularly useful to reconstruct this picture of tundra life as it is today and as it has evolved from the time of the transition. We then return to the sequence of the Yamal Nenets history. Chapter 3 covers the Russian conquest up to the Bolshevik Revolution, while Chapter 4 covers the period of Soviet authority up to the 1950s, when the peak of the Stalin era had passed. In Chapter 5 we trace the "strained dialogue" from the 1950s until the dissolution of the Soviet Union. Chapter 6 finds the Nenets and the new Russian state at the "tundra crossroads." In the Conclusion we return to the questions with which we began. Unless otherwise noted, the photographs in this book were taken by the authors between the years 1989 and 1996.

1

Rebirth of the Culture

Today the Yamal Nenets maintain the classical herders' culture based on reindeer. Nenets nomads seasonally migrate following the herds, repeating the natural rhythm of reindeer movement, directing the bulk of everyday activity toward reindeer, and relying on the products of this activity. Reindeer flesh, blood, fat, and marrow is their basic food; hides become tent covers, beds, and clothing; sinew is used for sewing thread; bones and antlers are made into handles, buttons, and utensils. Children play "reindeer" by throwing the lasso on one another, harnessing the caught individual into small sledges, reenacting scenes of camp life or a migrating caravan by using rocks as reindeer, wooden figurines as sledges, and dolls of ducks' beaks as people. The Nenets calendar consists of lunar months, the names of which are often directly (variants of the seven months) linked with herding: *sie nich iry*—false calving month, April; *ty nich iry*—(real) calving month, May; *nyavdy iry*—one-year-old doe's (calving) month, June; *selvy iry*—peeling (hairy film from antler) month, August; *khor iry*—buck's (coupling) month, October; *malkoms iry*—hornless (antlers falling) month, November; *yary iry*—knobs' (growing new antlers) month, January. A number of Nenets clan names are derived from the herders' vocabulary: *Ngokateta* means "owner of many reindeer";

Serotetta, "owner of white reindeer"; *Teseda,* "the reindeerless"; and so on. People and reindeer are inseparable even beyond life, as ritually slaughtered reindeer are believed to follow their masters after death.

It is impossible to think of the Nenets away from their reindeer herds. The Nenets, however, are recent pastoralists whose practice of large-scale reindeer breeding is hardly longer than three to four centuries. Their ancestors were skillful in taming and breeding reindeer since at least the early iron age, as archaeological data show (for example, harness parts from Ust'Polui site).[1] Those ancestors bred reindeer for transportation and used reindeer as a decoy for hunting, a practice that differs from large-scale herding as a secondary occupation from the economic mainstream. The transition from a foraging, subsistence pattern to herding occurred in some short period around the middle of the second millennium C.E. Ethnohistorical data show the absence of large herds in medieval times and the appearance of large herds at least by the eighteenth century. In Igor I. Krupnik's words, "In the mid- to late 1700s in the Eurasian Arctic zone occupied by Nenets, the population of domestic reindeer suddenly began to grow, and the herds increased surprisingly quickly. . . . Something approaching a 'reindeer revolution' took place over a hundred years, or during the course of only four to five generations in the human community."[2] Krupnik has attributed this transformation of the Nenets and several other Eurasian northern cultures to a convergence of ecological and social factors.[3] He was not the first[4] to notice the recent origin of arctic, including Nenets, pastoralism, but he first pointed out the "sudden" or "surprising" rapidity of the transition.

Debate concerning the emergence of large-scale reindeer herding in Northern Eurasia has been focused on two dimensions. (1) What produced the "reindeer revolution"? Was it a crisis in the former subsistence hunting system that pushed the Nenets to vastly increase their herds or, on the contrary, favorable conditions for enlarging the herds? (2) Did ecological or social conditions (or their convergence) play the key role in that transformation? Participants in this discourse have filled all the cells of this matrix.

1. *Ecologically critical circumstances*: "Climatic change increasing winter temperature which occurred in the first millennium AD would have to have caused a decrease in the total number of wild reindeer; that probably compelled people to change their traditional economic form," according to Khlobystin and Gracheva.[5]

2. *Socially favorable conditions*: The Russian state authority brought a reduction in intertribal warfare and established a rule of law that encouraged

and protected private property; this included ownership of reindeer. Without these conditions, Dolgikh reasoned, "[the property of] a wealthy man would be very soon expropriated by his own kinsmen. Besides, a big reindeer herd would be a permanently desired object for neighbors, and the clan of the wealthy man would have to conduct perpetual warfare."[6]

3. *Ecologically and socially favorable conditions*: Krupnik showed that "stable cooling phases [which are particularly positive for reindeer and their fecundity] clustered recurringly during the late 1500s to early 1600s, throughout most of the 1700s, and the early [and 'right through the middle of the'] 1800s, as well as the first decades of this century."[7] According to Krupnik's approach, the first period coincided with the Russian invasion of Siberia and attendant conflicts, epidemics, and forceful relocations, which could not be suitable for development of a pastoral reindeer economy. Rather, it was during the second period that occurred alongside "the entrenchment of government power, the development of trade throughout Siberia, and attenuation of intertribal conflicts" that reindeer pastoralism burgeoned in the Eurasian arctic. "The *ecological* aspect of the mechanism of transition to large-scale reindeer herding should have been fairly universal, while the *social* factors in this process probably varied among different peoples in their local environments and historically specific circumstances."[8]

4. *Socially critical impact*: The natives' desire for autonomy from newly established Russian power raised the importance of mobility to retire to remote tundra areas, and this in turn required larger herds. Simultaneously, overhunting and the consequent scarcity of wild reindeer led to reorientation of the native economy from foraging toward pastoralism. The core transition occurred in the 1600s. This is the view put forward by Golovnev in some previous works.[9]

What kind of ecological stress could be strong enough to induce tundra hunters to "suddenly" and "surprisingly quickly" change their subsistence pattern? Given the conservative nature of foraging societies, it seems reasonable to accept Khlobystin and Gracheva's view that an ecological crisis triggered the change, although not in the first millennium. Their position does not explain why the reindeer revolution occurred in a short period whereas the climatic conditions appeared at different times throughout both the first and second millennia C.E. The 1400s or 1600s, which Krupnik marked as adverse climatic periods, would be more plausible.

In arriving at his position (reason No. 3), Krupnik focused on domestic instead of wild reindeer, therefore his dates correspond to favorable climatic periods—roughly the 1500s or the 1700s. Krupnik's final choice of the 1700s, however, was not based on climatic factors: The two ecologically similar periods produced opposite results owing to different (accordingly, adverse and favorable) social conditions. At a time when the Nenets kept only a few domestic reindeer for transportation, favorable ecological change would have mostly increased the wild reindeer population rather than that of the small number of transport (usually castrated) domestic reindeer. In this case hunting would have flourished, instead of declining and being replaced with another means of living. There is further questionable stand in Krupnik's scheme. He determined the mid-1700s to early 1800s as the narrow window when pastoralism began to be practiced in Northern Eurasia. But the actual appearance of pastoralism exceeds these bounds: large-scale reindeer breeding is known to have been practiced in Scandinavia from the 1600s, and in the lower Yenisei, the transition period from foraging to herding lasted 150 years, from the late 1700s to early 1900s.

Russian scholars (Dolgikh, Gurvich, and others [summarized in reason No. 2]), who preferred to talk about the social impulse of reindeer-herding pastoralism, emphasized the auspicious circumstances—first of all the state support of private property in the 1600s. But the "classic pastoralists," the Nenets and the Chukchi, conducted warfare or rebelled against Russian power until the late 1800s. The permanent confrontation, explicit or not, was scarcely conducive to either a social alliance between natives and the state or to stable and "lawful" respect of property rights.

If we accept the Dolgikh and Gurvich standpoint, then we would expect the largest herds to be concentrated near settlements under Russian protection. As we know, however, the largest reindeer herds and richest owners' migration routes were located in remote tundra areas (for example, wealthy Nenets usually occupied northern coastal territories of Yamal, Gydan, and the European tundra. Explorers and the Nenets themselves explain that rich herders, in comparison with poor ones, are able to make long migrations, and they like this space. Such a simple explanation seems to be true both today and in former times. Since the Russians established administrative outposts in Northwestern Siberia in the late 1500s and early 1600s (Obdorsk on the lower Ob in 1595; Mangazeia on the lower Taz in 1601), Nenets who owned more or less sizable herds could retire to remote areas and avoid political submission and taxation. As is well known from chronicles, the Nenets (Samoyeds) engaged in military raids, fiercely persecuted Russian adherents, and resisted baptism; in short, they were firm defenders of their lands and customs. For a long time Samoyeds, especially those in the remote tundra, remained practically independent from Russian administrators. The real base for their social and economic autonomy became domestic reindeer.

This position (reason No. 4) does not entirely reject ecological change as a complementary factor. Adverse climatic conditions in the 1600s could have caused a reduction in the wild reindeer population, hastened overhunting, and broadened seasonal migration. These hard conditions could have strengthened a trend toward enlarging the small domestic reindeer herds for transportation. Adverse ecological change for tundra reindeer is closely connected to warming periods.[10] Hot, dry summers, with their accompanying hordes of mosquitoes, drove both wild reindeer and reindeer hunters north; therefore the ecological impulse for Samoyeds to leave the comfortable southern tundra-woodlands and move north could have coincided with the social pressure to escape from Russian outposts to remote areas. There, in the cold (mosquito-free) northern coastal tundra, hunter-herders found a favorable climate during a generally adverse period.

The odyssey of the Nenets gods parallels the historical path of the Nenets people from the forest boundary to the far-coastal tundra. The goddess Paemal Khada (Old Woman of the Edge of the Mountain) is said to have traveled from the southern forest border to the northern end of the Ural ridge, where her sacred place appeared. The goddess Yamal Khada (Old Woman of the Edge of the Land), whose form was that of a white reindeer, similarly journeyed in another direction across the Yamal Peninsula to the arctic coast. Stories of both women contain fragments connecting them to the transition period discussed earlier. According to legend, Paemal Khada, for some time, had served the Russians and sailed on their boat; people of the clan Ngokateta (Owners of Many Reindeer) followed Yamal Khada in her odyssey.[11] The myths indirectly confirm a synchrony of Russian contact and the shift of the Ngokateta to the north.

Another myth traces the way of another Nenets god, the patron-spirit of the Yaptik clan. The name of this clan in Nenets is close in meaning to "strong bone" but has no exact translation. The Yaptik clan is known among the Yamal Nenets from the earliest census ("tax book" of 1695). Lands used by this clan are located mostly on the remote northern, largely coastal areas of the Yamal Peninsula. Legendary ancestors of the clan are depicted as "living in a hole," hunting caribou and sea mammals, and hosting dwellers of the underground, a mysterious people called Sihirtia. The Yaptik clan became known by the "ungovernable" temper of its kinsmen; many shamans originated from this clan, and it is widely reputed to have been the hearth of "revolts" (Nenets, *mandalada*) during the Soviet era.

All Nenets clans have their own patron spirits (*haehae*) called by the name of the clan. The Yaptik clan's patron has a special designation: *haesie* (instead of *haehae*). This designation signifies his prominent position among other spirits. Yaptik-haesie has an "earthen" location as well as a "divine" one. According to legend, he originally was a son of sky god Num. He once descended onto the earth and lost his way back in a blizzard. He is considered to be the junior brother of the mighty spirit Pongarmae Iriko (Old Man of the Country of Winds or Old Man of the Frozen Land) who lives in the Far North. Being son-in-law of the Khanty god Ort Iki, Yaptik-haesie used to visit Khanty religious feasts in the lower Ob, in the southern boundary of Nenets lands. According to tradition, the strongest shaman from the Yaptik clan annually carries Yaptik-haesie's image, a sculpture wrapped in rags, in a special sacred sledge throughout the whole tundra from south to north. Yaptik-haesie's mission is to travel all over the Nenets' country and look out for people's well-being. The former sacred residence of Yaptik-haesie, as it could be interpreted through archaeological data (from evidence of dog sacrifice), was on the lower Ob River near Obdorsk.[12] Today his principal sacred place is on the very northern cape of Yamal, near the "tent" of the goddess Yamal Khada.

The legend of Yaptik-haesie is well-known among the Yamal Nenets. What follows is the version told to us by Ngoet Tadibe, who lives on Yaptik-cape (Yaptik-Sale since 1993) of the Yamal Peninsula. The story (*lahnako* in Nenets), "Five Yaptiks," tells of the conversion of a Yaptik kinsman into the god Yaptik-haesie. This is also a story of re-creation of the world, of the Nenets' transition from a foraging to a herding culture. As the story begins, five Yaptik brothers appear to have very little "culture": they have few reindeer; they are just hunters, not reindeer-breeders; they are symbolically dying. Then the eldest Yaptik leads his brothers against Nomadic Man, the god Ilibem-Baertia, who gives them another lifestyle based on pastoralism: reindeer-herding. This is the culmination of the plot, the point of rejecting the old (foraging) tradition and establishing the new (herding) one. This is the scene of conflict between men and god, Eldest Yaptik and Junior Yaptik.

There are many other remarkable features in the "Five Yaptiks" story that reveal the Nenets' manner so as to evaluate properly the "reindeer revolution." The story conveys the major sacred concepts depicting reindeer herding's emergence as the gods' gift to people. It touches on the scientific puzzle about the origin of the Nenets' pastoralism and acquaints the reader with a typical example of the Nenets' oral tradition.

Five Yaptiks

Five Yaptiks[13] have a mother and a sister. Nobody knows when the five Yaptiks began to sleep. It was the first snow of autumn, His snow.

Eldest Yaptik said to his mother, "Lift up the corner of the door." The mother lifted the flap of the tent. "It's too early," said Eldest Yaptik and slept again. Nobody knows how long he slept before he woke and said again, "Lift the corner of the door." She lifted. "Oh, it's time to get up; it's time to go hunting. Wild reindeer of Nartsoolapta perhaps have rested,"[14] he said.

His mother replied, "You haven't any food." She went out, then returned bringing five goose stomachs. She threw these into the cooking pot. The pot boiled. The five Yaptiks ate the five goose stomachs and went outside. The five Yaptiks have ten domestic reindeer; they harnessed five and rode away.

They rode a while. They shot the wild reindeer and loaded them onto their sledges. Eldest Yaptik said, "It's enough; let's go home." They came home.

They began to sleep again. The summer passed. Then the winter and one more summer. The meat of the wild reindeer was gone. It was the fall when Mother said, "Children, the pot is empty."

The Eldest said, "Lift the corner of the door, I'll see." He peered for a long time, then said, "It's not a time for hunting," and dropped off to sleep again. He slept for a while and his light slumber ended. He said to his mother, "Lift the corner of the door." She lifted. He watched, then he said to his mother. "It's time for hunting. On our Nartsoolapta, the reindeer have rested."

They harnessed the sledges and left again. When they filled their sledges with wild reindeer, they returned home.

The five Yaptiks slept again for three years, and all that time not a hair moved on their *yagushkas*.[15] They didn't hunt at all. The meat ran out. The fall came once again and snow fell. Eldest Yaptik said to his mother, "Lift the corner of the door." She lifted. He looked and said, "Now it is not the time for hunting." And Eldest Yaptik went to sleep again.

The mother took five legs of geese. She said, "These are the last morsels." They ate the goose legs and went out. Each of them harnessed two of their reindeer; they harnessed all ten.

The five Yaptiks rode a while, then stopped at the mound that hangs above the sea.[16] Eldest Yaptik, watching, said "What is happening?" The wild reindeer of Nartsoolapta began to move as though the whole land was moving. At the foot of the mound, one large tent stood. Eldest Yaptik beat furiously three times on the skin on his sledge, tearing it into three parts. He headed toward the tent, stopping near the *si* side of it.[17] Eldest Yaptik could see that the tent was about to be moved away. Eldest Yaptik said, "You took our hunting place. Now we are beggars.[18] You grabbed our spot. You are wicked."

The man replied, "I atoned for my guilt." He tied to their sledges reindeer for harnessing and other antlerless reindeer for meat. "Take these reindeer. I occupied the land for that." They departed.

After some time, they stopped. Eldest Yaptik released the gift reindeer and those of his four brothers. Eldest Yaptik hit the ear of one reindeer; all the reindeer went away. Junior Yaptik's thoughts are walking. "These reindeer are a gift. Why do I have to release them?" Eldest Yaptik said, "If you don't release the reindeer, after we kill that man, we shall come back and kill you." Junior Yaptik thought, "It's a pity I have to free these reindeer," but he unharnessed them. Junior Yaptik followed his brothers reluctantly.

In the head of the caravan Eldest Yaptik was riding. He stopped and took his bow.

Nomadic Man said, "What's the matter?"

Eldest Yaptik replied, "The matter is you are riding on my land. It would be better to kill you now."

Nomadic Man said, "That would be very bad for you."

The four Yaptik brothers took their bows. The arrows poured around Nomadic Man. He said, "You four Yaptiks annoy me." He took his bow from the right side of the sledge and shot his arrows toward the Yaptik brothers. Each of four brothers owned one of his arrows, and their heads were thrown away. Nomadic Man said, "Junior Yaptik, what shall be done with you? Probably it would be better to kill you too." And he killed Junior Yaptik. After that, he departed.

It is unknown when Junior Yaptik's eyes opened. He awoke and watched. His brothers' sledges were overturned, but his sledge was still standing.[19] His brothers' reindeer were dead, but his were still grazing.[20] He harnessed his reindeer. He rode. After some time, his two reindeer struck their noses into the moss.[21] He left his sledge and went by foot. He was tired and began to creep with his back forward. Soon his back encountered something. He glanced over his shoulder. There was a tent. He entered the tent, and his two eyes gazed into the fire. One side of the tent was empty. On the bedding side, an old man was sitting. Near the door, an old woman was sitting. Opposite the entrance in the *si* place, a young woman was sitting. The old man asked him, "Who are you?"

He replied, "Once, I was Junior Yaptik."

"Where are you going?"

"Where can I go? I lost the way looking for warm fire. I lost my tent."

"You found a warm fire. You have come into the tent. You have found a hearth. Go to bed."

Junior Yaptik reached a bed. The old woman boiled the pot. The old man said, "Junior Yaptik, where is your land?"

"I don't know where my land is."

The old man said to the young woman sitting in *si* place, "Now you have to go to your brother and ask him for his little Sihirtia[22] reindeer— would he give this one to Junior Yaptik? If he would, Junior Yaptik would be able to leave."

Junior Yaptik ate and slept. Then, the old man said, "Junior Yaptik, you slept for seven days. The woman who went for reindeer has come back already. Do you want to leave?"

Junior Yaptik put on his clothes and went out. The small Sihirtia reindeer's legs looked as thin as grass. The sledge was so small that only half of Junior Yaptik's buttocks could fit. He led his small Sihirtia reindeer to the camp's border[23] and rode. After a while, Sihirtia reindeer stopped. Junior Yaptik looked for what caused his reindeer to stop. There was no tent. On the sunrise side of the spot, he saw the edge of an earthen reindeer horn.[24] Junior Yaptik pulled the horn, and a door opened. He looked inside. Inside everything was shiny. Junior Yaptik's eyes were joyful. He saw an old man and old woman in this earthen tent.[25]

The old man asked, "Who came in?"

The old woman answered, "Who may come in? That one living on the other side of earth—Junior Yaptik probably."

The old man said, "Junior Yaptik, are you coming from a very far land? Where are you going?"

"Where may I go? I was led here by my reindeer. Who are you?"

The old man answered, "I am Sihirtia old man."

Junior Yaptik took the place near the old man and fell asleep. He slept for seven days. Then the old man said, "Junior Yaptik, we can't live together any longer. Leave us and take my daughter with you. However, she cannot live on the light land. You will meet her in your sleeping dreams."

Junior Yaptik went outside. The old woman said, "Junior Yaptik, wait." And she began to look for something in her corner. She found there a little cradle and gave it to him. He put the thing onto his sledge and rode away.

He came back to the previous tent and stopped near the *si* side of the tent. He freed his reindeer, took off his *sovik*,[26] and put it under the skin cover of the sledge. But he touched there, under the skin, someone. Junior Yaptik said, "You, stand up, beside the sledge. How did you get here?"

She replied, "You took me from the tent. Now you can't abandon me here between two lands."

The thoughts of Junior Yaptik were roaming. While he stood there, the woman entered into the tent. Another woman brushed the snow off her.[27] The old man said, "Junior Yaptik, once you didn't want to release antlerless reindeer. I think that four Yaptiks may be dead. Maybe you don't need them."

Junior Yaptik answered, "I don't care if you are displeased with them. They may be dead."

The old man said, "Maybe you need one more Yaptik alive. Next to eldest is more kind than eldest. The other three Yaptiks, let them be dead. My Junior Yaptik,[28] you should stay here tonight." Junior Yaptik agreed.

Morning came. From outside his wife[29] called, "Junior Yaptik, the sledges are harnessed. Let's go. Won't you get up."

The old woman entered the tent to heat the pot.

The old man said, "Junior Yaptik, look at the woman sitting on the *si* side. Now she is yours. In the future, she will keep your affairs. And you, Junior Yaptik, don't be foolish like your eldest brother was."

The old man harnessed two reindeer for Junior Yaptik's sledge hitching Sihirtia reindeer to the middle of it. Junior Yaptik led his sledge along the edge of the reindeer herd. Not far from him was a female reindeer with a lone antler, very thin, without meat. The old man said, "Won't you take this little thing with you as a present."

Junior Yaptik replied, "If you give me, I will take it." He drove this old female reindeer nearer to his sledges. As the caravan departed, the old female reindeer came closer to the caravan. She was joined by one reindeer from the herd, then another, thus thirty reindeer followed him. Probably she was their mother.

Junior Yaptik went a while. He saw his first tent-site far in the distance. He came to that place and said, "Let's put our tent here and stay here." Later, Junior Yaptik said, "It would be good to visit my mother." He departed to another nomad camp.

When he arrived, his mother and sister boiled the pot. His mother said, "Junior Yaptik, you were absent for a long time. How much land you must have traveled."

Junior Yaptik answered, "I was lost."

The mother said, "Your brothers died, their heads thrown away."

Junior Yaptik said, "They fell themselves. They behaved badly, and I too have been dead."

Junior Yaptik ate and returned to his tent. Morning came. Junior Yaptik's thoughts were roaming, "At one time, we were five Yaptiks. Where are my brothers now?"

He saw his next-to-eldest brother's two reindeer grazing and the sledge standing. But his brother was laying still. Junior Yaptik kicked his brother with the toe of his boot and said, "You seemed to be a strong man when you tried to fight in vain. Now get up."

His brother arose whistling[30] and said, "Oh, it seems to me I was sleeping."

"You weren't sleeping; you were dead. Your dead brothers are lying here too. Who knows how long they have been dead. Only their bones are here. You see how bad it is to fight in vain. You died because of the foolishness of Eldest Yaptik. Your brother caused all of you to die."

The two Yaptiks rode together. They rode not so long a time and arrived at the tent of Junior Yaptik. On both sides of the tent were beds that had been prepared by the two women. Junior Yaptik went to the side of Sihirtia daughter and said to his brother, "Go toward that second side. From now on, you will be called Eldest Yaptik. Tomorrow you'll go and bring our mother and sister here. Here, two tents will stand."

Eldest Yaptik brought his mother and sister with him. Two tents were standing. Their sister lived with Eldest Yaptik, their mother with Junior Yaptik. Three years they lived in such a way. The fourth year, snow fell. Sihirtia daughter gave birth to a daughter and a son. They grew up day by day. Very soon the son reached the age of a man, and the daughter reached the age of a woman.

Junior Yaptik's wife said to her husband, "It is time to send Sihirtia little reindeer back to its home, to its earth, but it is impossible to send it without some gift. Send your daughter as a load of its sledge."

Junior Yaptik said, "Let it be if you say so. Dress your child."

Sihirtia woman dressed her daughter in new garments and said, "Daughter, be good in your new home and obey your grandmother."

Junior Yaptik's daughter left. She led the little reindeer to the edge of camp and let him run. Sihirtia little reindeer flew toward the sky as a spark and disappeared behind the rain clouds.

Junior Yaptik sat on his sledge near *si* place. He said, "I have sent back Sihirtia reindeer, but the old man gave me two more reindeer. By these two reindeer I will be able to ride to far lands." Junior Yaptik stared toward Nartsoolapta. There wild reindeer were moving like domestic ones. He looked on the other side. Innumerable reindeer roamed there too. The reindeer mother was there, surrounded on each side by a hundred reindeer. Junior Yaptik said, "The old man gave me life [*Vaesako baertm Ilebts*].[31] If Eldest Yaptik hadn't tried to kill Him, Eldest Yaptik would be alive now. But he was a fool. Let him be dead."[32]

Junior Yaptik said to his brother, "Eldest Yaptik, you need to leave me. I will stay here, and this land will be a sacred place. From now on, Eldest Yaptik, do not be like your Elder brother was, or you will have the same fate."

Eldest Yaptik nodded: "Junior Yaptik, I won't be like Eldest Yaptik."

Junior Yaptik said to him, "From this place, you have to move your camp seven times.[33] Then you will see a cape pointing north. Beneath this cape you will find a place for your tent. You must live there. Each autumn when the snowfall begins, you must return here with your sacred offering. I have said everything. Go."

Eldest Yaptik left him. And arriving at the cape looking to the north, he built his tent. There Eldest Yaptik lived three years. At the third year when the snow fell, Eldest Yaptik recollected, "Oh, I have forgotten something. Junior Yaptik told me to bring a sacrifice every autumn."

The word[34] passed, going to Junior Yaptik.

Junior Yaptik sat near his sacred sledge thinking, "What happened to Eldest Yaptik? Maybe he has become a rich man and forgotten me. If he comes here at last, as he reaches my sacred sledge, he will fall on his hands and will lay there for seven days." Junior Yaptik entered his tent, ate, and went to sleep.

Junior Yaptik's wife went outside. At noon she saw someone driving; offerings were laying there on the sledge. It was Eldest Yaptik. He arrived and attached his sledge to the nose [front end] of Junior Yaptik's sacred sledge. Eldest Yaptik said, "First, I'd like to ask Junior Yaptik where I should offer these reindeer." He took two steps from his sledge and fell on his hands. At once his eyes became as ice on the lake. For seven days, not one hair moved on him.

Seven days passed. Junior Yaptik said, "Where is Eldest Yaptik? Did he make a sacrifice?" He went outside. The sledge of Eldest Yaptik was not unloaded. Junior Yaptik kicked his brother with the toe of his boot. Eldest Yaptik raised up whistling and said, "What happened? Why were my eyes closed?"

"I told you to come here every autumn. My sacred sledge needs sacrifice. The sacred sledge didn't receive anything for three years. Perhaps you achieved such a good life that you didn't remember my words." Junior Yaptik said these words and went into the tent.

Eldest Yaptik slaughtered his seven reindeer in front, at the nose of the sacred sledge, and he went around the tent following the solar path. Then he went away. The word ended.

Junior Yaptik turned into Yaptik-haesie; his mother, into Ya-Miunia. His son became a Nenets and went to live in the land of Eldest Yaptik.

Who are the heroes of the legend (Nenets legends, like thrillers, uncover the real faces of characters at the very end)?

Yaptik-haesie, the god mediator between divinities and people, supports people in the most difficult period, the winter. It is noteworthy that the sacrifices to him are offered at the time of snowfall. He plays an intermediary role between north and south—the sacrifices are offered to his sledge because he is the eternal traveler. By his journey, he connects all the mythological spheres with the human world. As the dying-resurrecting spirit, he often endures for the sake of people, being frozen in a blizzard or killed by a divine arrow. In "Five Yaptiks" he initially appears as Junior Yaptik.

Ya-Miunia, the goddess of childbirth, is the patron and protector of all women in their motherhood. She traces the destiny of each person from birth until death. She leads people through *po*, the mythological door between the living world and the world beyond. She is the womb from which newborns come, and she receives the dead. She renews the human life cycle, providing souls to be reincarnated from the dead into newborns, from ancestors into descendants. Her embodiment on the Yamal Peninsula is Yamal Khada. In the story she plays a role of the Yaptik brothers' mother, endowing the chief hero (Junior Yaptik) with "earthen force."

Ilibem-Baertia, the god-giver of reindeer and well-being, taught and continues to teach people to be real herdsmen. He is one of the images of the sky god Num. Being a mediator between nature and culture, he plays the role of culture-maker, converting wild reindeer into domestic ones. In the story he appears as Nomadic Man, who first killed the Yaptik brothers and then gave Junior Yaptik a new life, a herd of reindeer, and a daughter as a wife to be keeper of the celestial will among people. Summarily, he gave Junior Yaptik "divine force."

Sihirtia, the legendary small people once gone and still living underground, are considered to be the Nenets' predecessors on the tundra, sometimes hostile but more often friendly. They can appear on the earth only at night or in a mist. Underground they pastured earthen reindeer (mammoths), whose "horns" are used for the door handles of their pit houses. They seem to be skillful blacksmiths and magicians, presenting iron or bronze objects to people. In "Five Yaptiks" Old Man Sihirtia gave to Junior Yaptik a small magic reindeer and a daughter. Since then, Junior Yaptik borrowed the "lower force" of the Sihirtia underground world. (The Nenets' god-heroes passed over all the worlds, entering into alliance with the masters of the different worlds.)

As we trace a Nenets' myth, it is almost impossible to spot the moment when people suddenly become gods. Each legend describes the conversion of people into gods after some long-suffering way. Ritually, people play roles of gods; mythologically, gods play roles of people. "Five Yaptiks" begins with the image of people who sleep and eat the stomachs and legs of geese. They are just hunters who have a couple of transport reindeer for each man. These people die. Their culture also dies upon encountering another "divine idea." Perhaps Eldest Yaptik was killed without a chance to be resurrected not just because of his temper or because of Nomadic Man's all-absorbing mercilessness but because he had to be annihilated as guardian of the old culture. Even his name was transferred, so that his younger brother became "Eldest" Yaptik. At the story's end people live in tents surrounded by "innumerable reindeer." Good-for-nothing Eldest Yaptik has become so rich that he has forgotten his sacred debt—to sacrifice reindeer to the gods. This is an object lesson for people: they should not forget those who made them wealthy. One more of Yaptik-haesie's (Junior Yaptik's) precepts was for people (Eldest Yaptik and others) to live on "a cape pointing north"—that is, on the very north of the land. Here we can correlate the mythological story and scientific discourse.

Even the tone of this tragic drama with a happy ending depicts the cultural transition as a temporary death. The picture of the empty pot, the winter sleep, and the battle and defeat can be understood as a "deep crisis" that shook the tundra hunters and compelled them with their gods to change their lifestyle and move their tents onto "a cape pointing north." The story withholds the external reasons of crisis, focusing instead on the main idea uncovered in Junior Yaptik's vision: "There wild reindeer were moving like domestic ones." Other Nenets folktales depict those outside influences through scenes of competition between a Nenets shaman and a Russian physician, of Nenets warriors fighting with the czar's servants, and of warfare with perpetual reindeer chariots.

Nenets folktales tell stories of battles for and the theft of reindeer. This contradicts common Nenets ethics, which condemn any sort of theft. Indeed, the large reindeer herd was not yet an ethical object; it was an innovation. At the same time, stealing reindeer appeared in a rank of military normatives insofar as the tundra warrior was encouraged to become a reindeer thief in order to reduce the enemy's power and ensure his own invulnerability, especially against Russian authorities. Reindeer robbery was a means of accumulating a herd. Most likely, the "heroic" aspect of battling for reindeer directly enhanced the prestige of the new economic core and provided a "surprisingly quick" increase in the herd population. Since then the Nenets have considered only reindeer herders to be "real people"—Nenei Nenets.

Arctic pastoralism, at least as it applies to the Nenets, was provoked from outside and, from the beginning, deliberately opposed the invaders' sedentary lifestyle. The difference between the two cultures was so essential that they could never understand each other's values and goals. The Russians expressed their power by building a fortress on the lower Ob; the Nenets, by leaving the lower Ob River for the northern tundra. For the Russians, security was a stable plot, whereas for the Nenets it was a moving herd.

In some respects this misunderstanding allowed the two cultures to coexist. Even today, Russian administrative centers in the region are located on the forest-tundra border (Salekhard is the center of the Yamal-Nenets okrug; Yar-Sale is the center of the Yamal district), while the richest reindeer owners migrate in the northern Yamal tundra. One Yamal Nenets elder, Nikolai L. Ngokateta, said that nowadays the tundra is governed simultaneously from two directions, by the Nenets from the north and by the Russians from the south.[35]

Once again the symbols from "Five Yaptiks" reappear: "a cape pointing north," the ever-moving sledge of god Yaptik-haesie, and the "innumerable reindeer" around a nomadic tent. These emblems of folklore contain a rank of ethnic values, and it is not surprising that the legend is so popular among Yamal reindeer herders. The story of how hunters became pastoralists is today the story of what is an essential core of the Nenets' nomadic culture. Since the Yaptik brothers' ordeals, the Nenets have traveled a long historical road, changing and correcting their ethical, economic, and spiritual patterns. Nonetheless, in most cases those changes were not cultural breaks; perhaps there was some remedy within the Nenets' culture that served to heal the cracks, or maybe the Nenets inherited this immunity from their ancestors, who had lived through the crucial "transition period."

2

Nomadic Life: Men and Women in the Context of Traditions

"Look at the woman sitting on the *si* side. Now she is yours. In the future, she will keep your affairs." This is what the god life-giver said to Junior Yaptik in "Five Yaptiks." According to legend, it was the life-giver god's will that woman be the trendsetter of a new reindeer-herding culture among the *Nenets*—the "people."

The myth demonstrates the centrality of gender roles in culture-making. All the alliances entered into by the hero, Junior Yaptik, were mediated by women. From his mother Junior Yaptik borrowed his "earthen" force; through the daughter of god Ilibem Baertia, the "upper" one; through the daughter of Sihirtia, the "lower" one. No mythological action avoids gender symbolism. Following oral tradition, this chapter presents Nenets nomadic lifestyle in the context of gender relations.

Current Nenets culture consists of at least two layers. One is of nomads living on the tundra and keeping their traditions; another is of villagers living on the line between indigenous tundra and urban societies and cultures. Here we focus on the nomadic culture still existing among herders on the Yamal tundra. The following portrait is not a snapshot of everyday life but a cultural model based on religious and ethical notions of tundra dwellers. Today, some customs might be followed or avoided (depending on personal inclination), but these ideal behavioral types and patterns predominate. Most nomadic Yamal people, and especially the aged, adhere to them in ritual and in day-to-day life.[1]

Gendered Space and Sacred Power

When a Nenets nomad camp begins its migration, a woman leads the caravan, while a man, on his light sled, drives the reindeer herd and chooses the route. The man determines the site for the new camp; the woman sets the first object—sheet iron for the hearth—on the tent foundation. The open tundra is the male sphere of action; the space of the home is that of the female. As I. P. Bolina, talking with anthropologist V. I. Vasil'ev, once said, "Where it's warm, there's always an old woman; where it's cold, there's an old man."[2]

Actually, despite the separation of the tent into male and female spaces (*si* and *nio*, respectively), to some degree the whole space belongs to the woman. It is no accident that girls usually play their games inside the tent, whereas boys play outside. After returning from the tundra, the man, who, with the woman's help, has changed into domestic ("female") clothes, spends most of his time sitting or lying down. While observing the relations between husband and wife around the hearth, one is sometimes tempted to define (not very precisely) the dwelling of a man as "the tent of his wife."

The house is the symbolic point of intersection between forces of the universe and humans. Construction of the tent begins with the placement of the hearth. Probably this act combines the idea of covering the underhearth "hole" to the netherworld with metal, the idea of symbolically marking the center, and also the historical origins of the tent, which initially was "a campfire hidden from the wind."

The hearth (a fire in the summer; a small iron stove in the winter) is literally at the center of the tent, so each dwelling "corner" is equidistant from it. In whatever way people distribute themselves indoors, they are still sitting or lying "around the fire." It is the woman who gathers the firewood, sets it out to dry near the door, splits it with an ax, and lights the fire. In legends she talks with the fire, listens to its crackle, and announces (or conceals) the news it has brought. A fire that crackles or flares up means that enemies are approaching or that guests from other worlds are about to appear.

The *symsy* pole is treated as sacred because it holds the cooking assembly over the fire (the horizontal poles *ti*, the hook *pa*, the kettle *ed*); smoke rises along the pole, passing through the upper window on its way "from house to heaven." The *symsy* pole is customarily marked with seven carved heads or faces; in a shaman tent it was crowned with the mythological bird Minlei.

The woman conducts all rituals connected with the domestic fire and the *symsy* pole. In the late 1920s, when V. P. Evladov and his companions spent the night in Nenets tents, they observed (while pretending to be asleep) that every night before going to bed their hostess would make the smoke ritual over the hearth and the sacred pole: "During the ritual the woman makes some kind of deep, throaty sounds resembling a reindeer's '*khork*.' These sounds are barely audible."[3] This sound (more like "kku," made deep in the throat) can be heard today during purification rituals. Such rituals, called *nibtara*, are conducted by Nenets women when new grass appears in the spring, when the reindeer shed their winter coats, after birthing and death, before long trips (especially to sacred places), after touching any "impure" object, and after visiting villages. During the ritual, smoke is passed over each object and person of the camp.

Data about making ritual smoke suggest that the role of "keeper" of the holy fire and smoke belongs to the woman. This is all the more remarkable given that, in most cases, the woman has to make the smoke over herself, or over anyone who needs purification because she has been at fault. Crossing the space between the hearth and the *symsy* pole is one of the most common sins committed by women, although both the hearth and the *symsy* pole would seem to be "female" sacred things.

Customarily the woman may place herself on any side of the fireplace or sacred pole and may touch either. Furthermore, setting up the *symsy* pole, lighting the fire, and observing the daily smoke ritual are the woman's duties, not the man's. Perhaps it isn't woman herself but her *step* that constitutes the sin that the Nenets call *kheiwy*. A woman's step is capable of breaking the sacred link between the hearth and *symsy*.

According to Nenets traditions, the woman must not step over a lasso, a *khorei* (the stick used for driving reindeer hitched to a sled), male clothing, weapons, hunting and fishing tools, or a harness. Nor should she cross the path of a moving caravan. All these actions can bring evil not upon her, but upon the man and the family's reindeer and possessions. When this kind of evil is brought upon a person, an animal, or an object, the Nenets say that the "power" or "life" then leaves them. If a woman wants to do a man harm, she

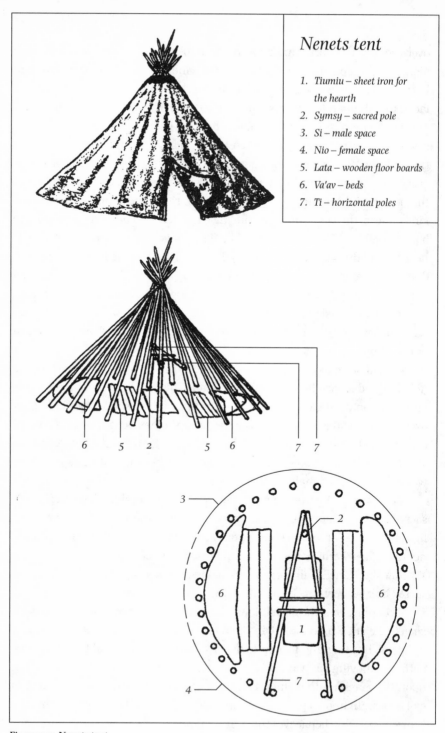

Nenets tent

1. *Tiumiu – sheet iron for the hearth*
2. *Symsy – sacred pole*
3. *Si – male space*
4. *Nio – female space*
5. *Lata – wooden floor boards*
6. *Va'av – beds*
7. *Ti – horizontal poles*

Figure 2.1. Nenets tent

steps over his things (first and foremost the *khorei*) with deliberate ill-intent. Legends tell of heroes who have overcome an enemy but cannot kill him because of the latter's shamanistic ability to instantaneously close his own wounds. The hero then calls a woman (usually his sister) to help him; he asks her to step over the enemy's body. This causes blood to flow from the wounds, and "real death" ensues. According to I. Lepekhin, when a dead man is brought out of a tent, the women step over the corpse "to make it impure, so that the impure-one could never again raise himself up." When the funeral procession arrives at the graveside, the women cut the belts "in which the dead man [is] entangled, making as they did so a little hole in each part of his clothing."[4]

Thus woman is endowed with the capacity to give death as well as to give birth. The organ possessing this "gift" is "child-making" and "life-taking" in equal measure. Its name (*pasy*) is a profanity, spoken more often than not by women themselves. Today it comes up when people quarrel or "exclaim in surprise"; however, if one recalls that "word magic" is a Nenets tradition, its original sorcerous intent cannot be ignored. *Pasy* probably has the same root as names denoting the most fearsome of diseases: *posa* (cholera), *poso* (small-pox), and *posabtsio* (plague).[5] In this context, the meaning of the stem *pa* (*po*) is related to the notion of transition ("passageway"), symbolizing a break in the circle of life. Both birth and death belong to the category of "break." We can say that the woman's "step" belongs there as well.

The Nenets consider a woman's legs a "shameful place." A daughter-in-law must not show her naked legs to her father-in-law, and the father-in-law, in his turn, must not look at them. According to Nenets Yuri K. Vaella-Aivaseda, "A Khanty woman covers her face and hair with a scarf; a Nenets woman covers her legs."[6] This also explains why the Nenets regard women's boots and the sled (*siabu*) used for carrying them as "impure" things. Legend has it that once an enemy's severed head is thrown onto the *siabu*, the foe is defeated forever. The "impure" sled, which combines the magic features of the under-the-hearth sheet iron and women's boots, is not just a "dirty thing"; it possesses a "low" power, *haeivy* (*haebiaha*), which is no less significant than the "high" ("male") power (*haehae*) that is concentrated in the sacred sled (*haehae han*). Therefore *siabu* and *haehae han* must never stand next to each other. They are the "poles" of the camp and stand at opposite sides of the tent.

These objects confront each other as man and woman do. The man should never touch *siabu*, nor should the woman touch *haehae han* (where the patron spirits *haehae* and men's weapons are kept). The man's place in the tent is *si* ("far from the entrance"), and the woman's place is *nio* ("near the entrance"). An imaginary line drawn from the fireplace through *si* to the outside will come out at *haehae han*; a line drawn in another direction (from the fireplace through the *nio*) will point to the *siabu*. These are the dimensions of male and female space in the dwelling and in the camp—dimensions originating, then diverging, from the center, from the hearth.

At the hearth these dimensions also converge. The conjugal bed (*va'àv*) sits in the space between *si* and *nio*. Both *si* and *nio* have the same literal meaning—a "hole" or "passageway." The sleds *siabu* and *haehae han* are equal in status. In camp they flank the tent; in a caravan *siabu* follows the woman's sled (*ne-han*), and *haehae han* follows the man's sled (*ngaedalyos*). Words denoting "sacred might" show this similarity: The feminine form sounds like *haeywy* ("low"), and the masculine one like *haehae* ("high"). When pronouncing *haebyoda* ("sinful") and *haebidya* ("holy") in quick succession, it is easy to make a mistake.

The primordial "hearth," which was the source of the notions *haehae* and *haeywy*, as well as of *hae'* ("thunder") and *hae* ("deep/whirlpool"), was most likely a symbol of some "living force" that filled all space—from the female "bottom/low place" and the male "top" to the very limits of the sky and the waters. Apparently this force has all the properties of fire—its warmth and brightness, its capacity for kindness or ill-will, its location in the center of the home. Fire accompanies all ritual and therefore serves as the language of the universe. Yet in Nenets, fire is called *tu*.

Actually, however, there is another "fire." It, too, is warm and red; it, too, is part of the language of ritual sacrifice. Its Nenets name, which contains the polysemantic root *hae*, is *haem* (*haebir*), or "blood."

Giving birth and taking life (of animals in the hunt or enemies in a fight) are both accompanied by bloodshed. According to legend, an enemy dies as soon as blood spurts from his "unhealed" wounds. The shaman who cuts himself with a blade during sorcery allows no blood to flow (his "wounds" must close immediately). A woman is able to give birth as long she bears the monthly "marks of blood" (in one tale a female Yamal shaman had never had children because she "had never had menses").

The blood (*haem*) that gives birth and death alike is also the "spirit" that opens and closes a person's life and serves as "power" (food) for the gods. The Nenets smear blood on the masks of the higher spirits; they leave drops of blood at abandoned campsites and sprinkle blood on the runners of sleds as a kind of ransom to the forces of the underworld. They pour blood into the water to pacify the raging elements. They strangle sacrificial reindeer with a lasso because the sacrifice must not have any bloody wounds; only unspilled blood is "alive" and pleasing to the gods. People themselves "must drink warm blood"; otherwise, according to Nenets beliefs, humans are doomed to die of cold on the tundra.

Woman, a source of blood, can break off human life, but she can also give it; she can weaken the sacred force of the *symsy* pole but also strengthen it. And woman can either confront or indulge the "dark" forces by standing at the dwelling's threshold. For this very reason, the woman's space in the *chum* (*nio*) is adjacent to the doorway.

The opposite part of the tent (*si*) is considered the man's: here the men sit and sleep. To be exact, it is not so much the man's space as sacred space; this is where the Nenets keep the box that is home to the patron spirits, and this is where they place the *symsy* pole; from here through *si* (but not through the door, *nio*), they carry out the little table used for ceremonies beside the sacred sled. This is the calmest part of the *chum*, shielded from people's constant bustling, from gusts of cold air or mosquitoes, and from dogs running about. *Si* is not merely the space –behind –the hearth meant for sitting or reclining. It is the entire space set apart by the length of the *symsy* pole. At the peak of the tent (where the pole tips cross) is the smoke hole, which the Nenets call *makoda si* (*makoda* refers to two main perches "standing on end"; *si* refers to "hole"). The sacred perch (*symsy*, *symzy*), by which the shaman climbs up to the sky and at which the summoned spirits gather, probably takes its name from the notion *si*. Mythological figures setting out to do battle with their enemies would leave the tent by flying out through this smoke hole. One might see in this the poetry of "heroic spirit" or a survival from some ancient time when the dwelling of not-yet-nomadic Nenets was a partially underground house with an exit through the roof (or with two exits—the everyday one in a wall and the "wartime" one in the ceiling).Whatever the case, *si* is considered "spiritual" ("smoke for heaven" rises out of it; "star time" flows past it, with the appearance of the Great Bear signaling that morning has come) and "masculine" (it connects the tent to the space of the open tundra).

The Nenets customarily set up a separate tent for a woman in labor, or the men may go elsewhere and leave her the whole tent. It is also the custom that the woman should not give birth where another woman has already done so.[7]

After a birth (just as after a death) the tent is moved to a different site. The former site is considered impure for a long time to come. If a birth or death has taken place in a house, the Nenets leave it uninhabited for several years.[8]

If one puts aside the vague notion of feminine "impurity," a place where a woman gives birth might be termed "sacred." In any case, places where there has been "much shamanizing" have the same forbidden status, and an "ordinary" tent must not be pitched there. We might speculate that labor and childbirth are themselves a kind of shamanizing. Here the woman not only summons the spirits but bears them within herself. "The instrument of sorcery" is her womb. There are amazing analogies between childbirth and the sorcery of "night shamans." In the course of shamanizing, "wild nature" comes into the human world through an empty kettle as if through a woman's belly. This is the "force" linking the woman's "low place" with the spirit of a hollow stump or a hole in the earth. This is the "impurity/sanctity" that men can neither control nor know, and that, as woman's "step," both frightens and attracts them. Herein lies the sacred mystery of "life creation" with which shamans try to commune.

According to popular opinion, communication with the higher gods is the prerogative of men. In Nenets tradition, women must not approach a sanctuary; their "temple" is the tent. Hence the prejudice that "high" religion is the sphere of men, whereas a set of minor (domestic) superstitions is women's. In Nenets spatial beliefs, however, the tent is a no less important dimension than is the expanse of the tundra. In some respects the tent is more significant; it is "near" rather than "far."

All collisions between worlds are played out as a struggle for possession. Beliefs depict all kinds of conquest in terms of overt or covert ownership of women. Mythical "strange people" may be endowed with all sorts of curious traits (they may eat moss, live underground, have one eye or three), but they nevertheless retain an ability (or even a heightened urge) to couple with "real people." In folktale and ritual the woman is a "door" to another country. Her "step" can turn people into enemies. As a result, both war (the passion to possess) and peace (possession through real or symbolic marriage) are, either implicitly or explicitly, a reflection of gender relations.

Male spirits of the light or dark worlds, omnipresent though they might be, are always "somewhere outside"; female images, however, exist "somewhere inside." In legends they are less active and noticeable but certainly present. Furthermore, men undertake heroic feats all for the sake of women; they are the object of men's deeds. Higher and lower gods may "pour out" their force into the world, but the goddess "gathers" this power into herself—apparently to "give birth" once again.

The idea of female spirituality might be expressed as the ability to bear life, and male spirituality as the ability to give it motion. The feminine pantheon is concentrated in the "home" and the masculine one in the "field." They are opposed and linked in equal measure. Or perhaps it is a case of the tighter the real link between male and female, the more pronounced the opposition, and only in alternation—coupling, breaking apart—can the rhythm of full-fledged life emerge.

The Rhythm of Activity

A number of observers have expressed surprise at the dreariness of daily life in a Nenets camp or Khanty settlement. M. A. Castren once remarked, "Ostiak [Khanty] for the most part live day by day, therefore one word—*chat*—signifies both 'day' and the necessities of life."[9] Indeed, the meaning of day-to-day work and social ritual consists in maintaining yesterday's well-being, in renewing the usual seasonal activities, in repeating the annual migration cycle, and so forth. Nevertheless, this monotony has its own "living" rhythm, expressed in two natural dimensions—alternating environmental conditions and the "exchange of energy" between man and woman.

Both Nenets mythology and everyday mentality deliberately set aside "real" time. For example, a folklore character may lie half-dead ("half-eaten by mice") for one to three years before reviving. A folklore battle, chase, or nonstop journey might take equally long. On the eve of a decisive fight, a hero's dream can last seven days—or three years.

Nor are the Nenets inclined to be exact in accounting for short stretches of time. The common expression *yed pihva* ("the kettle has boiled") does not so much measure time as mark a ritual of behavior—a pause used to separate one action (or state) from another. For instance, in scenes from legend, "Lamdo keeps silent for as long it would take to kindle a fire" or "They are silent for as long as it would take to boil a kettle."[10] Sometimes such a "measure" is used to stress immeasurability (for example, heroic strength): in the Forest Nenets folktale "Tyliku," the hero and a giant compete at tug-of-war with a mammoth "stick" for as long as "a kettle boils"; then when the "mammoth horn" breaks, they tug at an iron rod "for as long as a little kettle and a big kettle boil." (Actually such contests—*ngyhydarma*—last only a few seconds.)

In the words of Nenets Avvo Vanuyta, he who hurries on the tundra hurries to his death. The Nenets particularly enjoy anecdotes about someone who, in a rush, has bumbled something. They like to tell folk parables (*va'al*) about unlucky "hurriers." In one of them a partridge says, "Tomorrow I'm going to get up early." She makes her snow tent for the night and falls asleep. During the night her tail freezes to the snow; at sunrise something frightens her, and she tears out her tail as she flies away. That's why the partridge has no tail. As the parable teaches, Don't announce to the world that you are going to get up early tomorrow.[11]

The same attitude applies to those who insist on finishing a job before night comes. The Nenets consider it bad manners to be overly zealous in the evening—"There'll be a tomorrow, won't there?" In one *va'al* a woman wagers with the sun to see who is the quicker. Just as the sun's rim appears above the earth, the woman starts sewing a *yagushka*, which she intends to finish by that night. Half a day passes, and she has almost finished half of the *yagushka*. Night is approaching. Fearing she will not finish in time, the woman sends her children to see how high the sun is in the sky. They come back and tell her that it is sinking lower and lower. Just as the sun is about to set the woman is almost done with her sewing. "I finished my sewing," she says at last and begins to put on the new *yagushka*. At that moment her children come in and say, "Mother, the Sun has set." As soon as the words are said, the woman drops dead. And so the Nenets say, "*Syahard Haeradm ner nertimchu*" ("Never compete with the Sun").[12]

Anybody who has been sitting in a small northern airport for a couple of weeks and watching the calm faces of passengers in *yagushka* and *malitsa* as they wait for some unknown flight, might wonder: Are these the same Nenets who dash along on their reindeer-drawn sleds, who once a week (if not more often) pack up all their belongings and migrate to a new camp? How can a taste for lifelong wandering and a talent for endless waiting coexist in human character?

But let the fog lift over the airstrip or some faraway North Yamal cape, and it's time for action. Once boarding is announced, a Nenets will just happen to end up in the helicopter first and might even help the out-of-breath and inexplicably late "visitor" load his bags. In the nomad camp, where the helicopter lands briefly, a Nenets will immediately switch into a new rhythm, and while the guest fights the wind kicked up by the helicopter blades, the Nenets will manage to put on a new *malitsa*, change into a different pair of fur boots, and tell his relatives the news. In a matter of minutes the woman who has just arrived kindles a fire and puts on a kettle, while the man might immediately harness his reindeer and drive out to the herd to spell the tired herdsman.

The Nenets will hurry if they need to heat tea for guests, if the herd scatters in the fog or stampedes at the howling of wolves, if they need to set up a new camp after a long migration. In camp, the herdsman for the most part lies or reclines on his bed inside the tent, sits on a sled, walks around in unhurried fashion, or just stands, his hands hidden in the depths of his *malitsa*. He might meanwhile plane, sharpen, drill, mortise, smoke, or scratch himself, but he does all these things calmly. It is the women who make sudden movements—grabbing up children who are crawling toward the fire, quickly opening and closing the tent door (to keep out mosquitoes and frosty air), cleaning the table or utensils, and making or stripping the bed.

But women must stand calmly when they hold the rope that forms a corral for men to cut reindeer out of the herd. The men at the moment are transformed—they run from place to place, abruptly jumping and throwing the lasso; if they miss they rapidly reel it in, if not they start wrestling with the recalcitrant (and sometimes enraged) reindeer. Even in the bitterest cold they work without cowls or mittens.

The same swiftness of movement is common to men when they hop onto a sled pulled by eager reindeer, when they paddle a boat through high waves, when they throw out or take in a fishing net, when they grab a rifle from under a deerskin spread on their sled, when they compete at tug-of-war or jump over sleds. All these movements are brief, and are followed by a long stretch of "slow-motion" behavior.

The "slowness" has its own rhythm, predetermined by external reality, a reality that cannot be made "faster," that might in fact suffer damage or even turn hostile if dealt with too hastily. For example, testing fox traps too often is senseless—and might well reduce the fur harvest. Reindeer graze best when given complete freedom to move about and find their own food. For men or women, temperance of movement guarantees the "temperature" of both body and soul. Getting overheated leads to freezing in the winter or mosquito attacks in the summer. People "find" a rhythm in nature, instead of imposing one onto the environment. They don't hurry anybody or anything; they don't try to drag anything out or divide it up. If they do "invent their own time," it is obviously "not real"—which is why the legendary hero sleeps for three years and then chases or is chased for just as long.

Usually a nomad camp stays in one spot for no more than two weeks in the winter, one week in the summer, and two or three days in the spring or fall. The women spend about a hour in the wintertime or half an hour in summer setting up and taking down the tent. In legends the heroic woman strikes the tent so rapidly that she seems to just "walk around it." It isn't befitting for men to participate in this ritual, and besides, as V. P. Evladov remarked, men "don't know how to set up a tent well." Thus an unmarried Nenets man, "even if he owns enough reindeer, but has no woman in his household, considers himself unable to migrate, because there is no one to put up the tent."[13]

Most daily scenes follow the same pattern: when the woman is active the man is not, and vice versa. The custom of not helping each other is based on a practical rule ("Don't get in the way") and a ritual one ("Don't touch each other's things [field of action]"). This principle structures the culture: each person occupies her or his *own* place and is endowed with her or his own skill, which is quite sufficient for carrying out her or his *proper* duties. That is why the behavior of a guest who rushes to help his hostess chop firewood is perceived as humiliating for him and tactless toward her.

This is also why observers' laments over the "hard lot" of the northern woman "who is forced to work day and night" have an absurd ring. According to tundra etiquette, it's the other way round: an idle woman looks inept, disharmonious, and unattractive. If a woman wants to please a man, she first of all starts to work. Even a blind old woman will try to sew up to the very end of her life. The movements of women govern "the life of the *tent*," just as men's activity determines "the life of the tent on the *tundra*."

Men and women "switching on and off" by turns create the continuous internal rhythm of tundra life. The Nenets themselves don't consider their daily life monotonous—it is a matter of alternating effort, with each person temporarily taking on the responsibility for the common well-being.

3

Endurance: Chiefs against Rulers

"**F**rom now on, you will be called Eldest Yaptik," Junior Yaptik commands the next-to-the-eldest of his brothers in "Five Yaptiks," which illustrates an intrigue that is typical of Nenets heroic folklore. In such stories the younger relative "suddenly" assumes a senior role that had previously belonged to an older one. In fact, Nenets legends usually begin with the eldest brother leading a military band but end with the youngest becoming the winner over the innumerable enemies. One can see here some traces of ultimogeniture, which undoubtedly has been part of the Nenets' cultural values and practices. At the same time, these legends illustrate the flexibility of the Nenets leadership, its "democratic" or egalitarian character. Military chiefs appear and disappear, depending on circumstances; they could be few or many, men or women. This social ability to produce at once as many head warriors as necessary seems to be one of the Nenets' main "secrets of invincibility."

Russians who crossed the Ural Mountains to Siberia encountered different social traditions and military tactics. Tatars in the south were quite well known after centuries of Tatar-Russian confrontation and relationship. Middle-taiga Ugrians (Khanty) were less familiar but fairly manageable because they usually occupied fortified defenses and regularly dispatched detachments headed by native "princes" to raid their neighbors. The traditions and tactics of northern nomads, however, were considered mysterious and abnormal, as nomadic bands could suddenly scatter in the tundra like spilled mercury and then just as suddenly reappear. They had no fortresses or regular chiefs. For a long time the Russians had no strategy "to conquer a tundra"; therefore they chose to govern the tundra nomads via mediators—Ugrian leaders. The riddle "how to conquer a tundra" is still unresolvable on Yamal for anyone except the Nenets.

The Russian invasion and subsequent military subjugation of the native peoples of Siberia took place in the sixteenth and the seventeenth centuries.[1] To better understand the evolution of interaction of Russian/Siberian administration with northern native institutions, a Russian historian, Viktor A. Zibarev, has divided centuries of intensive interaction between Russians and indigenous peoples into three successive periods: direct rule (1580–1720), indirect rule (1720–1822), and the system of native rule (1822–1900). The first period might also be called the stage of military governors' rule. During that period native groups were registered in Russian forts and settlements for taxation (Russian: *iasak*). The Russians themselves collected the *iasak* and frequently took natives hostage to guarantee that other family and clan members would come to pay the tax (and liberate the hostage). During this period, Russian authorities, for the most part, did not intervene in the lives of the northern peoples. In the second period, that of indirect rule, all taxpayers were assigned to a local group (*ulus*) or clan headed by a local native leader (Russian singular: *rodonachal'nik*); under this system local mediators collected the *iasak* for the Russians. In the third period, reforms of Siberian governor Mikhail Speranskii established a system of native governance (with administrative, fiscal, and judicial functions) as a component of the Russian state machinery.[2]

These divisions highlight mostly the Russian state position and emphasize the evolution of government administration. To broaden the range of social relations between the Russians and Siberian natives that characterize the pre-Soviet period, we use other terms for nearly the same successive periods of (1) conquest, 1600s; (2) Christianization, 1700s; and (3) "legalization" of Russian authority, 1800s.[3]

The first period, which we call the "epoch of Ermak" (after the head of a Cossack detachment that was first sent to "conquer" Siberia in the 1580s), was the last time the chiefs of most native peoples played their customary sociopolitical roles. The local military confederacies' resistance to Russian troops seemed well-organized from time to time. Thus, for example, the Pelym Mansi crossed the Urals to make preventative strikes on the Russian fort Cherdyn, while a Khanty "army" of about 2,000 warriors fought on the Irtysh River against a detachment headed by a Cossack named Bogdan Briazga. The Sel'kup of the Pegaia Orda (Horde), in alliance with the famous Siberian Tatar leader Khan Kuchum, offered stiff resistance to Russian troops from the Surgut and Narym areas, while Samoyeds defeated a detachment headed by the Russian prince Miron Shakhovskoi in the lower Taz River.

During the tumultuous seventeenth century, some of the key political/military centers of Northwestern Siberia, such as the Pelym princedom and the Pegaia Orda, were defeated, while a powerful Koda (Khanty) princedom was incorporated into the administrative system of the new colonial government (see Map 4). The native "small princes" (Russian singular: *kniazets*) and "aristocrats" or "best people" (Russian plural: *luchshie liudi*) gradually became the "local elders" or "chiefs" (Russian singular: *starshina*), playing the role of intermediaries between the Russian state and the aboriginal people. At the same time, in regard to the native societies' internal affairs, the attention of the indigenous leaders tended to shift from the military-political to the religious arena. Explicitly or implicitly, shamans began to assume leadership roles, especially in those societies where shamanistic power had traditionally been an attribute of military chiefs.

From the indigenous peoples' viewpoint, the eighteenth century was a period of enforced baptism by the Russian Orthodox Church. That new stage of the Russian government's assertion of its control over Siberia could be called the "epoch of Filofei Leshchinskii," after the archbishop of Tobol'sk, the first to organize a campaign of mass baptizing of Ugrians and taiga Samoyeds. During this time many non-Christian ritual and ceremonial sacred sites were destroyed, and churches were built on them. Not surprisingly, this was also a time of persecution of shamans and the consequent considerable weakening of their influence. The Russian state's insistence on the "illegality" of the shamans' social status gradually elevated the influence of alternative "legal" leaders—the starshinas.

The nineteenth century could be called the "Speranskii epoch," so named for the Siberian governor who codified, developed, and was responsible for enforcing the 1822 statute "On the Administration of Non-Russians in Siberia" (*Ustav ob Upravlenii Inorodtsev*). That statute combined local customary law and Russian civil law into one system. In so doing, Russian authori-

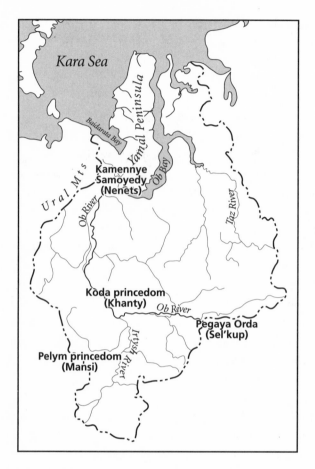

Map 4.   Princedoms in Northwestern Siberia

ties co-opted the native sociopolitical structures by allocating local governmental functions within the Russian administrative system to native leaders.
By legitimizing those leaders, the 1822 law allowed the Russian authorities to
regulate their activity "in accordance with the state law." Thus the Speranskii
reforms became one of the major steps in subordinating indigenous leadership to the Russian state.

Deviating in time and intensity, these processes occurred all over Siberia.
In Northwestern Siberia the periods had "classic forms" among the Khanty,
the Mansi, and the Sel'kup. On the contrary, tundra Samoyeds, the Nenets,
demonstrated their unique (and, to the Russians, peculiar) ways throughout

the three epochs: neither military raids, mass baptisms, nor administrative maneuvers of Russian authorities reached their proper goals on the tundra.

Epoch of Ermak

While Ermak battled in the southern taiga against the Tatars and their Mansi, Khanty, and Sel'kup allies, the northern tundra endured its own travails. A foreign boat was wrecked in the Ob estuary in the early 1580s, and all the crew was killed by Samoyeds. That news was reported to Moscow authorities by a captured Tatar, Prince Mametkul. Most likely the unfortunate seamen were English. At least as early as the mid-sixteenth century, the English had endeavored to reach the Ob River via the northern seas; notably, an English poet of the era devoted a few lines to Samoyeds, who attracted everybody with their treasure of sables. By one opinion, Samoyeds dealt harshly with visitors after learning of Ermak's raid. But it could be just a custom to attack any suspicious stranger. In 1556 a Russian coastal dweller, Loshak, having met an English boat led by Stephen Borough and traveling through the Kara Strait (*Karskie Vorota*), advised its master not to be careless in sailing farther, as Ob Samoyeds "are seeking every possible way to shoot down all the people who don't speak their language."[4]

Loshak told the English captain in detail how to reach the Ob estuary by sea and seemed himself to know well both the route and Samoyed customs, and perhaps their language as well. Many other accounts testify to the familiarity between Russian northerners and Siberian Samoyeds in this "pre-Russian era." Northern Russians from Great Novgorod discovered a way to "Midnight's lands" in the eleventh century or even earlier: the first record in the chronicles of their visit to Ugrian and Samoyed lands is dated 1092. Later on Russian northerners and coastal inhabitants contacted Western Siberian peoples. Sometimes there were military or tax-collecting raids; for example, Novgorod Governor Iadrei headed a failed expedition 1193;[5] for the most part, however, interaction was confined to an intensive private fur trade. It is not surprising that the special trade firm Iugorshchina (the name derives from "Ugrians") existed in Great Novgorod in the 1300s. In Siberia, Northern Russians (people from the Northern European region) were referred to as "walking people" (Russian plural: *guliashchie liudi*) or "trading people" (Russian plural: *promyshlennye liudi*). They seemed to "walk" and "trade" independent of political authorities, and sometimes they even formed alliances with their enemies, Samoyeds and Ugrians. In 1193, for example, a Russian man, Savka, participated in battle between Novgorod and Ugrian troops on the side of the latter.

In 1607 Russian officers registering taxpayers on lower Enisei for the first time listed a Samoyed clan under the name of Iasha Vologzhanin.[6] Vologzhanin literally means "dweller of Vologda," one of the biggest Northern Russian cities. Ethnographer Boris O. Dolgikh, searching for any folklore analogies to this fact, found a Taimyr Samoyed (Nganasan) story about a Russian boy, Kurzhanik, who was adopted and brought up by Samoyeds. Whether or not Iasha and Kurzhanik were the same person, it is notable that at least one Northern Russian could be a forefather of a Samoyed clan. It is hard to say on which side Iasha or his successors might have allied in the struggle between the Russian authorities and Samoyeds. In 1600, not far from Iasha's clan location on lower Taz, the detachment of the Russian prince Miron Shakhovskoi was defeated by Samoyeds. In any case, "walking" North-ern Russians retained their opposition toward Moscow governors after the long-term hostility between the Novgorod Republic and the Moscow Grand-Princedom.

Paradoxically, of all Samoyeds, the most northern dwellers in Western Siberia had the deepest and longest contact with Russians, and these relations lasted over five centuries, up to the eve of Ermak's "conquest." But those were particular Russians, free traders from the Novgorod Republic, who preferred to respect native traditions rather than suppress them. The Great Novgorod was finally defeated, and its inhabitants were cruelly massacred by Ivan the Terrible's Moscow army in 1570. In the late 1500s Moscow troops appeared in Siberia.

Siberian Samoyeds probably knew enough about current political changes either from their European relatives (the Samoyeds living west of the Urals) or directly from Novgorodians. At least, they were ready to meet Moscow messengers beforehand, and they triumphantly met them on the lower Taz in 1600. And then, in the course of the seventeenth century, Samoyeds openly warred against Russians, while in the taiga the struggle had already taken a different shape, one without revolts. The famous Russian his-torian Sergei V. Bakhrushin pointed out, "The Berezovo [Yamal, Ural, and Lower Ob] Samoyeds had not been registered in the 1600s even approximately, because in fact the government's power did not extend over tundra adjacent to the Lower Ob." The annual caravans shipping bread from Tobol'sk (an all-

Lakhati Yaptik, an elder of the Nine Yaptik camp, northern Yamal.

The authors (middle) with archaeological team at Mys Kamennyi on Yamal, July 1992.

Vladimir Ngoet Tadibe and Andrei Golovnev in the *chum*.

Tents at the Nine Yaptik camp, northern Yamal.

Women's guardian spirits of the *chum*.

Lidia Kiripova correcting the translation of "Five Yaptiks." Note the arrangement of women sitting close to the door and men reclining on the bed. The guardian spirits of the *chum* (women's gods) can be seen on the bedding next to the women. From the left: a neighbor, Lidia Tadibe, Ngoet Tadibe, and Boris Tadibe.

The greatest sacred place on Yamal, the "Seven Tents," northern Yamal.

A sculpture depicting the face of Yaptik-haesie, lying in the moss, northern cape of Yamal.

A patron spirit of the Seroteta clan.

Old Man Tadibe with his collection of knives. The handles are hewn from reindeer antlers.

The tent of Yamal Khada, "the Old Woman of the Edge of the Land."

Edeiko Ngokateta (guardian of the "Seven Tents" sacred place) and Andrei Golovnev by the "Seven Tents" site.

A Nenets herder roping reindeer, northern Yamal.

A Nenets couple in winter dress.

A Nenets mother and child, western Yamal.

A woman's sledge (designed to carry women and children in a caravan) in winter camp.

Putting up the *chum*, Yaptiksale.

A typical Nenets reindeer camp on the Yamal Peninsula, Yaptik-Sale tundra.

Raising the cover (Nenets, *niuk*) onto the tent frame.

Women of the Ngokateta clan.

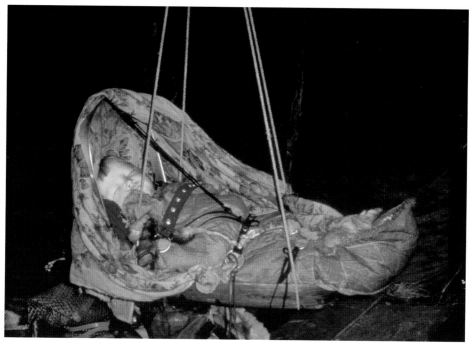

A Nenets baby in a traditional cradle.

A sacred place on the island of Litke.

Lidia Tadibe scrapes a reindeer hide in the August sunshine. Her son Boris carves a Nenets toy.

Siberian administrative center) to Mangazeia (a Russian fort and trade post on the lower Taz) were often attacked by "bellicose Samoiad." In the 1660s Taz Samoyeds beat Russian tax collectors and traders in Mangazeia, while Ural and Yamal Samoyeds prepared a raid on Berezovo. In April 1679, 400 Samoyeds laid siege to Obdorsk for six days. In the 1690s, after a campaign by Mangazeia's governor against Samoyeds on the Pur River, kinsmen of the Samoyeds came upon Mangazeia, captured soldiers with their wives and children, beat them with sticks, and threw their dead bodies into the river. Russian officers complained of the Samoyeds' fierce practice of cutting noses and fingers off of their dead enemies, and were rankled by the impossibility of capturing them, because, faced with defeat, Samoyeds preferred death to surrender.[7]

That was a hectic time of mobile warfare, a time to increase reindeer herds by all possible means. The maneuverability of Samoyeds was a headache for Russian governors. Bakhrushin, quoting from Russian archival documents, wrote, "The slightest cause—and they [Samoyeds] take flight like a flock of birds frightened off by a man. In the Berezovo region, the administration attempted to capture just a few Samoyeds to be *amanat* [tax hostages], and 'those Samoyeds who were in Karachei [clan], those nomad-folk, dispersed right away to Mangazeia and to Enisei and to Piasida [Taimyr Peninsula] and other remote rivers.'"[8] The Khanty, forest dwellers, explained the specific temper of their tundra neighbors to Russian officers: "They, Samoyeds, are people of savagery and freedom."[9]

Samoyeds acquired a reputation reflected in the titles of Russian chronicles—"*vorovskaia Samoiad*" (Samoyeds robbers), "*nemirnaia Samoiad*" (bellicose Samoyeds), and, on the nearby Taz River, even "*krovavaia Samoiad*" (bloody Samoyeds). Those epithets were not applied to the Nenets' southern neighbors, the Khanty, the Mansi, and the Se'kup, or at least they were no longer used in the 1600s. Nevertheless, the southern neighbors had no less military experience. As Castren, a prominent nineteenth-century specialist in Uralic ethnology, has noted,

> Long before they were visited by Ermak, primitive Siberian peoples had already acquired a great deal of experience in the bloody fun of war. . . . Blood was often spilled as a consequence of internecine conflict between clans within the same tribe. The entire region was involved in a . . . *bellum omnium contra omnes* (Latin: "war of all against all"). . . . Eventually a few

separate families within the same clan or tribe would unite and elect a chief or prince for their entire group.[10]

Archaeological surveys have verified the existence of fortifications every-where in the forests of the Ob River region. In the areas occupied by the Khanty, the Mansi, and the Sel'kup, fortifications date from the early Iron Age and the Middle Ages (700 B.C.E. to the 1600s C.E.). Ugrian and Sel'kup folklore contains numerous references to military conflicts headed by "princes." Such groups as the Koda Ostiak (now called the Ob-Atlym Khanty), the Pelym Vogul (the Southern Mansi), and the Pegaia Horde (the Narym Sel'kup) each had a reputation for being the most bellicose among their neighbors. Their "capitals" were governed by "grand princes" whose own status as well as those of their satellites, called *bogatyr* (Russian for "mighty warrior"), were based on heredity and rank. Russian officers very seldom, and if so, most likely mechanically, called Nenets leaders "princes." But almost no traces of fortifi-cations have been found in the Western Siberian tundra.

It is risky to analyze the historical roots of native leadership in North-western Siberia from the archaeological finds known today, or from medieval chronicles that often used vague and uncertain terms. Different scholars could interpret the same data in opposite ways. For example, Bakhrushin con-sidered it possible to speak about "Ostiak-Vogul feudalism."[11] In contrast, Nikolai N. Stepanov[12] and many other scholars after him saw no basis for sim-ilar evaluations and characterized the traditional social relations among the indigenous peoples of Northwestern Siberia as archaic, very simple, and poorly developed. Perhaps the same contradiction would appear after a suffi-cient number of tundra archaeological sites have been excavated. Combined with folklore characteristics,[13] however, the sketchy data can be used to trace certain features of Samoyed and Ugrian war styles.

Both Samoyed and Ugrian military ethics contrasted sharply with the morality of everyday life. All imaginable forms of violence against the enemy were allowed and even encouraged, including treachery, thievery, assault, and murder. References to scalping, burning, and human sacrifice can be found in myths and historical tales.

The specific features of a native way of life, such as Nenets pastoral nomadism in contrast to the relatively sedentary existence of the Khanty and the Mansi, had a major impact on the distinct norms and styles of Samoyed and Ugrian warfare. Ugrians used sophisticated methods of defending their fortresses. In the summer they deployed boats on the rivers and annihilated enemies as soon as they arrived. In fact, the sighting of an unknown boat in the distance could trigger an alarm. A visit by strangers was considered to be an invasion, unless the "guests" behaved in accordance with particular social norms that signaled their friendly intentions. An *urt* (chief) who saw himself as the strongest in his region would construct his fortified settlement on the highest ground, while persons below him in status would settle on lower ground. One of the features of Ugrian warfare is particularly remarkable: according to folktales, the death of the chief inevitably led to the destruction of his settlement and the dispersion of its inhabitants. As the foregoing characteristics demonstrate, the forest-dwelling people living in isolated and close-knit communities had clear ideas of the boundaries of their own lands and the lands of others.

Nomadic Samoyeds (the Nenets), who often came across strangers on the tundra, had their own customary "ritual" for recognizing and testing potential foes. A standard sign of a challenge to fight was someone knocking on the pole of a person's tent. Usually this "knock" was accompanied by the words "Would you like to be killed inside the tent, or would you come outside to fight?" For the Nenets, unlike Ugrians, the idea of a foreign invasion into their territory was not sharply defined—consequently, we find no fortifications on the tundra. Here battles were conducted in the open space. According to Nenets' tales, the best method of defense was a rapid preventative raid against the enemy. Generally speaking, for the Nenets, defense against an enemy meant protection of the residents of a camp and their reindeer herd rather than protection of a particular area of land. Escape was not necessarily seen as defeat, but only a tactical maneuver, as is typical of many other nomadic societies. In Nenets folklore, a fighter rarely waged warfare alone, and a leader's fall never signified inevitable defeat. On the contrary, the more frightening the folkloric image of a hero's death, the more triumphant was his relatives' eventual revenge against his killers.

In Nenets tales, an army's size was described symbolically by means of large numbers—"ten times ten times three," "nine times nine times seven," and so on. In describing an actual gathering of warriors (*mandalada*), the Nenets would use such metaphors as "the troops' movements looked as if the earth itself was moving" or "mosquitoes droning" or "the tundra wavered under the feet of warriors." The Nenets had no permanent military leaders. Instead, their many potential war leaders (*saiu erv*), under special circumstances of warfare or revolt, could become actual military leaders. Those chiefs, like leaders of group hunts (*serm paertia*), could be replaced on the march under certain circumstances; for instance, after they lost the way, or if the reindeer showed unusual anxiety, or if some other bad omen had happened. That feature of nomad society, a kind of social flexibility, of "democratic military leadership," denied the Nenets' enemies a complete victory. Russian reports of victory in the earliest campaigns against peoples of "Midnight's land" used the terms "lay siege," "capture," and "occupy" in regard to Ugrians, but they only used "kill" in regard to Samoyeds. During a military expedition across the Ural Mountains in 1499–1500, Prince Semeon Kurbskii's detachment is reported to have occupied forty-one Ugrian *gorodoks* (little fortresses) and captured fifty-eight Ugrian princes; in addition, Russian warriors "killed fifty Samoyeds on the Kamen [Urals] and took two hundred reindeer."[14]

This explains why societies of forest-dwellers (for example, the Khanty), in comparison with those of the tundra (for instance, the Nenets), offered greater resistance against the Russian invaders and eventually suffered greater defeat. Among the forest people, the "aristocracy" was defeated first and then partially transformed into the high-ranking servants of the new rulers.

The end of Ermak's epoch was not the end of warfare for Samoyeds. In the early 1700s they remained nominally registered under Russian sovereignty. Undefeated, tundra Samoyeds had used the time to adapt their culture for new conditions. Their adaptation took the form of a transition to pastoralism. Perhaps their preparedness for this quick transition in some respect had been developed during the long period of contacts between Samoyeds and Northern (Novgorod) Russians. Those contacts could be a sort of social vaccination against the later powerful Moscow pressure.

It is not surprising that Russian authorities exercised their power in the tundra in an indirect way. In the early 1600s, the Moscow government had declared Khanty prince Vasilii Obdorskii (the forefather of the Taishin dynasty) to be ruler over all Obdor country "'till the coast of the Arctic ocean." But Prince Vasilii had been hanged by Russians in 1607 or 1608, as had his grandson Ermak in 1663, both for attempts to raise rebellions. All the other representatives of the "governing" clan in the 1600s (Mamruk, Molik, Gynda, and Tuchabalda) demonstrated more conformity with ideas of Samoyeds than loyalty to Moscow, although in 1679 Prince Gynda traveled to

Moscow to ask for support against Samoyeds.[15] The main reason that Obdor princes observed Russian laws was for the privilege of collecting tax on behalf of Moscow. Gradually the ruling Khanty clan, staying on the border of confrontation, became the real mediator between Russians and Samoyeds. The clan later received the name "Taishin," after its representative Taisha, son of Prince Gynda, was christened and given the name Aleksei. But that happened in another epoch, in the early 1700s.

Epoch of Leshchinskii

Cossack Ermak had never visited the tundra (or we know nothing of it), but Bishop Filofei Leshchinskii did. In 1726 he reached a northern frontier of the forest, sailing a boat from Tobol'sk to Obdorsk. Only God knew this travel, and this year was the last for the famous Siberian baptizer. From the time this brilliantly educated Ukrainian priest had left Kiev in 1702 for Tobol'sk (at the order of Emperor Peter the Great) to lead the Siberian diocese, a whole era passed. His life in Siberia, spanning almost a quarter century, was overshadowed by conflicts with conceited Tobol'sk governors, by political discord between Ukraine and Russia, and by his own temporary retreat from his post as metropolitan and his renunciation of the world to enter a monastery. Nonetheless, Bishop Filofei (then Monk Feodor) did not retire from his major goal—to spread "enlightenment" all over Siberia. He and his confederates built there thirty-seven churches and baptized nearly forty thousand pagans and adherents of other creeds.[16]

In the early 1700s, a few Western Siberian indigenous people converted to Christianity, mostly those of the clan of Ugrian prince Alachev from Koda. In 1600 one Obdor prince was baptized while visiting Moscow under the name of Vasilii. On returning home, he at once forgot Orthodox precepts and loyalty to Moscow. He was soon executed. All his descendants in the 1600s (Mamruk, Molik, Gynda, and Tuchabalda) remained heathens. On December 2, 1706, Emperor Peter ordered the Berezovo *voevoda* to ask two Khanty princes, Sheksha from Liapin and Tuchabalda from Obdor, whether they would like to be baptized, but instructed him not to use force. Both princes refused.[17]

At the end of the same year, the emperor charged metropolitan Filofei to bring Christianity to the Khanty and the Mansi. His instructions were "to burn and destroy all the idols and heathen temples, wherever found, and on those places to build churches, chapels, and to put up the icons." Those who would like to be baptized, "to release from all previous years' [tax] arrears and give them out from the state treasury caftans, shirts and bread." In 1707 Filofei sent several missionaries to Berezovo Khanty, but they were not sufficiently successful. Most Khanty, "due to their affection towards their fathers' belief, would not even hear about new faith, and received and *saw off* the missionaries embitteredly."[18]

In 1710 Peter I repeated his demand with a remarkable addition: "Those of Ostiaks [Khanty] who would show resistance to this great sovereign's decree, should be punished by death."[19] In 1712 Filofei (at that time called Feodor), accompanied by interpreters, assistants, and dozen of Cossacks, sailed from Tobol'sk to the north. Beforehand, instructions had been sent to local authorities "to gather *inorodtsy* [natives] in places close to the [Ob] River."[20] That was the start of a new policy of enforced baptizing of Western Siberian natives, and of a new relationship between them and the authorities, and even among themselves, henceforth separated into Christians and heathens.

The baptizing went on year by year, advancing northward. In 1714, after missions succeeded in southern regions, Filofei arrived at Berezovo. The Khanty (Ostiak) and the Mansi (Vogul) had as usual been gathered from all the neighborhood ahead of time and "accepted christening without resistance." Six Ugrian princes initially came through the ritual. Among others there was Taisha, son of Gynda, from Obdor. Accompanied by his wife, Taisha entered into the Sos'va River "as into Jordan" and then received the new name Aleksei. Thus Christianity reached Obdor natives.[21]

Three years later, in 1717, Filofei decided to march into the heathen stronghold, the Obdor area. Officer Nikita Paltyrev received a command to leave Berezovo for Obdorsk, and there, ahead of time, to gather Ostiaks from the area and to detain those who were in town already. Paltyrev fulfilled his task, and Filofei saw from aboard a crowd on the Ob River bank. But Ostiaks "did not allow him even to land."[22] Prince Taisha-Aleksei watched the scene from his residence. It was his revenge for "swimming" in the Sos'va River. Historical sources unanimously named him the provocateur of the Ostiaks' rebellion.

Filofei retired and returned to Tobol'sk. Prince Taisha launched a counterattack. In 1718 he directed his younger brother Mikishka with a detachment of Samoyeds to go south, "to take vengeance on the newly-christened for their betrayal of *iazychestvo* [heathenism]." Taisha encouraged his brother, "Wherever you find prince Semeon of Liapin [one of the six newly christened princes], right away lift him up on the spears, but do not let his blood drop on the earth, and then put him to death." Samoyeds brutally raided the Ostiak converts. On the Liapin River they robbed villages, beat men, "violated women and, naked, threw them into snow"; they "killed two men to death, and disemboweled the dead, ripped open their chests, cut out their private parts and put them into the mouths [of the dead]." Prince Semeon pleaded for Russian authorities to take him out from Liapin to Tobol'sk.[23]

Samoyed raids against the "faithless" rolled over the whole Berezovo region. The official reports from the 1720s are full of troubled news. In 1722 Obdor Samoyeds "robbed and killed christened Ostiaks" on the Kunovat River. Another band of 130 Samoyeds raided settlements on the Liapin River again and smashed the small town [*gorodok*] of Prince Semeon. They plundered a church and burned the town itself. Some of the inhabitants were killed, and their corpses were "barbarously maimed." Moving along the Liapin River, Samoyeds killed Ostiaks, "took the crosses from them and tied [the crosses] to the tips of *khorei* [Nenets: long stick to drive harnessed reindeer]; they dragged on the ground the holy icons tied to the sledges."[24]

In 1720 Filofei Leshchinskii hustled about, trying to obtain the release of all the newly christened from any taxation. In 1722 he petitioned the Tobol'sk governor to defend Ostiaks against Samoyeds. Berezovo officers received an order to guard the Ostiaks' villages and to send several Cossack detachments to the northern territories. After a while the Cossacks brought to Berezovo *amanats* (hostages) from Samoyed tribes of both sides of the lower Ob. Some Samoyed leaders were captured as well and publicly executed. Samoyeds Tereva, Kel'ta, and Gaicha were whipped. The "chief ringleaders" were hanged on the places of their crimes—Punzy and Nemda in Obdorsk town, Kharka in Kazym town, and Obyndia in Liapin town. After that, Samoyed rebelliousness seemed to calm.[25]

In 1726 Bishop Filofei again sailed to Obdorsk, to the land of the Samoyeds. Perhaps he understood that this could be his last expedition. As he had nine years earlier, he looked at the Ob River bank crowded by nearly a hundred natives. This time the boat crew was prepared to overcome any hindrance to land. The boat moved alongside the shore, and Filofei "started to persuade [the crowd] to leave their idols and to worship the true God," but the heathens "shouted at him, cursed him, and at last shot arrows at him and his companions; since then the elder had to leave Obdorsk."[26] The last duel of the Siberian Baptizer against Samoyeds had been lost.

Bishop Filofei and his "godson," Prince Taisha-Aleksei, died at about the same time. The heirs of Taisha also were christened, but with particular attention from authorities. The godfather of Vasilii Taishin in 1742 became the Tobol'sk governor Sukharev. The newly christened prince was presented with a red caftan and two shirts. Leaving Tobol'sk, he asked the governor to send a priest with him and to build a church in Obdorsk. At home the prince, followed by the priest, was met by "unfriendly" Samoyed and Ostiak kinsmen, who, upon seeing the prince cross himself, were ready to kill him.[27]

The church was built in Obdorsk in 1746 and later hallowed by the name of Vasilii. A century later, while visiting Obdorsk for trade, Samoyeds circled the church, threw silver coins into the yard and offered fur for icons. In 1899, during liturgy when all the Christians were inside, fifteen Samoyeds sacrificed a reindeer nearby. They did so because the church was erected on an ancient place sacred to Samoyeds.[28]

Until the end of the eighteenth century, Russian attempts to baptize Samoyeds and Northern Ostiaks (who were close to Samoyeds in lifestyle and beliefs) became more rare, although they were renewed many times during the following centuries. A policy of "soft" baptizing was substituted in the late 1700s in the period of "enlightened absolutism" of Empress Yekaterina II. In 1789 the Russian Senate decreed a halt to missionary activity in the northern and eastern territories.[29] At the same time, secular authorities increased in power. In 1767 Yekaterina II solemnly confirmed all previous privileges of the Obdorsk prince Taishin and officially ennobled the Ostiak clan.[30] The *iasak* reforms of 1763–69 banned the practice of taking tax hostages and transferred the right and responsibility for *iasak* collection to local native chiefs and elders.[31]

Involuntarily or deliberately, political changes reduced the influence of local shamans, who had played leading roles in confrontations with the Orthodox Church. They were replaced with "legal" leaders subordinated to Russian authority. The hard years of "religious wars" were behind. Samoyeds, having won the duel with Bishop Filofei, strengthened their system of religious leadership. Let us trace roughly the features of shamanistic patterns of northern Samoyeds (the Nenets) and their taiga neighbors.

Among the Nenets, three categories of shamans existed: the *vydutana* (*sevndana*), who appealed to the upper/sky spirits; the *yangangy*, who communicated with the ghosts of the lower world; and the *sambana*, who were capable of penetrating the land of the dead and conveying the souls of the dead into it. The Sel'kup shamans were divided into the *sumpytyl'kup* (from *sumpyko*, "to conjure in the light"; that is, in a tent with a burning fire) and the *kamytyryl'kup* (from *kamytyrko*, "to conjure in a dark tent"). Among the Khanty there were the *arekhta-ku* (from *arekh*, "song"), the *ulom-verta-ku* (from *ulom*, "dream"), the *nyukyl'ta-ku* ("conjuring in the dark"), the *isylta-ku* ("healing man"), the *pankal-ku* ("the man who eats the fly-agaric mushroom"), and the *chirta-ku* or *yolta-ku* (from *yol*, "sorcery"). The Mansi shamans were divided into the *koiupyng nyayt* ("conjuring with a drum"), the *nas-pengne nyayt* ("summoning patron spirits of the clan"), and the *mutran nyayt* ("harmful magician").[32]

The division of the shamans into the "light" and the "dark" ones did not mean that one brought good and another evil. In fact, Sel'kup informants assert that the two types of shamans supported rather than competed against each other. Both groups protected the people, with the "light" ones appealing to the forces of the above (sky spirits) and the "dark" ones to those of the netherworld. Under certain circumstances, a "white" shaman could turn into a "black" one, and vice versa. According to the Kazym Khanty, this could happen if an "upper" shaman appealed to the spirits of the below to bring disease upon his people's enemies (for example, at the start of a war). Therefore a community's white shaman could be seen as a black one by its enemies.

The impact of Christianity on shamanism was most pronounced in the forest zone, especially among the Mansi, whose shamans even borrowed Christian attributes and tended to turn themselves into the intermediaries between the new official religion and the traditional indigenous one. Because of strong Russian influence, the shaman in Mansi society acquired a similar reputation to that held by clairvoyants in Russian Christian communities. Among the Khanty, shamans usually did not advance as a special social category. According to popular opinion, every man "could shamanize a little," and real shamans differed from other people only by possessing higher religious skills. This allows us to describe their shamanism as "democratic."

In contrast to Ugrians, the Sel'kup regarded the shamans as the "masters" of distinct domains, people whose influence spread over an entire set of interrelated social institutions and relationships. According to Prokofieva, the last "great shaman" among the Taz Sel'kup was David Kalin, who at the turn of the century lived on the Khudosey River, a tributary of the Taz River. Referred to as Tama Ira, he was considered to be "the force that controlled everybody in the neighborhood." The people of that area carefully examined every success or failure of their spiritual leaders. Frequent failures doomed a shaman to losing his relatives' trust, while success gave him incontestable authority. The Sel'kup conducted their annual festivals during duck migrations, when shamans performed their new songs and the community made a decision about enlarging or diminishing the size of their shaman's drum, depending on whether the conjurer's power was seen as increasing or diminishing.

The Nenets shamans were usually highly respected and cloaked in mystery; any important events, including wars or natural calamities, presupposed their intervention. Shamanistic talent was an obligatory feature of a great leader. Nenets mythology usually depicts heroes as being capable of flying through the sky and bringing themselves back to life. In folktales and personal recollections, the appearance of real historical leaders sometimes has miraculous attributes.

During the Russian colonial era, the social roles of the Samoyed shaman differed greatly from that of the Ugrian, with the former enjoying the status of "the sovereign of his neighborhood," and the latter reduced to a lowly status. Various outside influences weakened the Ugrian shamans. Conversion to Christianity and other external political pressures were more detrimental for Ugrian peoples, who were more accessible to outsiders. Various other factors from within the native culture itself, however, could also be responsible for this weakening: in Samoyed nomadic and semi-nomadic societies, the shaman had played the same role as the chief aristocrat (prince, *bogatyr*) played in Ugrian societies. Leadership among Ugrians had more of a "civic" character than leadership among Samoyeds, whose leaders were, first and foremost, shamans. That is why the Nenets system of "democratic" military leadership paralleled the Khanty system, which we have called "democratic" shamanism.

In "religious wars" between christened Ugrians and pagan Samoyeds (the latter were accompanied by northern Khanty) we can see many traits derived from shamanism. Cutting off fingers, taking out hearts, forbidding a victim's blood to drop on the ground, throwing naked bodies onto the snow, and other horrifying actions were not actually targeted to the Khanty as a people. Rather, they were acts of exorcism to expel the evil spirit of Christianity. Samoyed successes provided growth of their shamans' warrior status. Finally, it became clear to Russian authorities that further religious pressure on stubborn heathens such as the Samoyeds could bring contrary results; thus they changed their strategy. Meanwhile, the nomadic Samoyeds, at least in comparison with their taiga neighbors, emerged as successfully from this second round of interaction with the Russian empire as they had the first one. In the seventeenth century they advanced in warfare and mobile reindeer herding; in the eighteenth century they strengthened the religious frame of their culture.

Epoch of Speranskii

The 1822 Statute on Administration of Non-Russians in Siberia, initiated and compiled by the Siberian governor-general Mikhail Speranskii, declared that "non-Russians who confess no Christianity have freedom to perform worship by their law and rituals." The Russian clergy was required in missionary activity to treat non-Russians "by mild rules, only by persuasion and with the least compulsion."[33] Although this position was addressed particularly to *kochevye* (nomadic) and *brodiachie* (wandering) non-Russians, the latter, *brodiachie*, to which Samoyeds were ascribed, immediately experienced religious shock. In 1827 the mission headed by Archimandrite Veniamin devastated the greatest Samoyed sacred place, located on Vaigach Island, burning and destroying there more than four hundred idols.[34] At the same time, most of the Samoyeds in the European tundra were christened. Five or six hundred fled over the Urals to the Obdor tundra.[35] Obdor Samoyeds and Ostiaks were on the edge of a new religious revolt. They planned to gather at the Obdorsk fair and "to beat all the Russians to death and to do the same with those non-Russians who wore their hair like Russians" (heathens wore plaits). A Samoyed elder, Paigol, who had recently been given a red velvet caftan by the authorities, came to the governor saying, "For what have I been given this red caftan? I did not do anything special. If it is to baptize us, I do not need the caftan."[36]

The Orthodox Church attempted to extend Archimandrite Veniamin's mission to the Siberian tundra. In 1828 a special mission was established in Obdorsk. But Samoyed chiefs and the Obdorsk prince Matvei Taishin hindered all the actions of priests. After five years, in 1833, missionaries returned to Tobol'sk with a list of only seventeen newly baptized. It was not a good time for further experiments in conversion. From that time, a cascade of rebellions rolled over the Obdor tundra. The religious confrontation became complicated by new administrative norms.

Speranskii's 1822 statute stirred additional controversy in lower Ob relations. The statute tried to incorporate indigenous customary law within the Russian legal system. Speranskii, an intimate advisor of Emperor Alexander I, who appointed him governor-general of Siberia, was, as portrayed by biographer Marc Raeff, an enlightened advisor and governor whose interest and concern for natives earned him a good reputation among them.[37]

The statute brought a uniform law for all of Siberia and defined the powers of the native administration and its interrelations with Russian authorities. At the same time the law distorted the preexisting customary indigenous system by creating administrative divisions not existing in the nomadic native encampments. The law did not provide a real channel for interacting with native leaders, and its implementation triggered conflict.

Significantly, the statute divided the native population into three categories: *brodiachie* ("wandering": migrating throughout the year from camp to camp), *kochevye* ("nomadic": changing residences seasonally), and *osedlye* ("settled": living in villages or settlements), with each category having a different tax policy and law.[38] The Nenets were included in the first category and exempted from most taxes. Their southern neighbors (the Mansi, the Khanty, and the Sel'kup) were attached to the "nomadic" group. While exempted from payment of fur tribute, they were subjected to a local tax. Some southern groups of Khanty, Mansi, and Sel'kup (which were considerably mixed with Russian and Tartar) were assigned to the category of "settled" natives and classified as state peasants. The latter were subjected to a tax that was sometimes ten times greater than what natives previously had paid; thus many settled natives went to extremes to show that they were really "nomadic."

The Obdorsk Ostiaks (Khanty), who had been classified as "nomadic," protested the differentiation in classification and taxes between them and the neighboring "wandering" Samoyeds (Nenets). The Samoyeds, for their part, being officially separated from "nomadic" Ostiaks, used this opportunity to establish their own administration, thereby removing themselves from the rule of the Obdorsk Ostiak Prince Taishin.[39] Even in 1821, before the statute was completed, seven Samoyed chiefs had refused to be subordinated to the Ostiak prince and had paid *iasak* directly to Russian authorities.[40] After implementation of the statute, Samoyeds elected their own "chief elder," Paigol Nyrmin, who on this occasion was given the aforementioned red velvet caftan.

As told by traveler and physician Franz Beliavskii, Paigol was elected owing to his "venerable old age" (he was ninety) and his position as an elder of the largest clan, Karachei. One of Paigol's three wives, originating from the European tundra and fluent in Russian, played an important role as interpreter for Samoyeds. Paigol and Prince Taishin occupied opposite poles of the Obdorsk tundra community: some of Samoyeds supported and paid taxes to Paigol, while others continued to deal with Taishin.[41]

In 1827 Russian navigator V. Ivanov arrived in Obdorsk for a hydrographic expedition on the Yamal Peninsula. Paigol decisively refused to assist the expedition with transport and guides, even for payment. He asserted that the navigator had been sent "to measure the lands for the purpose of later taking these lands away [from Samoyeds]." (The Speranskii statute had proclaimed state ownership of all the land and then "granted" possessory rights to the natives.) Prince Taishin, contrary to Paigol, ordered the expedition to go forward, declaring it "sacred, because it contains the will of the Khan [Sovereign]." Ostiaks and Samoyeds loyal to Taishin led the expedition through all of Yamal. Taishin won that round. A while later, the prince once more gained the upper hand over the Samoyed elder when he obtained an order reascribing Obdorsk Ostiaks to the same category as Samoyeds: "wandering."[42] Paigol seemed to lose power step by step. He soon died, and Samoyeds found themselves under Prince Taishin's rule again.

While the elder Paigol confronted Prince Taishin in Obdorsk, another leader appeared in the remote tundra. Vauli Piettomin, from the Neniang (Mosquitoes) clan, gathered a "band of robbers." In early 1839 Vauli was captured and brought to Obdorsk by Taishin's adherents. The prince reported to Russian authorities that the captives had robbed other Samoyeds and Ostiaks (supposedly loyal to Taishin) over a period of ten years. Vauli and his companion, Mairi Khodin, were whipped (given twenty lashes publicly) and exiled to Surgut.[43]

In September 1839 Surgut officer Shiriaev informed Berezovo authorities that Vauli and Mairi had escaped from Surgut and were headed to Obdorsk. Berezovo authorities hastily set an ambush on the approach to the lower Ob towns, but rebels avoided the Russian forts at Berezovo and Obdorsk. Vauli appeared in his clan's land, the "Lower Side" (the lowlands east of Obdorsk). He declared himself "chief elder" (*glavnyi starshina*) over all non-Russians of the Obdor *volost* (district),[44] thus claiming Paigol's former position and, further, that position still held by Taishin. Moreover, Vauli proclaimed himself "*parangoda* of Lower Side." That would have seemed to the Nenets a pretentious move (they had previously applied this title only to the czar), but Vauli, a powerful shaman, had considerable leadership capabilities.

Vauli acted decisively. In 1839–40 his band grew to 400. He replaced two official Samoyed chiefs and declared his program to lower prices for Russian bread and other trade items and to reduce taxes from two polar foxes to one. He sent his messenger to Obdorsk with an order to cease tax collection until he himself arrived there for the winter fair. According to records of that time, Obdorsk dwellers (mostly Russians) and Ostiaks were frightened by these events; "each of them was in fear of being killed, or at least, robbed."[45]

Chief officer (*ispravnik*) Skorniakov urgently arrived from Berezovo to lead the campaign against Vauli. Plotting to trap Vauli in Obdorsk, he called on Prince Taishin to pretend fear of the Samoyed chief. He then spread a rumor of Taishin's readiness to yield to all the rebel's demands and sent the Russian merchant Nechaevskii, a trading partner of Vauli, to locate the Samoyed rebels and inquire of their intentions. Being hospitably received, Nechaevskii expressed his respect for Vauli's power and invited him to be his guest in Obdorsk. Vauli responded with an order for the prince to meet him.

Vauli's band of 200 stopped about 100 miles from Obdorsk, waiting for the prince. On January 13, 1841, Prince Taishin and ten clan chiefs arrived at Vauli's encampment. From the beginning, Vauli treated the Ostiak prince as a Nenets master might have treated a lowly worker. He cursed him and reached to strike him with a reindeer antler; only the interference of Nechaevskii saved the prince. Either the prince was in fact frightened or he played well the role prescribed by Skorniakov. He bowed at Vauli's feet and kissed his arm (the ten chiefs did the same) and offered to yield his position as prince of Obdorsk or to pay tribute to Vauli. Enraged, Vauli declared Taishin stripped of his power. Prince Taishin and the chiefs, familiar with the bellicose habits of Samoyed shamans, expressed complete accession and narrowly escaped from Vauli's camp.

A few days later Vauli moved closer to Obdorsk, stopped a mile short and called again to the prince. Ivan Taishin arrived immediately. Vauli confirmed again the prince's demotion from power. Taishin again demonstrated his obedience and invited Vauli to his Obdorsk home. Vauli followed, escorted by forty Samoyeds. He stopped in front of the prince's residence, leaving half his escort outside with sledges and armor, and entered the house with the other twenty armed only with knives. Seeing the clan chiefs gathered, Vauli denounced the prince.

Meanwhile, chief officer Skorniakov personally appeared in the house. He took Vauli's hand and led him outside. One of Vauli's guards tried to attack Skorniakov with a knife but was stopped by a saber. Cossacks and Russians then surrounded the Samoyeds and disarmed them. Vauli was cruelly beaten, bound, and imprisoned.

Later, during an inquiry, Vauli and his adherents testified that they had a plan "to occupy Obdorsk at nightfall, burn the church, enter house after house, knifing and robbing all the Russians, and then, retire to the Taz and Yenisei rivers [far to the east]."[46]

The military minister of Russia, Count Chernyshov, informed Emperor Nikolai I of those events. Governor General of West Siberia, Prince Gorchakov banished Vauli, Mairi Khodin, and Vauli's other companions-in-arms. Vauli, sent to Eastern Siberia, never returned.[47]

In the 1840s and 1850s another wave of revolts crossed the tundra. This time it was centered in a remote area on the lower Taz River. Shaman Pani Khodin, brother of exiled Mairi Khodin, headed the rebellion. Pani ordered Samoyeds and Ostiaks not to pay taxes and to seize the reindeer of Prince Taishin's adherents.

In 1856 the rebels were captured by Samoyeds and Ostiaks loyal to Taishin. The captors broke Pani's left hand and fingers (which were considered to be the source of his shamanic power) and transported him to the Bere-zovo jail. The only further account of the incident indicates that the prisoner Pani was christened under the name of Ivan.[48]

Gydan Nenets today recount their legend of shaman Pani according to which, after his arrest by the Russians in the mid-nineteenth century, he was imprisoned in the faraway city of Omsk. There he was killed and buried deep in the ground. The shaman, however, did not die. Having come back to life in the underground, he found a spiritual helper, the master of the netherworld, Nga, and both returned to the tundra. During the ten years that the shaman spent under the earth, he turned into a giant covered with white hair. People occasionally saw his huge tracks in the snow and sand and recognized his body "higher than a tent." Those who had seen his companion, Nga, were said to collapse, as if dead. The legend states that Pani returned to find and kill the kinsman who had betrayed him, and after that to deal with all non-Nenets newcomers.

In the 1840s and 1850s Russian authorities were searching for a manageable way to govern Samoyeds. One high-ranking clerk, Obolenskii, sent to resolve administrative matters in Obdorsk, contemplated that "up to now, 32 Samoyed clans were considered to be lower than Taishin clan; if now one Samoyed were appointed to be chief over all the Samoyeds, one of the 32 clans would dominate and so become equal with the Taishin clan." Then "other clans would be offended, and any tribal governance would be impossible since it [leadership] is maintained entirely by esteem and influence."[49]

It is hard to say whether conflict with Samoyeds would have eased had Prince Taishin exerted his power moderately, but after the rebels' insults, the prince used every opportunity to demonstrate his high rank, to Russians as well as to natives. In 1852, shortly after visiting St. Petersburg, the prince, wearing all the Russian garments and regalia he had received in the capital, met the missionary Averkii, who had come to his summer residence, Gorno-kniazevsk, near Obdorsk. Greeting Father Averkii on the bank of the Taishin River, he said that neither czar nor bishop in St. Petersburg had told him about any baptizing. Therefore, he ordered, "Go back to Obdorsk. I do not permit Ostiaks to be christened, and I do not provide you any transport." He and the seventy Ostiaks with him cursed Father Averkii. Working himself into a rage, Prince Taishin struck the missionary's guard, a Cossack, twice in the face. That created a great scandal in Obdorsk. The Russian officer Yuri Kushelevskii arrested Taishin and imprisoned him in the prince's own residence, locked in shackles. The prince and his relatives raised a clamor. Finally, the prince won, and Kushelevskii was brought to trial and discharged from his post.[50] Kushelevskii, at his defense, pointed out Samoyeds deep distrust of Taishin. Years later Yuri Kushelevskii published a book that presented the first public positive view of Samoyeds. It contains quite good data on Samoyed customs and folklore, and favorably compares Samoyeds to Ostiaks.[51]

After the Kushelevskii-Taishin conflict, several Samoyed elders began to look for a direct alliance with Russians against Prince Taishin. Some Samoyeds asked to be baptized under the patronage of high-ranking Russians. In the early 1850s, for example, a chief of the Khudi clan, being christened, acquired as "godfather" the Russian Grand Prince Mikhail (brother of the Emperor Alexander II). Samoyed Vyrmy (from the Lamdo clan) traveled to Tobol'sk to be baptized under the patronage of a distinguished Tobol'sk merchant, Stepan Bronnikov.

At the same time, Samoyed elders appealed to Tobol'sk and St. Petersburg officials for administrative autonomy from Ostiaks. In 1864 I. Sedleev, chief of the largest Samoyed clan, Karachei, traveled to St. Petersburg seeking separation. In 1865 Samoyeds finally were legally parted from Ostiaks; the position of their chief elder (earlier held by Paigol) was renewed, and Paigol's grandson, Paivolo, was elected to this post. Prince Taishin remained head over only the northern Ostiaks.[52]

From then until the Soviet era, the role of official Ostiak and Samoyed chiefs (princes and starshinas) remained relatively stable. Both the Samoyed and the Ostiak chiefs collected tribute and served as judges. They were responsible for collecting taxes and keeping taxpayer records. The chiefs were entitled to receive 2 percent of the tax collected. The native courts were also led by these chiefs. Decision making was based on the traditional or customary law. Judges conducted their deliberations verbally and had discretion in establishing their own style of procedures and their own reasons for making decisions. The native courts presided over all matters affecting the indigenous population with the exception of issues related to anti-Russian rebellions, premeditated murder, violence, robbery, and theft of state or communal property.

Despite an obvious Russian influence on the institutions of traditional leadership, one could still recognize specific Ugrian and Samoyed features in the new administrative system. The positions of the Khanty and the Mansi princes and starshinas were more entrenched, owing to their own dynastic system, than those of the Nenets. Among the latter, military and economic task-force leaders changed frequently and easily. The Nenets' starshina was usually a rich reindeer herder (Nenets *teta*) who owned his own pastures and was designated *serm'paertia* (literally "a conductor of business" or a leader of an economic task force) or the head of one of the camps. The starshina's position could be inherited by a son from his father, but only if the latter had a good reputation and the former was seen by his kin as being an appropriate heir. For example, in the beginning of this century, the head of the Seroteta clan, named Hambi, lost many of his reindeer and became poor. His kinsmen regarded this as a bad sign, and after his death the position of clan starshina passed not to one of his sons but to another member of his clan, Eremzi Serodeta.[53]

In the mid-1800s, while the rebellion headed by Pani still rumbled, a critical turn in the relationship between Russians and Samoyeds occurred, triggered partly by Yuri Kushelevskii's "pro-Samoyedic" (and counter-Taishin) actions. More important, this turn was a consequence of new economic activity. Not accidentally, the Russian merchant Bronnikov (godfather of the Samoyed Vyrmy, from Lamdo clan) became a godfather to Samoyeds in a wider sense. Russian merchants initiated a "fishery revolution" on the lower Ob. Previously, the fishing grounds at the mouth of the Ob and in Ob Bay were economically inaccessible for lack of suitable equipment and a market for the fish. Russian merchants provided both; they supplied nets, big boats, and salt for conservation, and they arranged for distribution of the catch. Russian fishermen, seasonally brought from southern sites and villages, usually headed the fishing crew. Steam navigation, developed in the Ob basin in the mid-1800s, added impetus to the commercial fishing. The lower Ob quickly attracted immigrants. Komi-Zyrians from west of the Urals first appeared in Obdorsk in 1853; by the early 1900s about 100 families had settled on the lower Ob. By 1925 their population increased to 3,810. Simultaneously, Russian and Tatar professional fishermen streamed to the lower Ob, and by 1908 they numbered 1,308.[54] At the turn of the century, export of fish products from the region totaled 600,000 pounds and brought merchants up to one million rubles in profit.[55]

In more southern areas of the upper Ob, the fishery boom in the 1800s did not produce a dramatic change. In forested areas, the Khanty and the Mansi had since ancient times used various weirs and short nettle nets for mastering the shores of the Ob River. These waters were productive, but not so rich as fishing grounds closer to the mouth of the Ob. Not surprisingly, the Khanty and the Mansi mostly retained the fishing grounds for their own use; upriver from Obdorsk, the Russians controlled ("rented") only one-sixth of the best fishing grounds. At the same time (1914–16), almost four-fifths of the richest "net-fishing sands" at the mouth of the Ob River and Ob Bay were rented by outsiders. New, mixed patterns of economy and land use appeared in the lower Ob. For some Nenets and northern Khanty—specifically, those who did not have enough reindeer to migrate across the tundra—commercial fishing offered an attractive economic alternative. In the late 1800s about seven thousand natives on the lower Ob and Ob Bay participated in this new activity.[56]

Formerly, the outside contacts of tundra Nenets were generally restricted to the winter Obdorsk fair; by the mid-1800s, however, the contact zone had broadened over all the year and over all the forest-tundra borderland. Nenets who became seasonal fishermen comprised a new layer of mediators between tundra nomads and settlement dwellers. That layer located near the Ob and speaking different languages (at least four: Nenets, Khanty, Russian, and Zyrian) gradually emerged as a polyethnic satellite of Russian settlements and authorities. Nenets fishermen remained semi-nomads, using their small rein-deer herds in the winter and delivering them to herders for summer pasturing. In some respects they turned into "semi-Nenets," having lost the core of their reindeer-herding culture. Those semi-nomads were doomed to play a key role after the October Revolution in 1917.

Each epoch that Samoyeds (the Nenets) endured had its peculiar features, but each ended restlessly. The military confrontation that emerged in the epoch of Ermak (1600s) sporadically flared over the next two periods of Russian colo-nization and spilled into the Soviet era. Religious conflicts that appeared sharply during the epoch of Leshchinskii (1700s) echoed later when Commu-nist ideology instead of Christian missionaries endeavored to suppress indige-nous religion. In the third epoch (1800s) the Speranskii reforms attempted to fold native leadership and native decision-making processes into forms that could be understood and manipulated by Russian administrative authorities. Only partly successful, the reforms instead created new administrative prob-lems among natives—problems such as those played out between Prince Taishin and Nenets leaders.

In the period of Russian colonization, Nenets culture changed most, not due to, but counter to Russian efforts. Nevertheless, the Russians influenced at least two transformations in the Nenets economy, the first in the seven-teenth century, with the appearance of large-scale reindeer herding, and the second in the nineteenth century, with the emergence of commercial fishing. If the first strengthened the Nenets, the second had the opposite result, split-ting them into nomads and semi-settlers.

4

Ordeals: The Last Rebellions

"**Y**our dead brothers are lying here too. Who knows how long they have been dead. Only their bones are here. You see how bad it is to fight in vain." This is what Junior Yaptik says to his next-to-eldest brother at the end of "Five Yaptiks." One could probably say the same words "in vain," recollecting natives' uprisings against Soviet power in the 1930s and 1940s. But the events occurred despite the native leaders' efforts to stop them. It scarcely could have been possible to persuade indigenous people not to wage war against the new authorities, especially in the critical period of the 1930s.

One cannot quite say that the Revolution of 1917 and the Russian Civil War of 1918–20 had no effect on native peoples. Rather, the real meaning of such concepts as "Soviet authority," "counterrevolution," and "*kulak*" did not become clear to them until sometime later, in the mid- to late 1920s, when measures were undertaken to nationalize land, confiscate the property of rich herders (*kulaks*),[1] and "expose the shamans." Between 1918 and 1921 the natives had not yet realized just what, not so very far from their settlements, those detachments of White, Red, Red-Green, and other "white people" were fighting for—all the more because natives' trade partners and acquaintances in Russian towns and villages included both supporters of the revolution (exiles, poor people) and opponents (merchants, the clergy, and so on).

More often than not native peoples were drawn into military actions against their own will—either battles were fought on their territory, or else they ended up serving as guides for one Russian detachment or another. That is why Nenets and other native names can be found (albeit rarely) on the casualty lists of both sides.

The facts available on organized, armed uprisings by native peoples during the Civil War years (including the so-called SR-Kulak Revolt)[2] are few. We do know that in 1921, in the Lar'yak District (eastern Khanty area), "a counterrevolutionary rebellion took place, in which as many as ten local native *kulaks* took part, killing two Communists, one of whom was an Ostiak. (The rebellion was not put down until a month later, by sailors.)"[3] Several local uprisings of "shamans and *kulaks*" occurred in the forest area near Obdorsk in 1921. The Yamal Nenets sometimes call this period a *mandalada*, "a wargathering of the whole land." Nevertheless, until the late 1920s, the northern territories mostly remained apart from the centers of revolutionary activity. The Nenets, Khanty, Mansi, and Sel'kup seldom encountered the new regime until several years later.

Creeping Sovietization

In November 1917 the Soviet Congress adopted "The Declaration of the Rights of the People of Russia," which proclaimed the "Free Development of National Minorities and Ethnographic Groups Inhabiting the Territory of Russia."[4] This officially ended the colonial rule that had existed since Speranskii's reforms of 1822, but practical application was postponed until the years following the Civil War. Preoccupied with other concerns, the central government exercised no real authority over the northern regions in the immediate postwar era and did not attempt to rein in exploitation of natives or to alleviate the harsh effects of civil war. The reindeer herds had declined disastrously owing to raiding, increased slaughter to prevent starvation, and anthrax epidemics. Pleas and "panicky reports," primarily from ethnographers in the field citing the dire conditions of the native population, reached the People's Commissariat of Nationalities (Narkomnats), which historian Yuri Slezkine has described as "the one organ in Moscow that could claim jurisdiction in the matter."[5] But Narkomnats itself had few resources. The Section of National Minorities within Narkomnats in 1922 formed a polar subdivision that commissioned an investigation of options for rule by peoples of the North.[6] Three alternative projects were designed:

1. Creation of protected territories in places inhabited by aboriginal people, similar to the Native American Indian reservations of the United States and Canada;

2. Formation of a government organization to deal with Northern matters; and

3. Formation of nomadic Soviets and the convening of Congresses of the Soviets of Native Clans and Tribes.[7]

Petr Sosunov, who headed the Polar Subcommittee, was sent to Samarovo in Tiumen Province to organize the first conference of tribes of the polar North. The delegates to this summer conference adopted a resolution favoring formation of a special polar federation in Northwestern Siberia. Provincial newspaper articles even discussed creation of a Polar Republic of the Khanty, the Mansi, and the Nenets.[8] Although proposals to grant autonomy to northern peoples would appear to be compatible with the official declarations of rights of national minorities inhabiting particular territories, such proposals were in fact treated as heresy. Sosunov was arrested and jailed for promoting formation of autonomous regions.[9]

Although the Russian government squelched reformers' efforts to allow native self-government, it adopted measures to address the most serious social concerns. Decrees canceled all debts of native hunters to traders in 1920, banned the sale of alcohol (at least between 1923 and 1925), and exempted natives from state taxes and labor obligations. Medical services increased, and grain was distributed in areas of famine.[10]

In 1923 the central government abolished Tiumen Province (Tiumen-skaia Guberniia) and merged its territory into the newly formed Ural Oblast, with Sverdlovsk (formerly and in the post-Soviet period named Ekaterinburg) as its center. The former territory of Tiumen Province became Tobol'sk Okrug within the Ural Oblast. The Tobol'sk Okrug included the districts of Aleksandrovo, Berezovo, Kondinsk, Obdorsk, Samarovo, and Surgut. Former northern townships (*volosti*), including native townships,[11] were reorganized into forty rural settlements (*selskii sovety*). Thus three levels of regional and local authority exercised control over native affairs. Council meetings of "deputies" elected executive committees for each of the three levels. Among the deputies of all these councils were 169 natives: 154 Khanty, 7 Nenets, and 8 Mansi.[12] Among the nomadic populations, clan chiefs or family heads continued to exercise authority.

Policy, however, was still directed from the center in Moscow. After abolishing Narkomnats on June 20, 1924, the presidium of the All-Russian Central Executive Committee of the RSFSR (VTsIK) established the Committee for Assisting the Peoples of the Northern Peripheries, commonly known as the Committee of the North. Twenty-six northern nationalities, numbering from 150,000 to 160,000 people, were to receive state "protection" under its jurisdiction. The fate of the territories populated by northern natives was debated within this committee. "Protectionist" or "conservative" committee members argued that native people exemplified a kind of "primitive communism." They advocated establishment of reserved lands, prohibition against new settlers, a ban on sale of alcohol, limits on private trade, creation of nomadic schools with native teachers, and provisions for food, clothing, and medical services.[13] The dominant members of the committee, the "radicals" or "progressives," however, believed that a "primitive" and nomadic life was incompatible with Communist doctrine and collectivization.

In the territories inhabited by northern peoples, peripheral or borderland Committees of the North were also formed in the autonomous republics and provinces. Tobol'sk, as the regional center of Northwestern Siberia, had a Committee of the North attached to the Tobol'sk Okrug council from 1925 to 1932. By 1926 new organs of Soviet power and authority—clan councils (Russian singular: *rodovoi sovet*), district native congresses, and district native executive committees—with far wider jurisdiction replaced prior clan authority and native administration (*inorodcheskaia uprava*).[14] Clan councils were to familiarize the population with the lawmaking process, ensure availability of supplies and tools, assist in the creation of cooperatives, supervise compliance with hunting and fishing laws, deal with questions of "enlightenment," guard the health of the people, and support the social order.

Although clan councils, consisting of a president, a vice president, and one council member, were elected by means of open voting for a one-year term, "exploitative elements"—princes, shamans, rich reindeer herders— were denied the right to vote and participate in the councils. The role of women in these organs of government increased, as women and youth received the right to vote and be elected. The councils operated without pay. No fewer than 400 voters, consisting of clan, band (*vataga*), and settlements inhabiting a common territory, organized district native congresses. Conducted once a year, these congresses elected executive committees (*tuzrik*) to act during the year. These new organs of Soviet power thus pushed aside indigenous leaders, altered gender roles and relations, and exerted outside authority into economic and social spheres previously left to the indigenous systems of governance.

Regional native councils (Russian singular: *tuzsovet*) were created among the Sos'va Mansi; the Khanty of Shuryshkary, Balko-Pim, Trom-Yugan, and Nazym; and the Nenets of Taz, Yamal, and the Urals in 1926–27. By mid-1928, 11 native districts (with *tuzrik*) and 49 clan, settlement, and *vataga* councils existed. In 1929 the number of native councils rose rapidly, to sixty-four, and by October 1930, seventy-two native councils existed alongside thirty-one village councils, as shown in Table 4.1.

Soviet authorities from the 1920s began to explore prospects for economic development of the northern regions. Russian rulers, traders, and merchants had been interested in use of the northern waters to access Northwestern Siberia long before the Soviets came to power. Russian authorities had even outlawed travel on the Arctic seas because merchants buying furs from natives impeded collection of *iasak*.[15] Early in the 1920s, the Committee of the Northern Route (Komseveroput)[16] initiated field expeditions that located coal

Table 4.1. Native councils (*Tuzsovety*) of the Tobol'sk *Okrug* in 1930

Tobol'sk *Okrug* districts (*Raiony*)	Number of village councils (*Sel'sovety*)	District centers	Number of native councils (*Tuzsovety*)
Obdorsk	4	Kushevat	7
		Synia	6
		Tazovsk	3
		Ural	5
		Shuryshkar	6
		Yamal	7
Berezovo	5	Kazym	11
		Sos'va	13
Surgut	4	Balyko-Pim	3
		Trom-Yugan	2
		Ugot-Yugan	5
Samarovo	12	None	None
Kondinsk	6	Karym	4
Total	31		72

Source: Zibarev 1968, 138.

and oil deposits and surveyed fish and sea mammal resources of the Barents and Kara seas.

The first Kara trade expedition was conducted between June and July 1920. More than 9,000 tons of wheat and 5,400 tons of raw materials were exported to England and Germany from Siberia via the Irtysh and Ob rivers.[17] Agricultural machines transported from England and Germany arrived in Siberia while food, fur, skins, flax, and other goods were exported from Siberia. The main task of Komseveroput, reorganized into the Northern Siberian State Stock Company of Industry and Transport in 1928, was to transport lumber from the Yenisei and Ob river basins to obtain hard currency.[18]

As economic activities expanded, Soviet authorities became interested in the prospects for social change among the indigenous peoples. In those days bold social experiments *became priorities*. In the summer of 1926 the Tobol'sk Okrug Committee of the North selected the Kazym River, inhabited by the Khanty and forest Nenets, as the first potential site for such an experiment. Vasilii M. Novitskii headed the Kazym-Nadym Delta expedition "to study opportunities for colonization (by the Kazym people) of the Nadym River area, which aimed to exert a cultural influence on nomadic reindeer-herders."[19] Novitskii noted that, among the "semi-sedentary native population of Tob-North," which he believed was "dying out," "indifferent to progress," and "listless by nature," one native people that "stand out by virtue of their staunchness in the struggle for survival, their colonizing abilities, their lively, unlistless nature, their search for new ways to organize their lives, their artistic inclinations, their healthy spirit and body" are the Kazym. He considered these people to be "the only native group (with the exception of the Samoyed reindeer herders) within the borders of the TobOkrug[20] that . . . is neither dying out nor ruined by capitalist culture. . . . [It] is rather powerful economically, inasmuch as it carries on all three forms of indigenous economic activity: fishing, hunting and reindeer breeding (forest type). This group does not just sit at home in Kazym; instead, representatives of it travel widely through nearly all of the native TobNorth: one can meet them in Samarovo, Maly Atlym, Kondinsk, Berezovo, Surgut and even Obdorsk. (They float timber down river from Kazym to Obdorsk.)"[21] As Novitskii recorded,

That is why the local Committee [of the North], as it sets itself the task of—roughly speaking, in naturalists' terms—moving toward "improving the indigenous species," must focus its attention exclusively on the Kazym people as the group that is the most viable and least assimilated. And, through the Kazym, moving toward a recovery in spirit and body, toward cultural progress, for the entire semi-sedentary (and even nomadic) native population of TobNorth.[22]

The researchers were in for a disappointment. In August of 1926, Novitskii presented a report to the Committee of the North in which there was no longer any trace of that initial "colonizing" optimism. The author noted with particular regret that "the native attitude toward already existing cooperative ventures is one of resentment"; that "trapping and fishing equipment is supplied to the populace at extremely low levels"; that "except for the occasional visit by a medic from Berezovo, there is an absence of medical care, and the population is left (in terms of doctoring) to its shamans, domestic gods, or else 'the Russian God' by way of the Polnovat priest." Among other proposals, Novitskii suggested reinforcing the Kazym native Soviet with cultural workers and opening a local native school. He was convinced that "the natives will go to school, but they need a boarding school and a teacher who knows the language."[23] Neither Novitskii nor Kazym residents themselves suspected at the time just how acute the conflict over schooling would become.

Enlightenment through education was a main feature of the Soviet doctrine. Education in the post–Civil War period, like administrative rule, served the purposes of the Bolshevik party—to inculcate Marxist-Leninist values among northern "ignorant and uncultured" nationalities, who were to be enlisted in the building of socialist society. Beginning in 1918, a special board coordinated cultural and educational work among national minorities, and an educational committee directed departments of public education and "enlightenment" of nationalities. In August 1919 the "conservatives" and "progressives" who had fought for control of the Committee of the North presented opposing views in a conference dedicated to organizing "enlightenment" of the non-Russian people. The conservatives (protectionists) favored self-determination (allowing national minorities to make their own decisions regarding school development), while the progressives (radicals) argued for complete ideological and organizational uniformity in education as a "revolutionary necessity." For the latter, language differences, specific living conditions, and national differences were not relevant considerations. As in government affairs, the "progressive" view prevailed in schools throughout Russia (not only in the North).[24]

In education, the top priority of the Committee of the North was to introduce compulsory primary schooling (at least the first four grades). Following this objective, the committee began to prepare the first alphabet books in the Khanty, Sel'kup, and Nenets languages in 1926.[25] At the same time a few natives were sent to a special "northern workers' faculty" near Leningrad, which served as a base for a future teacher-training institute for northern nationalities.

At this stage, trading posts (Russian singular: *faktoriia*) played a key role in the northern economy and life; thus primary schools were attached to them. By 1921 such posts had opened in settlements throughout the Obdorsk area: on the Yamal Peninsula (Yar-Sale, Novyi Port, and Shchuchie), on the lower Taz River (Khalmersede), on the Ob lowlands east of Obdorsk (Khae), and in the northern taiga (Muzhy, Kushevat, and Shuryshkary). In later years, their numbers grew rapidly (see Map 5). Each *faktoriia* had a bakery and tea room as well as a warehouse that supplied people coming from the tundra with relatively cheap goods. *Faktoriia* workers visited the most remote nomad camps to trade provisions for pelts, furs, and so forth.[26] Until the 1930s, schooling remained a subsidiary activity of the trade posts; "enlightenment" remained at the experimental stage.

Likewise, new economic reforms, particularly cooperatives, existed mostly on paper. The first cooperative of hunters and fishermen, Northern Cooperative (Severnyi Kooperator), founded in 1918 in Obdorsk, listed 1,700 Samoyed (Nenets) and Ostiak (Khanty) as members. After the failure of this and other attempts to form giant cooperatives, Soviet authorities sent special research expeditions to figure out how the collective units might be firmly organized among northern hunters and breeders. The Ural Oblast administration sent Vladimir Evladov to the Yamal Peninsula to lead an expedition in 1928–29.

The expedition was to be a "multifaceted investigation of political-economic conditions of life, everyday activity, customary law of Yamal nomads, flora, fauna, reindeer herding, fur hunting and fishing, trade-exchange relations, production and consumption, activity of trade-storage organizations."[27] Conducting long-term, year-round research, Evladov noticed political tensions mounting between Yamal herders and Soviet authorities. Responding to Evladov's concerns, Obdorsk clerk V. F. Vashkevich exclaimed,

> "Here we have a lot of affairs apart from studying Nenets. The main [task] is reindeer, how to put them to service to build socialism; we'll deal with the Nenets later."
>
> "Does it mean that animals are more important than people? Are we

building socialism for reindeer or for people?" Evladov asked.

"Your Samoyeds pull all our economy back to primitive society. . . . It is necessary to break down all this patriarchality. We must first levy big taxes on rich men," responded Vashkevich.

". . . If they rebel?"

"We needn't curry favor with them."[28]

Despite the growing antagonism, the 1920s remained a time of political discussion. Decisive actions, such as those of Sosunov in the political sphere and Novitskii in the social sphere, only touched the Siberian North. This was

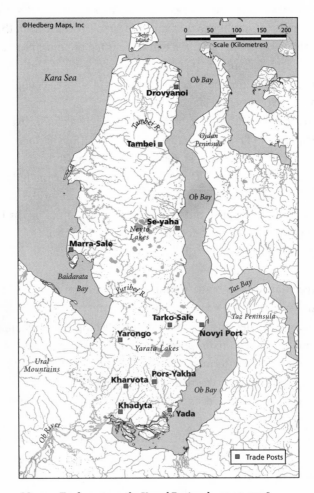

Map 5. Trade posts on the Yamal Peninsula, 1935–1936

an experimental and preparatory period. These first steps in Sovietization only slightly influenced the life and culture of natives, although they laid the foundation for significant changes in the next period.

Galloping Sovietization

The 1930s brought administrative and economic intrusions on a scale not before seen. On December 10, 1930, the Presidium of the VTsIK passed a decree "regarding the organization of the national unification in regions of disbursement of the small peoples of the North," and on January 7, 1932, the Presidium abolished the Tobol'sk Okrug and created two new northern okrugs, the Ostiak-Vogul Okrug, with its center in Samarovo, and the Yamal Okrug, with its center in Obdorsk.[29]

Although the okrugs bore their names, natives were minorities in them and therefore had little chance of influencing government decisions. Moreover, during the elections for representatives of the new regions and districts, 1,569 Khanty, Mansi, and Nenets were declared "class-hostile elements" and thereby deprived of the right to vote. At the same time, clan councils were replaced with "territorial" and "nomad" councils.[30] These political divisions reduced the functions and importance of local government and the role that indigenous leaders might play in decision making. At the same time, the layers of bureaucracy between native villages and central authorities increased. The real purpose of the okrugs was to provide a structure for rapid fulfillment of Soviet reforms.

Alongside the creation of new political divisions, Soviet authorities began to open the North to industrial-scale development for the extraction of natural resources; this was accompanied by a huge influx of outsiders. The Soviets' real power in the North was shown in 1933, with the establishment of the Main Administration of the Northern Sea Route (Glavsevmorput).[31] Building the infrastructure that would open Northwestern Siberia and other parts of the Soviet North to trade and industry, like the opening of the American West with the construction of the transcontinental railroad, had an enormous impact on the indigenous population.

As envisioned by the early planners, the "Northern Sea Route" encompassed a massive communication and transportation network joining the Arctic Ocean with the Siberian rivers that flowed into it. Development of water transport in the Ob North, via the Kara Sea and along the Ob and Irtysh rivers was accomplished in two stages: the first (1920–33) encompassed exploration and research, and the second (1933–38) focused on the exploitation of resources.

During the second stage, Glavsevmorput came to govern the whole Asiatic North above the sixty-second parallel and to affect the lives of the native peoples of Siberia as no governmental organ had done before. The purpose of Glavsevmorput was to establish the Northern Sea Route from the White Sea to the Bering Strait and then equip that route, keep it working properly, and provide for safe navigation.[32] Within a few years the VTsIK USSR issued a decree liquidating the Committee of the North and transferring its functions to Glavsevmorput.[33] The special attention given to concerns of the indigenous population was no longer deemed necessary; thus administration and modernization of native affairs was incorporated into the general plans for developing the Northern Sea Route. In the mid-1930s, 65 percent of the expenses of the okrug were provided by Glavsevmorput. By the end of the 1930s Glavsevmorput monopolized the use of natural resources throughout the northern Ob region. Beginning in 1931, the newly organized state forest products enterprises (*lespromkhoz*) developed the timber industry with bases at Berezovo, Surgut, and Khanty-Mansiisk;[34] regional shipping activity expanded; and the fishing industry grew rapidly.

From 1930 to 1934, more than 50,000 peasants from the Azovo-Chernomorski, Volga, Ural, and southern Siberian provinces were deprived of their property and resettled on land of the Ob North. These *spetzpereselentsy* (special resettlers) were sent to the areas of new construction and forced to work. They provided most of the labor to construct the city of Khanty-Mansiisk, as well as the Belogorski wood-processing plant, the fish-processing factories in Obdorsk and Samarovo among other locations, and the cultural stations at Kazym, Sos'va, Taz, and Yamal.

Building these cultural stations (Russian singular: *kultbaza*)[35] had been a project of the Committee of the North in the late 1920s; the intention was to organize economic, cultural, and educational activity among the native population. In the early 1930s the cultural stations became the responsibility of Glavsevmorput. The cultural stations clustered social services around centers of trade. In general, they were supposed to provide medical, educational, veterinary, and other services to the native population. They were also expected to eliminate illiteracy, teach "modern" hygiene, introduce natives to Communist doctrine, and teach them how to become "modern" members of the socialist labor force. State-supported boarding schools were established at the stations. At the same time, the Soviets experimented with traveling schools, known as "red tents." These were few in number; their influence in the region was overshadowed completely by the boarding schools.

Construction of the Yamal cultural station at Yar-Sale was finished in 1932. Its director, Mikhail M. Brodnev, described in his memoirs the difficulty of starting up this station and the boarding school:

> People in the kultbaza staff did not know the local conditions, did not speak Nenets, and only a few Nenets could at that time speak Russian. How . . . could the work begin? [We agreed that] every specialist has to go to a nomad camp, live there two to three months, become acquainted with the native lifestyle, participate in economic activity, keep good relationships with the Nenets. Such a "christening ceremony" passed over all the specialists, teachers, medics, and most of all the specialists on tundra economy.
>
> . . . We sent people to the camps to gather children [to bring them to the boarding school], but they came back without pupils; the Nenets refused to deliver their children to school. The first year, with great effort, we collected seven children. . . . The most frequent reason for refusing was: "You will spoil the child, he will live in your house, diverted from the tent; he will be afraid of smoke [in the tent] like you Russians are afraid of it; you will teach him to write and read, but not to pasture reindeer, to trap foxes; what sort of Nenets would he become, an odd man for tundra, how would he survive?"[36]

The cultural stations became the base of a new sedentary way of life on the tundra. Not surprisingly, Yar-Sale became and is today the administrative center of Yamal. The stations were magnets for semi-nomads who before the Revolution engaged in the commercial fishery and after trade collapsed in the 1920s sought alternative connections to outsiders. Brodnev recorded the first steps of this transition:

> Many households which did not have reindeer settled on the kul't-baza; some of them worked here. Their tents stood in the center of the village. . . . We brought electricity to the tents. The master electrician had a lot of troubles. The Nenets customarily moved their tents from one place to another, breaking the wires, but then asked to make "cold fire" again.
>
> One time kultbaza workers, walking near such an electrified tent, heard urgent talk about "wise fire." They lifted the tent's cover and saw

one Nenets holding a cup to a lamp, then drinking some drops from the cup and saying something. Asked what they were doing, the Nenets answered: "we drink a little." . . .Workers who know Nenets well explained that "wise cold fire" [was] unknown and mysterious for the Nenets. In some respect they animated it, and so fed it with spirits [alcohol].

The workers of kultbaza decided to end those superstitions and led the Nenets to the power station. They explained the purpose of each mechanism, turned them on and showed the process of making "the cold fire." Then they demonstrated that fire can be used both for light and to operate an electric saw. Boiling tea and frying fish on the cook stove, they showed that fire is not only cold, but also hot. The Nenets followed attentively all those [demonstrations], and one old man said about the workers, "They are strong shamans."[37]

Brodnev's memoirs illustrate not only how these Nenets adjusted their beliefs and customs to technical innovations, but also how they adopted new economic activities that made sedentary life possible: "As soon as the horses appeared, the Nenets acquired skills to store hay, that provided the possibility to keep cows [and] found a dairy farm. A workshop on sewing fur clothing was organized as well; that gave women a chance to be involved in collective farm work." Those who owned reindeer and remained herders also felt the quick and decisive change in Soviet economic policy. Reindeer breeding became the target of early governmental efforts to reorganize labor and create collective farms (Russian singular: *kolkhoz*). In 1929 the first *kolkhoz* on Yamal was founded in Yar-Sale, with six Nenets households. By 1935 the number of collective farms in the Yamal District had increased to five including 104 families, with 2,815 reindeer.[38] A number of owners of large herds moved into northern Yamal at the end of the 1920s and beginning of the 1930s to escape collectivization, which had not yet reached northern Yamal.[39] Until the late 1920s most Nenets who reached northern Yamal in the summer returned south in the winter. In 1931 only half of them crossed to the south of the Neito Lake region of central Yamal; in 1932 only one-tenth migrated to the South. Soviet agents attributed this changed behavior to the attraction of three newly established trade posts on northern Yamal.[40] (See Map 5.) But the reasons for the Nenets to remain in the North were not so simple.

Never before had the Nenets experienced such close contact with invaders. Early in their history, the Nenets were able to escape the Russians and their allies by fleeing to the remote tundra, usually farther north. Now they were blocked. The Northern Sea Route Administration, in establishing trade posts throughout both the Yamal Peninsula (at Seyaha, Tambei, and Drovyanoi, for example) and the Gydan Peninsula (at Gydoyamo, and Napalkovo, for instance),[41] laid siege from all sides.

The Defiant North

The most significant native rebellions against Soviet authority occurred in the 1930s. Notable among those in Northwestern Siberia were those on the Kazym River (the forest Nenets and the Khanty), on the Tol'ka River (the

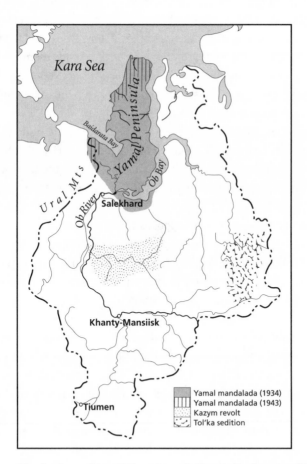

Map 6.   Areas of twentieth-century rebellions in Northwestern Siberia

Sel'kup), and on the Yamal Peninsula (the Nenets). (See Map 6.) In some respects the three uprisings can be considered a single Khanty-Sel'kup-Nenets rebellion against Soviet authority. Here, however, we trace the Yamal Nenets rebellion.[42] Thanks to recent publication of materials from Communist party archives,[43] it is now possible to describe these events using not only oral histories (which are often rather tangled and chronologically vague) but also documents (though permeated with the ideological "spirit" of the epoch). OGPU (later the NKVD and later still the KGB, the secret policy)[44] operatives who took part in suppressing these uprisings and who later were to evaluate them strove to produce as many proofs as possible that their opponents were "counterrevolutionaries," and hence the documents they compiled contain detailed factual—if tendentiously interpreted—information.[45]

Old Nenets often grow confused as they try to determine exactly how many rebellions occurred on Yamal during their time. One could hear of two, three, and even four—depending on how far back into his memory the narrator delved. At times it seems that there the *mandalada* (Nenets: war assemblage) never really ended, but instead would simply slip into a temporary lull.

An official memorandum from the end of 1934[46] notes, "Ever since the Yamal (Nenets) National Okrug was established (1931) and national Soviets were organized to replace the tribal councils (the majority of which were headed by *kulaks*) resistance by the *kulak*-shaman part of the tundra population has been spreading, becoming increasingly active, and taking ever more acute form." If in 1932–33 it was only individual, still rather unorganized factions of *kulaks* and shamans who opposed the organization of councils and tried to exert influence on the working people of the tundra, by the spring of 1934 these individual *kulak*-shaman groups had begun to unite and had, by the autumn of 1934, all enlisted in one single group they named "Mandolyda," which in Russian translation means "those assembled":

> "Mandolyda" activity is focused on almost the entire Yamal Peninsula and the eastern shore of Baidarata Bay; it includes some territory in the Priural District (the upper reaches of the Baidarata River, Yaro-to Lake, the Yarkuta River). The most significant concentration of tents comprising the Mandolyda organization is located in the area around Yaro-to Lake, along the Yuribei and Yarkuta Rivers. Some smaller individual groups do venture south of the locations indicated (Salita, Yada, and others).

The chief organizers and leaders of the *kulak*-shaman faction are at this time located in the northern portion of Yamal: these are Nyd Vanuito, organizer of the northern Yamal faction; the current leader Khatevo Okatetto (*kulak*); his assistant Veisaibi Okatetto (son of the *kulak* Tilyang Okatetto, who was tried and convicted in 1932).

In the southern part of Yamal (Nei-to and Yaro-to Lakes) the leader of a group which has united almost 250 tents is Yutola Serpiu (*seredniak*).[47]

In the Yuribei area a group comprised of around 80 tents is headed by Yamno Okatetto (shaman), Yanoto Vanuito, Yanauyti Vanuito and Khanzeko Khudi (*kulak*).

In the Priural region the main leader is one Solinter (surname and social origin undetermined); his second-in-command is Ilya Pyryrko (*seredniak*).[48]

The OGPU had its own peculiar language, in which the heroic-sounding Nenets *mandalada* became the rough-sounding *mandolyda*, which was used to classify Nenets movements as a "resistance group." One can understand the OGPU and Bolshevik officers—they had their own set of rituals, their own gods and sacrifices, and they interpreted what was happening according to their own customs. Still, we can look behind the "pathos of the class struggle" set down in official documents for the real causes of the rebellions.

The first to make their discontent with "reindeer and fur stocks" known were a Nadym "*kulak*" named Eko Anagurichi, owner of 3,000 reindeer, and a Yamal "*kulak*" named Mai Solinter, who owned 3,500 reindeer. The latter, on March 11, 1932, "in the presence of Nenets Tipchi Syrotetto and Semyon Syrotetto, declared to commissioners Vityazev and Anfuriev of the Khe Cooperative that he did not recognize the *bedniak* decree on confiscation of reindeer, that the *bedniaks* had no right to discuss any 'issue' concerning him or his reindeer. 'You've had a lot of commissioners, they've gotten nowhere and they won't get anywhere in the future. I can live without the Russians. I've got reindeer, I won't go hungry.'" On April 24, 1932, when handed a summons to appear in court on charges of exploitation of his hired men, Mai Solinter declared, "I don't recognize your judges or Soviet authority; I have my own laws." When the Nenets Rogalev insisted that he take the summons, Solinter attacked him with a knife but was disarmed. Later he gathered twelve men from neighboring tents, armed with knives, and sent a messenger to bring more people from neighboring camps.[49]

In 1934, owing in part to rumors of war on the Kazym and Tol'ka rivers but more to increasingly highhanded actions by Soviet authorities, a real *mandalada* did develop on the Yamal Peninsula. In some instances "those assembled" resorted to "passive" acts such as the blockade or sabotage of Soviet trading posts. For example, in the spring of 1934 "shipments headed for trading posts in the Yamal and Priural districts were dumped from the sled caravan and left in the tundra." In other circumstances more active methods came into play: "In northern Yamal . . . faction members . . .convened a 'people's court' (a *kulak* reprisal) for the chairman of the Tambei Natsoviet, Pibichi Okatetto and *natsoviet* [national council] member, *bedniak* Numi Tusida, who had categorically refused to join the faction. They stripped these comrades naked, rolled them in the snow, beat them, and then forced them to join the faction." The same treatment was meted out to members of the Shchucherechensky Council near Yaro-to Lake. In the Nadym tundra, Semyon Sigil'etov and others robbed a trading post on the upper reaches of the Nadym River, killing three Soviet commissioners.[50]

During the course of the *mandalada* the Neitin, Tambei, and Tiutei native Soviets were disbanded, and communications between district authorities and the northern Yamal trading posts on the Seyaha and Tambei rivers and the Drovyanoi Cape were blocked. Natsoviet (National Council) reindeer herds were seized and distributed among the Serpivu and Yaptik clans:

> In northern Yamal, and also on the Baidarata, fur trapping and hunting is shut down. The "Mandolyda" has forbidden working people to trap. "This year," say Mandolyda leaders, "is not a year for trapping; it is a year for talking with Soviet authorities."
>
> The chief demands presented by the kulak faction are:
> "Abolition of norms for issuance of foodstuffs and goods";
> "Purchase according to need, and for cash";
> "Down with *kulaks* and *bedniaks*—we are all the same";
> "Restoration of voting rights to shamans and *kulaks*";
> "We do not recognize the soviets and those elected to them, and we won't obey them; we will not elect new ones";
> "No trading posts, because too many Russians have begun coming here; get the Russians out";
> "We are opposed to Soviet laws and will not abide by them";
> "Release all Nenets from trading posts and councils";

"We will not send our children to schools."

These demands are in fact demands according to which Party and government would have to renounce all measures currently undertaken, and liquidate Soviet authority in the tundra.[51]

Indeed, the *mandalada* opposed all measures undertaken by Soviet authorities in the 1930s, not because the Nenets did not recognize Soviet authority from the start but because the latter's each and every action, point by point, ran counter to Nenets custom and tradition. Soviet "culture" was not simply different from Nenets; it seemed, almost by design, to be its exact opposite.

The following are excerpts from one participant's recollections of "sedition on the Yamal Peninsula" in the thirties. They come from "the other side," from Nenets Esiko Laptander, who joined the *mandalada* twice, both in the 1930s and 1940s.

By my count I must be 90 or 92 years old. I was born in the mountains, but spent my whole life on the Yamal. Now I live in the mountains again. There were a lot of times when I could have died, but here I'm still alive and don't know what will come next.

When the *mandalada* started I was migrating around the mouth of the Yuribei. The *mandalada* started on the Ob, crossed the mountains, Konstantin Rock, and went as far as the sea. I don't know the names of the Russians who took away the reindeer. They were just soldiers—Red Army men. I don't know what year that was either.

When the Soviets took power, Red Army men started coming to the tundra, to all the tents. Ten or fifteen men at a time, with rifles. Everyone was supposed to give them reindeer and harness. Rich, poor, it didn't matter—you had to give them reindeer and sleds. If you didn't, you were for the Whites, and they shot you right there. And if you did, then you had to take them where they said. Then you could come back home with your sled. The Red Army men were collecting people, one from each part of the tundra, taking them away to Salekhard for a meeting (*sabora*).

Then, some time later, another "affair" (*sertavy*) started. They said that people had to round up 300 reindeer from our tundra (Ust'-Yuribei) and give them up for free. People didn't want to give up their reindeer. There was one man—Yermechi Seroteta. He had 3,000 reindeer. He said to people, "That's not very much, 300 reindeer." And he gave up 300 males from his own herd, on behalf of everybody. That year passed.

Then it was the same thing—round up 100 reindeer and give them up for free too. And later it got even worse. The Red Army men started coming round to all the tents, looking for gold. If a person didn't turn in his gold, they took him away. They took away all the shamans. Some Nenets took the Red Army men around on their sleds. And they gathered the reindeer they'd taken into a herd and drove it off somewhere.

One time they came to the camp of old man Nyangi Khorolia, who had 3,000 reindeer. They wanted to take his reindeer. But the old man was dead, he'd been laid out on his sled until the spring. The Red Army men didn't believe that he was dead. They started unwrapping the sled, rummaging around the corpse. They found two polar fox skins and took them. They also drove off all his sons' reindeer. They left only a hundred head.

The next year they started taking away everyone's reindeer. I didn't have very many; at the time I was a herder for a rich old man. He had 2,000 reindeer. The Red Army men came, a Nenets named Yangasov was with them. So he collected the reindeer and left the old man only a hundred head. The old man was about to start his migration, and he didn't have enough reindeer to pull even one sled—the ones left were all young and untrained. . . .

Pretty soon people began driving up, one after another. One sled or two at a time. They're saying, "We need to assemble (*mandalas*). People are being taken to jail. For no reason. The shamans are all being taken away." More and more people came to our camp. Not far from us there was another camp—they went off to the north of Yamal, they didn't "assemble." They left for where it was quiet.

The *mandalada* elected two people as chiefs on the Yuribei. Their names were Yamna Seroteta and Khateva Khudi. They were good at talking to people—"didn't make mistakes."

Spring, summer and fall went by. It was the second snow since the *mandalada* began. Yamna Seroteta and five other men went to the mountains, to To-tse-khe Lake (in the Baidarat tundra), to the sacred mound Terenolva. Yamna Seroteta was a powerful shaman. He shouted [conjured] on Terenolva mound and said that people had to be called to a "holy war" (*khebidya sayu*). More and more people came. But some left.

. . .

News came that Red Army men were coming to break up the *man-dalada*. There were 100 of them. People started coming to our camp every day. Everyone gathered in Yamb Yvgnada's tent. Five sleds full of people came to our tent, among them Yamna Seroteta the giant. He asked us, "Who is it that's resting around here? Where's the other half of the people?" We answered, "They've gone around to neighboring camps." He started railing at us, "You're running around visiting, while we aren't even thinking about things like that. There is no one to graze the reindeer—everyone has joined the *mandalada*. Soldiers are marching on us, and you are in here resting!" Then he cooled down, and they left.

The sled teams were hardly gone when some others came—and Yamna Seroteta again. They spent the night in our tent. We asked, "Are the soldiers really coming?" He replied, "They are supposed to arrive tomorrow."

The next morning we had tea, and started rounding up reindeer to harness. I said to my father, "If we're going to assemble, we might as well all do it. If we're going to die, we might as well all die. Give me a sled too." My father replied, "Take one, go ahead."

Yamna Seroteta overheard our conversation and said, "This boy remembers my words. I should have spanked your ass."

"If you want to spank my ass, go ahead and try, I'm not afraid of you," I answered.

"You've got a stout heart. If you want to come with us, let's go."

We left. We came to Yamna's camp. There were five tents and lots of people there. They slaughtered a reindeer a day for meat. There were heaps of antlers from the slaughtered reindeer. There were so many people that the earth moved under their feet. You could hear rumbling under the earth from their steps. I thought that maybe 500 or 600 men had gathered. Everyone knew that today the soldiers were supposed to come.

Then many sleds came into sight. They went down a hill toward the river. They disappeared from view, and when they reappeared, they had already split into two parts and surrounded us. There were 50 of them, two soldiers on each. The sleds came to a stop. Soldiers with rifles got out and stood by the sleds. Several Russians without rifles approached us. There was a Nenets man with them named Nogo, a chief, he'd grown up among Russians. He said to us, "Break this up, stop the *man-dalada*. You can't beat the Russians anyway." Our people answered, "Release the people you've taken in, then we'll break up."

They started searching out our leaders—Yamna Seroteta, of course. He yelled out, "You need me? I'm right here!" The soldiers took him. They took Khateva Khudi too. They couldn't find two of the ones they wanted—they were hiding, lying down inside some sleds. That was Yanuta Vanuito and Norni Khorolia. All in all seven men were arrested.

About thirty Nenets men had brought the Russians. One of them, Portu Khudi, said to us, "Enough, break it up! Your people haven't been taken forever, they'll come back." They took the seven away. And then a blizzard started. It lasted two days. We would wake up in the morning— lots of sleds would be gone, all that was left were the circles [reindeer tracks]. People said, "What did we come here for, if there's nothing we can do anyway?" Each took his own reindeer and went his own way. And so the first *mandalada* dispersed.[52]

It wasn't in the Nenets' power to halt this machine called "the socialist offensive along the entire front," and in fact they didn't seriously try to do so. Following traditional tactics, they often let the machine "deal a crushing blow to an empty spot"—they would retreat, hide themselves in remote parts of the tundra, adapt to *kolkhoz* and administrative innovations, but maintain, with enviable persistence, their own way of life. It would seem that the punishment squads and brigades had made their triumphant sweep across the tundra and that the *kolkhozes* were finally "purged" of *kulaks* and new Soviets elected. Here and there, however, new "nests of counterrevolution" would "suddenly" be discovered. For example, in 1937 A. Puiko, chairman of the Yuzhno-Yamalsk native Soviet, was "exposed" for collaboration with *kulaks*.[53] In its turn, Soviet authorities missed no opportunity to strengthen their superior position using the economic power of Glavsevmorput and the political power of the OGPU.

The War within the War

By the mid-1930s Glavsevmorput had established a whole web of transport and communication facilities to "master" the North. All the activities of Glavsevmorput in Northwestern Siberia were directed from Omsk, an industrial city in the steppe zone located along the Trans-Siberian Railroad. From there Glavsevmorput operated thirteen meteorological stations, seventeen hydrological stations, two aero-meteorological stations, seven observation points, two information bureaus, and seven radio stations.[54] In 1935 a scheduled airline between Tiumen and Obdorsk further opened the northern Ob. Hydroplanes made experimental flights to trade posts and newly built settlements on the Yamal Peninsula.[55]

In 1936 Glavsevmorput launched a new economic activity—fur farming—opening the first fur farm in the region near the village of Katravozh in the Shuryshkary District. The farm obtained forty silver-black foxes from a state fur farm in Moscow, and after a year it began to supply foxes to other farms within the Yamal-Nenets Okrug.[56] Muskrats brought from America were acclimatized and reintroduced on the Polui and Pur rivers, where trade and hunting stations had been built. On the coasts and islands of the Kara Sea, Glavsevmorput established sea mammal hunting stations to harvest beluga whales.

The activities of Glavsevmorput in the Ob North encompassed practically every sphere of economic and social activity. Glavsevmorput assumed responsibility for the first three state farms in the Yamal-Nenets Okrug (on the Nadym, Pur, and Liapin rivers).[57] By 1940, 80 percent of the indigenous people in the Yamal-Nenets Okrug had been coaxed or coerced into 109 collective farms. Twenty of these were on the Yamal Peninsula. During the "Great Patriotic War" (World War II) reindeer owners of Yamal were ordered to deliver their herds to the collective farms.[58] During the years of the war, the herds on Yamal were cut in half largely for "defense needs." In 1941 private owners held six times more reindeer than the collectives. By 1943 the collectives owned nearly as many as private families, and the size of the combined herds had dropped by well more than one-third. (See Table 5.2 and Figure 5.1.)

The order to deliver their herds triggered the Yamal Nenets rebellion in 1943, as the Nenets demanded the liquidation of the *kolkhozy* and the return of their reindeer. Soviet authorities clearly sensed this mild but stubborn resistance. Possibly, their own never-quite-acknowledged powerlessness (something like that experienced by Orthodox missionaries in the nineteenth century, when they retreated in the face of the nomads' indifference to the "true faith") provoked attempts to show their might by any means possible, to frighten those whom they themselves feared. The repressions of the late 1930s cost quite a few tundra dwellers their lives: the Nenets compare 1937 and 1938, in terms of the number of victims, to a war, and they sometimes refer to that time as a *mandalada*. But massive repressions did not dissipate the authorities' fear of some mysterious tundra "counterrevolution," nor did they make the "nomad enemy" any more understandable or accessible. One can imagine just how difficult both living and working conditions were for OGPU-NKVD-KGB officers. Consequently, it is no surprise that the *mandalada* of 1943 was organized by the Yamal District KGB office itself.[59]

What prompted the KGB section head Medvedev to stir up this "revolt in the Yamal tundra" in the autumn of 1943? Was it some directive from higher up, some desire to demonstrate his vigilance, the need to settle private scores, or genuine apprehensions concerning a rebellion in the making? According to Nenets accounts of the time, the military was requisitioning reindeer in large numbers, and it may be that Medvedev knew that many Nenets were unhappy with the Soviet regime, and that the most unreconciled of them were migrating to the tundra of northern Yamal. It may be that he was acting quite professionally (for that era)—nipping a revolt in the bud, organizing it himself, the better then to crush it.

Medvedev chose Mans Yezyngi, chairman of the "Red October" *kolkhoz*, to carry out his plan. Through an interpreter (district doctor P. A. Shutkin), he managed to persuade Yezyngi of the necessity of calling a *mandalada* together. In Shutkin's words,

> Medvedev suggested that Mans Yezyngi visit the camps of Vengo Sele and Yaptik Satoku and see what their attitudes are, invite them to "assemble" and if they agreed, take them along to all the *kolkhoz* camps from Malygin Strait to Nei-to Lake, issuing a call to the *mandalada*. I reminded Medvedev that the situation in the tundra, given the lack of bread and miscalculations in taxes, might push some Nenets into genuine anti-Soviet activity and lead to dire consequences. . . . Medvedev answered that I didn't understand operations work and therefore was obliged to translate literally and exactly, and also to keep the content of this discussion secret.[60]

As was expected, Sele Vengo and Satoku Yaptik readily supported the idea of a *mandalada*. According to custom, the *pidtevy pya* (the stick on which personal signs could be marked in support of the gathering) was prepared and sent from camp to camp. The chief goal of the *mandalada*, they announced, was dividing up the *kolkhoz* reindeer—that is, returning them to their owners.

Caught up in his own rhetoric, Mans Yezyngi vividly described the forth-coming repressions. Nyda Vanuito, in his testimony, described the scene in his camp when the leaders came to visit in November 1943:

> After tea, Yezangi Mans, started saying that we should join the *man-dalada*. I asked, "Why? The Nenets don't need it." He answered that the Russians had decided to try everyone on the *kolkhoz* who wasn't working hard. This would be the punishment: they would take the guilty ones and hang them by their feet from a pole, douse them in kerosene and set them on fire. "Will the Nenets stand for that?" concluded Yezangi Mans. I said that people should work hard and then there wouldn't be a trial. Vengo Sele mostly kept quiet, and when he heard that Nenets would be set on fire, he looked surprised, and I understood that this was news to him.

Taking into account that Nyda Vanuito was slightly adjusting his attitude toward *kolkhoz* work for the prosecution's sake, his stance clearly illustrates the caution (or perhaps puzzlement) with which the tundra reindeer herders regarded this scheme. And in fact, the "provocateur" (as A. Petrushin calls Mans Yezyngi) was forced to return to Tambei without accomplishing any-thing.

In the meantime, Medvedev, sure of the operation's success, sent a telegram to the KGB district section in Salekhard: "On May 1, at the Kalinin, Stalin and Kirov kolkhozes, a *mandala* rebellion was uncovered. It is led by Vengo Sele and Yaptik Satoku. The rebels are dividing up the *kolkhoz* herds. There is threat of armed insurrection." After receiving word from Yezyngi that the Nenets were hesitating, Medvedev decided to settle their doubts once and for all—he took an operations group to Sele Vengo's camp and fired on it from a distance. This finally persuaded the Nenets that Yezyngi was right about Russian plans to kill Nenets for not fulfilling their quotas for fur and fish.

So the plan succeeded, and a *mandalada* indeed spread over the northern Yamal tundra. Another telegram went out from Tambei: "Group returned today, November 16, from the tundra. There was a ten-minute exchange of fire. No casualties. Situation serious. Request lightweight machine guns to be sent by plane. 'Mandala' has 200 men."

Soon the news of "revolt in the Yamal tundra" reached the Omsk Region KGB head, a Colonel Bykov, and even KGB minister Merkulov (although the latter seemed unimpressed by the report on the "Nenets rebellion"). At the regional level, however, the KGB enthusiastically began working out the operation. A Lieutenant Colonel Garanin, Bykov's second-in-command, flew to Tambei, escorted by several high-ranking officials and a company of machine-gunners.

An operations group of 50 sleds moved out of Tambei into the tundra. After capturing two reindeer herds and thoroughly terrifying tundra dwellers, they proposed that the "mandalists" assemble at Satoku Yaptik's camp. More than 150 men appeared, and according to a list confirmed by Garanin, Medvedev arrested 50 of them.

When the operations group (which had apparently undergone special training in neutralizing tundra bandits) began stripping the prisoners of their outer clothing and tying them to the sleds, some of the captives tried to run. The soldiers opened fire, killing seven and wounding seven more. The remaining Nenets were taken to Tambei. Meanwhile, Colonel Garanin, an experience spy-catcher, managed to search out and arrest "a resident agent of German intelligence," a certain Pliusnin who happened to be the head of a Glavsevmorput hydrographic group. If the KGB managed to beat Pliusnin into an admission of "cooperation with Hitler's intelligence organization and direction of the rebellion movement among the local populace," then what could confused and frightened Mans Yezyngi do but testify against every single one of the defendants, including Pliusin?

The "architects of victory" over the Yamal reindeer herders got their medals and, some time later, their five (Bykov), eight (Garanin and Yezyngi), and ten (Medvedev) years of labor camp. They were just chips in a much bigger game.[61]

All Northwestern Siberian rebellions of the twentieth century developed in nomad territory, while the sedentary natives tended to be either observers or Soviet collaborators. Notably, other centers of rebellion of 1934 among the Khanty, forest Nenets, and Sel'kup were Kazym and Tol'ka—taiga areas in which reindeer herding was the most developed, and the rebels were those whose lives were closely attached to herding, while the key figures representing Soviet power came from the villages. Reindeer herding provided a level of economic and social independence that allowed indigenous peoples not only to get along without "civilized" support but also to act in opposition to it.

Everywhere shamans played a leadership role in rebellions, and everywhere the suppression of rebellion meant capture and imprisonment of shamans. Twenty-nine of the Khanty and forest Nenets who were brought to trial in connection with the Kazym rebellion were shamans.[62] As Nenets say, "the shamans' drums stopped after the last war." What do they mean, the Great Patriotic War or their own fight, the war within the War?

It is an odd coincidence that leaders of the last rebellion and the leader of a Glavsevmorput hydrographic expedition became inmates in the same prison. The intense involvement of Glavsevmorput in the economic and social affairs of natives of the Ob North had ended in 1938, when the administration's economic and cultural branches were transferred to other government ministries. But one more significant act occurred before the end of the war. In 1942 the mining and geological branches of Glavsevmorput, which had continued to conduct surveys on the Yamal and the Taimyr, discovered gas and oil deposits in the Yamal-Nenets Okrug.[63]

5

Strained Dialogue

It is unknown when Junior Yaptik's eyes opened. He awoke and watched. His brothers' sledges were overturned, but his sledge was still standing. His brothers' reindeer were dead, but his were still grazing. He harnessed his reindeer. He rode.

Recollecting events of the last *mandalada*, Yedeiko Ngokateta recently said that most of the Nenets' leaders had been from the Yaptik clan. Satoku Yaptik, he recounted, had been arrested and severely beaten. His hip broken, Satoku was taken to Salekhard and executed there. He was said to have been later resurrected and reappeared on the northern tundra. In another vignette Shaman Ngaivodiu Yaptik was shot by several guns, but remained alive and escaped driving a white reindeer team that was mysteriously shaped from the snow. These stories have become new myths about Yaptiks. Yedeiko remembered one other, more realistic tale about a *mandalada* leader: Khasavamboi Yaptik had been arrested and imprisoned four times, and each time he found a way to escape. The last days he spent not far from Novyi Port, living in a pit house. The Nenets now treat the place of his house as sacred.[1]

The image of Khasavamboi Yaptik living in his pit house, having few or perhaps no reindeer, echoes the "precultural" portrait of the sleeping Yaptik brothers from our legend. As a consequence of the war, many Nenets returned to small-scale herding conditions as depicted in the beginning of "Five Yaptiks." As mentioned in Chapter 4, in the early 1930s a large number of herders moved north to escape collectivization. In 1943 this aggregation of people was stunned by the military suppression; then many reindeer owners were deprived of their reindeer. The northern tundra dwellers found themselves without any means of subsistence. According to Nenets' recollections, "At the end of the war there was a horrible famine." Authorities urged tundra dwellers to move to villages of southern Yamal, where they could survive. Many did relocate, settling in villages. Some of them later returned to northern Yamal. For example, Lachu Ngokateta made the long migration back, driving his remaining eight reindeer. Today his son Nikolai Ngokateta owns several hundred reindeer and has become a leader in the northern, Seyaha tundra.

Herders and Settlers

According to historical records, in 1947 Soviet officials closed eight collective farms of the former Tambei District in northern Yamal and relocated 335 households to southern Yamal.[2] From the early 1950s, Soviet authorities reorganized the collectives of Yamal, merging smaller farms into larger units. As a result of economic reorganization in 1961, the collectives of the okrug were consolidated into a dozen large state farms,[3] with the former "members" of the collectives becoming "workers" for the state farms (*sovkhozy*). Three *sovkhozy* were established in the Yamal District: Yamal'skii on the northern tundra (with its administrative center in Seyaha), Yarsalinskii on the central and southern tundra (with its center in Yar-Sale), and Rossia (now Panaevsk) on the western tundra (with its center in Panaevsk). (See Map 3.) In addition, two fishery plants, Puiko and Novyi Port, were endowed with reindeer herds. (See Table 5.1.)

Table 5.1. Number of domestic reindeer on Yamal, 1960–1994

Herd Location	1960	1980	1994
Sovkhoz "Yarsalinskii"	16,372	28,500	36,756
Sovkhoz "Yamal'skii"	3,899	18,000	15,787
Sovkhoz "Rossia"	15,175	16,520	17,513
Novoportovskii fishing plant	24,111	12,552	—
Puikovskii fishing plant	12,229	5,546	—
Total state-owned reindeer	71,786	81,118	70,056
Total privately owned reindeer	29,720	50,070	100,021
Total reindeer in Yamal District	101,506	131,188	170,077

Source: From archival data of the Yamal District department of the SPCU (Communist party) from the Yamal Museum in Yar-Sale.

These fishery plants, as well as the administrative center of the Yamal District, Yar-Sale, became the base of a new Yamal population, settlers or villagers who were largely "special resettlers" (Russian plural: *spetspereselentsy*) from southern Russia, Ukraine, Moldavia, and other republics. But many of those Yamal Nenets who were resettled after the war remained in southern Yamal, working in the newly established plants in Novyi Port and Puiko. In July 1994 we encountered an old man living in Siunai-Sale, on the southern coast of Yamal, near Yar-Sale. Like so many others, this man had been relocated from the Mordiyaha River, in northwestern Yamal, to a fishing collective near Novyi Port.[4] His wife recalled being beaten in those early days for being late to work at the fish-processing plants. (The regime of these fishery enterprises remained warlike for a time.) During "modernization" and development, the government relocated many natives from the tundra to villages to work in commercial fishing and processing.[5]

For those remaining on the tundra, conditions were also hard. The collectivization process begun in the late 1920s was completed in the early 1950s throughout the Yamal-Nenets area. From 1941 to 1950, the ratio of private to collectively held reindeer fell from 6:1 to 1:2. As the transfer of ownership coincided with the war years, the number of privately held reindeer plummeted: by 1950 private herds had dropped by almost 100,000 reindeer, to less than one-fifth the number that had been privately owned in 1941, while the total number of reindeer on Yamal had been cut in half. (See Table 5.2 and Figure 5.1.)

Table 5.2. Dynamics of reindeer on Yamal during the crisis (1940s)

Year	Communal	Private	Total
1941	20,865	122,080	142,945
1942	34,377	81,903	116,280
1943	43,766	43,962	87,728
1944	34,493	40,183	74,676
1945	34,363	34,427	68,790
1946	36,413	31,059	67,472
1948	42,919	21,552	64,471
1949	34,735	25,683	60,418
1950	45,169	22,412	67,581

Source: From archival data of the Yamal District department of the SPCU (Communist party) from the Yamal Museum in Yar-Sale. "Communal" combines reindeer of *kolkhozy* and state enterprises. "Private" includes reindeer owned privately by members of *kolkhozy* and independent herders.

Being on the edge of catastrophe, Yamal reindeer herding was saved by something of a miracle. Compared with most of Russia, where the intensive collectivization process lasted long enough to suppress the rural economy, on Yamal it lasted only a decade. Stalin's death in 1953 ended this epoch of open violence against traditional economies. Herders on Yamal found ways to save their herds even though the reindeer were officially delivered to "collectives" and later to state farms. The total number of reindeer on Yamal increased by almost 50 percent from 1950 to 1960 and had nearly doubled by 1980. (See Tables 5.1 and 5.2 and Figure 5.1.)

During the next decades, even though Soviet policy encouraged a sedentary lifestyle, the Nenets preserved their traditional nomadic style and steadily increased their herds. They devised ways to satisfy officials and retain their customs. One trick was to mix the collective and private herds to make it impossible for inspectors to know the actual ratio of private to common reindeer. Additionally, young herders, who were officially workers of the state brigades, pastured collective herds, and their old relatives, registered as "pensioners" or "hunters," pastured private herds. The two herds migrated side by side, so that it was impossible for authorities to figure out how many reindeer were privately held. Sometimes local authorities, even after having been

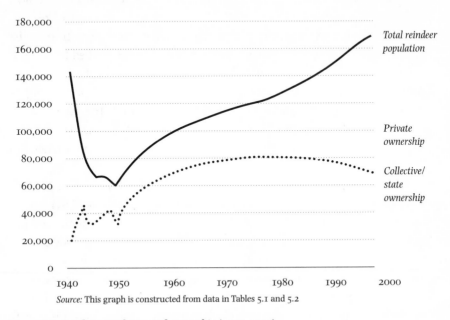

Source: This graph is constructed from data in Tables 5.1 and 5.2

Figure 5.1. Reindeer population and ownership (1941–1994)

informed of a "trick," let the situation be. Okrug and local authorities sometimes softened the demands of the central power concerning sedentary occupation and collective ownership. Private herds were allowed but limited in
size. In the 1970s each herder in northern Yamal could own eighty reindeer,
while southern herders were allowed only fifty. That was the law. The story of
Irimboi Vanuito as retold by his son Mikhail, is closer to reality:

> One time in the 1960s, people from the settlement came to my camp.
> At that time I had 1,500 reindeer. I invited [the people] into the tent, giv-
> ing a command to my best dog, Terenzia, to split the herd. In the tent, we
> talked [discussed the number of reindeer I was compelled to sell], and
> they agreed to leave me 150 reindeer. We rounded up the herd. They took
> all but 150. Later on when I rounded up my reindeer from the nearest tun-
> dra, I counted the herd as 600, thanks to my dog.

Some time later, when the herd had increased to 800, Mikhail recalled,
"Father said to me and my brother, 'Sons, we need to divide our herd into
three parts; that's the way to preserve it.'" (At that time, *sovkhoz* authorities
fulfilled the state plans in part by compelling herders to sell private reindeer at
low, fixed prices.) This story could be told freely today because, in the 1980s,
the government abolished laws strictly limiting privately held herds. This policy change produced a dramatic increase in private stocks only partly offset by
reductions in *sovkhoz* herds. In 1994 official statistics established herd numbers in the Yamal District at 170,077,[6] with 59 percent held privately.
Although overall herd numbers have grown by 23 percent since 1980, privately held reindeer doubled from 50,070 to 100,021, while the population of
state farm herds in the district declined from 1980 levels by only 11,062. The
trend is toward further reduction of *sovkhoz* herds as private ownership
increases.

The Soviets' settlement policy disrupted the Nenets' lifestyle in another
dimension. The rhythm of activity for the Nenets, which we described in
Chapter 1, was destroyed for those who became villagers. Off the tundra, the
space of male activity, men were deprived of their economic and social position. The overwhelming majority of village occupations were women's work
(from a traditional point of view), and this "new way of life" narrowed the
male realm even more. This became even more pronounced in taiga villages,
where "new types of domestic economy" (market gardening, fur farming, cat-

tle breeding) oriented exclusively toward women were actively promoted. The expanding system of village services (trade, medicine, and so on) provided mostly women's jobs. Moreover, in Soviet administrative functions the native women proved no less capable than the men, and sometimes more capable, because they were less prone to the chief "male" activity in villages—hard drinking.

Establishment of boarding schools as well as construction and operation of the *kul'tbaza* ("cultural bases") particularly affected children and their mothers. Once delivered (via boarding schools) from "the excessive toil" of bringing up children and processing "man's harvest" (from hunting, fishing, and reindeer breeding), women had the opportunity to finish high school and even seek higher education, to work in their chosen field, and to make money and take it to the store. Women left the cultural-economic circle of the tent and camp that was traditionally the woman's place.

By 1945 literacy among northern natives had reached only 6 percent. That a whole generation of natives had grown up during a quarter century of Soviet rule without being educated became a topic of concern at the regular party conference of the Yamal-Nenets Okrug in February 1945. The following year the Executive Committee of the Tiumen regional council of workers' deputies passed a mandatory education resolution and set fines and punishments for failure to send children to school. School directors also could be "warned," fined about 100 rubles, or sentenced to mandatory hard labor for one month for letting children miss classes without good reason.[7]

Despite these harsh laws, in 1952, six years after passage of a universal compulsory education law, 45 percent of the school-age children (329 of the 731 children) in the native population of the Yamal District did not begin school.[8] Some parents took their children away from school during the academic year, and some students ran away from the boarding schools.[9] While the administrative authorities frequently discussed questions of educating native children, they failed to analyze the reasons for parents' reluctance to send their children to boarding schools.

At the end of the 1950s and the beginning of the 1960s, the influence of schools on nomadic areas widened. Conditions in the schools had worsened as resources were stretched to accommodate the influx of workers brought to expand the industrial economy. In response, a 1957 resolution of the Central Committee of the CPSU addressed improvement of public education boards and called for full state support for study and the living needs of northern children. Rations and provisions of clothes and shoes increased, and the state assumed the entire expense of transporting children to and from boarding schools, regardless of the residence of parents. In response to the resolution, 42 new boarding schools accommodating 2,300 students were opened in the Yamal-Nenets Okrug.[10]

In the late 1950s the state finally had emerged victorious from the war between native parents and state school authorities over control of the education of children. It is difficult to see a winner in this war, however, for while the state increased enrollments and achieved widespread literacy, it failed to prepare significant numbers of future generations for legitimate participation in the industrial economy. While scientists and administrators debated the pros and cons of involving natives in industrial work, education of natives shifted increasingly to polytechnical schools. From 1971 to 1981 the number of elementary schools in the region was cut in half, and "incomplete" (eight-year) schools dropped by one-third, while the number of secondary schools rose sharply.[11] Schools in smaller settlements were closed, forcing children to go to more distant boarding schools. Services in small native communities in general were far worse than those provided in the large towns that housed oil and gas workers and their families. The dominant share of regional resources for medical, commercial, and cultural services were directed to the newcomer population. At the beginning of the 1980s in the Yamal-Nenets Okrug, Nenets children from the tundra were separated from other pupils in boarding schools. Many Nenets children were directed to "special classes" in which they were neither prepared for herding trades nor for skilled jobs in new economic activities.

The Age of Oil and Gas

While timber, fish, and fur production became important branches of the new economy, state run oil and gas monopolies effectively ruled Northwestern Siberia from the 1960s through to the 1980s as Glavsevmorput had earlier. Government policies facilitated these monopolies by authorizing high salaries and bonuses for workers willing to move north to construct modern cities, work in the oil and gas fields, and further the industrialization of reindeer herding and other traditional trades.

Northwestern Siberian oil workers produced the first million tons of oil in 1965; in 5 years production rose to 28.5 million tons; by 1975, to 143.2 million, and by 1980 to 307.9 million tons. Gas production, which totaled 3.3 million cubic meters in 1965, rose to 9.5 million cubic meters in 1970, to 38 million cubic meters in 1975, and to 160 million cubic meters in 1980. Thousands of miles of pipelines, roads, and railroads cut across the tundra and taiga. About one million tons of oil spilled annually from pipelines in the Tiumen region. By 1988, 11 million hectares (42,460 square miles) of reindeer pastures in the Yamal-Nenets and Khanty-Mansiisk okrugs had become unusable according to widespread reports.[12]

To make matters worse, industrial and military activities not only in Northwestern Siberia but outside as well transported air and water pollution to the tundra and taiga. Environmental pollutants including persistent organic pollutants (POPs), heavy metals, and radioactivity have come from the mining, metallurgical, chemical, nuclear, and military industries of Ekaterinburg, Chelyabinsk, Ust'-Kamenogorsk, Omsk, Barnaul, Biisk, Novosibirsk, Kemerovo, and Tomsk, as well as from more distant locales. "The largest releases of radioactive wastes in the world have been recorded over the last few decades" at sites including Chelyabinsk and Tomsk on rivers that flow into the Ob and at Krasnoyarsk on the Yenisei. Wastes totaling more than 100 million curies were discharged into lakes and rivers at one site, and billions of curies have been injected directly underground.[13] From the 1960s into the 1980s, the Soviet Union dumped containers and barges, as well as ships and submarines containing nuclear reactors both with and without spent fuel, into the waters of the Kara Sea off of Novaya Zemlya. Researchers are continuing to measure potential releases, studying whether and how the radionuclides migrate and attempting to determine how they might affect human populations and the ecosystem.[14] Between 1955 and 1990 the Soviet military conducted 132 nuclear tests on Novaya Zemlya, including 87 above-ground or atmospheric tests, 3 underwater tests, and 42 underground tests.[15] While a report prepared by the U.S. Office of Technology Assessment states that "almost all of the fallout was distributed globally, rather than locally," it does not rule out the probability that "close-in fallout may have been deposited over the Kara Sea" and perhaps by extension over the Yamal Peninsula as atmospheric transport was generally toward the east.[16] In addition, fifteen underground nuclear explosions occurred in the region for the stated purpose of increasing oil production in the middle Ob basin.

From the 1960s through the 1980s, the indigenous populations became marginalized in their homelands. The need for skilled workers in the oil and gas fields and the building of new towns to accommodate workers and their families led to a tripling of the population of the Tiumen Oblast between 1965 and 1990. The largest part of this increase was in the Yamal-Nenets and Khanty-Mansiisk okrugs, which increased sevenfold and ninefold, respectively. In 1897 indigenous peoples comprised almost 80 percent of the population of the region that became the Yamal-Nenets Okrug . By 1939 the Nenets, Khanty, and Sel'kup together were in the minority, and by 1959 they composed only one-third of the okrug population. With the okrug population almost doubling in the 1970s, the indigenous population (though still increasing in absolute numbers) dropped to 16 percent, and by 1989 the figure fell to only 6 percent of the population in their homelands. (See Table 5.3.)

This marginalization of the indigenous population was more pronounced in the regions of heavy exploration and development of oil, so that the indigenous populations in the Yamal and Priural districts still comprised roughly half the total population in 1989. (See Tables 5.4 and 5.5.)

Because all formalized systems of native self-government had already been eradicated, the demographic shifts over the last 100 years had particularly negative effects on the power and influence that native peoples could have on local and regional government. Development of oil and gas and displacement of the indigenous population took place without negotiation or discussion.[17]

Table 5.3. Indigenous population in the Yamal-Nenets Autonomous Okrug

Census Year	Nenets	Khanty	Sel'kup*	Total Population	Natives as % of Total
1897	4,368	4,106	48	10,686	79.7
1926	9,384	3,842	—	18,166	72.8
1939	13,454	5,367	87	45,840	41.2
1959	13,977	5,519	1,245	62,334	33.3
1970	17,538	6,513	1,710	79,977	32.2
1979	17,404	6,466	1,611	158,844	16.0
1989	20,917	7,247	1,530	494,844	6.0

* The sharp population increase between the 1939 and 1959 censuses can be explained by the fact that part of Turukhansk region was taken from Krasnoyarsk Territory and transferred to the Yamal-Nenets Okrug, forming the Krasnosel'kupsk region.

Source: Compiled by Alexander I. Pika and Dimitri Bogoyavlinsky from census data in Russia's state and departmental archives.

Revival of Leadership

As the era of glasnost arrived in the late 1980s, those ready to test the parameters of the new openness in the Soviet Union began with environmental issues. Khanty writer Yeremei Aipin penned a passionate and moving report of environmental destruction of the taiga by oil, gas, and timber interests, recounting how oil workers had stolen his father's boots, leaving the old man to trudge home on a January night in his socks; how loggers had taken his father's sledge and dogs (his only transport) during another winter; and finally how loggers had "cut down all the trees on the tribal cemetery thus

Table 5.4. Population of the Yamal District (Yamal-Nenets Autonomous Okrug)

Census Year	Nenets	Khanty	Total Indigenous Population	Total Population
1897	1320	3	1,323	1,338
1926	3229	4	3233	3,233
1939	5273	246	5519	8,430
1959	4533	147	4680	8,245
1970	5852	232	6084	9,727
1979	6251	289	6540	12,334
1989	7181	272	7453	15,119
1994*	8636	341	8977	15,507

*Figures for 1994 are from the Yamal District offices in Yar-Sale.
Source: Compiled by Alexander I. Pika and Dimitri Bogoyavlinsky from census data in Russia's state and departmental archives.

Table 5.5. Population of the Priural District (Yamal-Nenets Autonomous Okrug)

Census Year	Nenets	Khanty	Total Indigenous Population	Total Population
1897	507	1780	2287	2287
1926	1457	1070	2527	3551
1939	1623	1666	3289	6403
1959	1127	1219	2346	5466
1970	1793	1746	3539	5793
1979	1677	1571	3248	6080
1989	1930	1669	3599	6652

Source: Compiled by Alexander I. Pika and Dimitri Bogoyavlinsky from census data in Russia's state and departmental archives.

ruining [his father's] final resting place." The article appeared in *Pravda* in June 1989 and was later translated into English, drawing worldwide attention to the appalling destruction of indigenous lands in Northwestern Siberia.[18] The pleas of indigenous writers were supported by ecologists, geographers, and sociologists who had worked in Northwestern Siberia and had seen first-hand the impacts of oil and gas development. The crisis on Yamal thus became a focal point for the new environmentalism in the early stages of glasnost and before the demise of the Soviet Union. In 1989 indigenous people established a regional native association, Yamal for Our Descendants (Yamal Potomkam), to oppose the ecological destruction of the Yamal Peninsula, improve economic and social conditions, and increase self-government. Together with the newly formed State Committee on Environmental Protection, environmental organizations, scientists, and local administrative agencies, indigenous people pressed the government to halt development of the Yamal gas fields. In 1989 the government declared a temporary moratorium on full-scale development of Yamal gas and called for environmental and social impact studies.[19]

In the 1990s the government commissioned environmental and social impact assessments of alternative pipeline routes to move gas south from the west-central part of the peninsula. The moratorium on construction was never seriously implemented, but construction of the pipeline was delayed while, for the first time, alternative routes were examined and their environmental, social, and economic risks and costs were compared. Before the protests, plans called for gas deliveries to begin in 1991. By 1989 the deadline was pushed back five to seven years. Engineers had originally planned for ten parallel pipelines to transect the peninsula from Bovanenko to Novyi Port, cutting across the core pasturelands and valuable fishing grounds. Today these plans have been modified to an anticipated construction of three parallel pipelines (and possibly a "spare" fourth in case of loss of one of the others). The preferred route has shifted to cross Baidarata Bay, avoiding the central pastures.[20] Although construction of the railroad and road has continued, lack of financing has indefinitely postponed construction of any pipeline on Yamal. And although the Nenets and the Khanty compose only a small minority in their regions, they were able at the end of the Soviet period to tap into national and international public support that gave them political clout far beyond their slim numbers.

Other small signs indicate the reemergence of leaders who seek the pro-

tection of grazing lands and fishing grounds and the revitalization of indigenous self-government. Native associations and communities are also calling
for the return of local education to the villages and small settlements so that
the children will not be removed from their parents at an early age. Authorities on Yamal finally agreed to open a primary school in the small fishing community of Siunai-Sale in 1994, after many years of requests from the local
parents. The availability both of space for the school in an existing building
and of two native-speaking teachers was sufficient for the education department in Yar-Sale to open the school. In the view of administrators, the main
obstacle to the creation of more "small, compact schools" is the difficulty of
recruiting native teachers to live in the settlements. Perhaps in time, as natives
gain greater control of the education system, they will develop a new cur-
riculum, provide on-site training of village residents as teachers, and adjust
the criteria for teacher certification to meet community goals.

In April 1990 Nenets herders on the Yaptik-Sale tundra objected to the
placement of an exploratory drilling rig near the headwaters of a fish spawn-
ing stream that originates in Yarto Lake. At a local council meeting, Anatoly
Hudi explained, "If [the rig] is not delivered to another place, the water in the
river will be polluted, and all the fish from there reach Ob Bay. Besides, we
think in summertime, there wouldn't be a possibility to use tractors there
along the tundra or our reindeer would be disturbed."[21] The drillers did in fact
move the rig to the opposite side of the lake, away from the headwaters of the
stream, where the potential for pollution was reduced though not eliminated.
It was a small victory, but one that might not have occurred only a few years
earlier. In July 1992 the authors visited the then-abandoned drill rig, traveling
forty kilometers through winding streams to reach the headwaters, a small
blue lake on the far side of which the metal hulk loomed on a bank surrounded by sand and drill tailings. Behind the rig a strange-colored pond held
the liquids spewed up from the test well. Makeshift metal huts remained. An
occasional magazine photo flapped from the patterned wallpaper of shacks in
which the well drillers had briefly lived. These recent remains lie within sight
of the much more ancient remains of nomads who had left a more subtle
record of their regular presence on the lake's banks in occasional places of
exposed dark sediment.

To the south, the forest Nenets and the Khanty protested the destruction
of their homelands by oil development. Over a twenty-year period the traditional lands and waters of the Khanty and the forest Nenets had been devas-

tated by oil pollution and plundered by thousands of newcomers who helped themselves to wild mushrooms and berries, game and fish while the indigenous people were forced to survive increasingly marginal circumstances. According to the protesters, thirty men, women, and children (inhabitants of the Variogan taiga) had died over two decades from causes related to oil exploration, and many reindeer had been killed on the heavily used road between Raduzhny (an oil town in the taiga ironically named "Rainbow City") and the western Variogan region. Finally, in the summer of 1990, an oil truck hit and killed an old Nenets man's reindeer—his only means of transportation to hunting and fishing grounds, triggering a response that resonated around the world. Families from five clans in the area constructed a tent in the middle of a bridge that blocked trucks and machinery in both directions. Reports and photos of the protest reached Moscow and beyond. Native leaders from Moscow and Khanty-Mansiisk—Vladimir Sangi, Evdokia Gayer, and Yeremei Aipin—appeared at the blockade. The locals told how reindeer had not only been struck accidentally but intentionally; they were decapitated and their carcasses were left to rot. Locals gave accounts of the desecration of a Nenets grave and told how trucks had terrorized an entire native camp, destroying its storehouse, salted fish, and winter clothing.[22] "Compensation" for damage and destruction of lands and resources consisted of a bus and yearly payments of 300,000 rubles to the Yariogan village council. Yuri Vaella Aivaseda, a forest Nenets poet and local leader, became the spokesperson for the protest. He rejected offers of financial compensation and asked rather that the destruction cease. Aivaseda, who edited a local newspaper in forest Nenets, has been in the forefront of a cultural revival in his homeland on the Agan River, now surrounded by oil and gas fields.

Since the late 1980s a revival has taken place, but its direction is still unclear. The official leaders of the new movement for ethnic/cultural revival are often the people who had been brought up in accordance with the Soviet value system. Such persons believe that political goals are more important than the preservation and revival of the traditional native culture. Another major problem for Nenets leaders is to find ways to mediate between the nomadic and settled populations. The settled and semi-nomadic people of Yamal reside in compact groupings, consisting of a so-called ethnic village and its surrounding areas and governed by a rural council (Russian: *sel'sovet*). While the village administration is also the local government for the nomadic herders who are registered in that *sel'sovet*, the more important administrative office for herders is that of the state farm (*sovkhoz*), which may be located in a different village or town. The Yamal tundra is now divided into several "tundras"—Yaptik-Sale, Seyaha, Novyi Port, and others.

For Nenets reindeer herders, sedentary life in Soviet-style villages contradicted the essential principles of their traditional lifestyle; moreover, in their indigenous philosophy, sedentary life was regarded as a sign of bad luck, misery, and a lack of freedom. In earlier eras only failed herders and families who had lost their herds became village dwellers. At the same time, during the Soviet period some villagers acquired new skills and higher education or technical training, and because of this the village community acquired a new and, in some respects, higher status vis-à-vis the remaining nomads. As in earlier times, however, the tundra has remained the main production base and the source of traditional values and practices. Still, Nenets villagers have developed over the years a new type of community, one offering a way of life that differs considerably from that of the tundra. In the villages new clan formations have grown and occupied important places in the village social hierarchy.

Contrary to what one might have expected, our observations suggest that there are no sharp contradictions between the tundra and the village. In various respects they complement each other, exchanging useful goods and ideas. Although there has been competition for prestige between the tundra and village communities, both have produced their own cohorts of Nenets leaders.

In the so-called Yaptik-Sale tundra (the area surrounding the village of Yaptiksale), the Yaptik clan predominates, which is reflected in the area's name.[23] According to local cultural tradition, its members are considered to be the owners of area pastures. Secondary clans, such as the Salinder, the Niarui, and others, are represented in the tundra in relatively small numbers. Within the village, however, members of these clans are more numerous and have more power than the Yaptik, and because of this they provide the counterweight to the Yaptiks' influence in the tundra surrounding the village. The village, being more involved with commercial winter fishery than with tundra reindeer herding, seems to be a relatively autonomous community within the entire Yaptik-Sale region. About ten to twelve brigades of fishermen from the southern Yamal area (Novyi Port fish factory) are brought to the coastal part of the Yaptik-Sale area in the wintertime. At the time of our field research, Yaptiksale village served as an intermediary between the tundra Nenets and the Russian as well as some Nenets fishermen brought in from the outside. Remarkably, this intermediary role is being played mostly by the native women, who generally have more formal Soviet/Russian schooling than the native men and constitute the majority of the village's inhabitants.

The elite native group in this village consists of representatives of the Niarui clan. Three young, formally educated women from the same family occupy the key positions in the settlement, such as managing the "cultural" activities (for example, organizing "festivals of native culture," managing the work of the village community club, and so on) and serving as the secretaries of the local administrative officers—positions of some significance and prestige in these communities. Their mother is a distinguished elderly leader among the women of the village. She controls a great deal of day-to-day information and appears to be the main advisor for most of the villagers. In one case, her adult sons consulted her about to the possibility of visiting a local shaman. They also clearly see her as the chief judge of their bad actions (for instance, she was the only one capable of bringing an end to their drinking sprees).

Apart from the village, just across the river, lives this old woman's relative, known among the local people as a shaman. He purposefully maintains a lifestyle marginal to that of the community, which is expressed, for example, in his keeping a large pack of vicious dogs in his tent. According to an unwritten local rule, one could gain access to this shaman, a member of the Niarui clan, through the intercession of this old woman, who belongs to the same kinship group. For the villagers as well as strangers, the shaman himself personifies some sort of frightening force that adds support to his clan's authority and prestige.

Because of its alliance with this Niarui clan, the Salinder clan, which is heavily represented on the tundra, also enjoys high status. In fact, the aforementioned old woman's maternal relatives come from the Salinder clan, and she maintains close ties with its members living on the tundra. Representatives of the Salinder clan have a local reputation of being aggressive and prone to engage in conflicts. This reputation adds to their influence on the tundra as well as in the village. On the tundra, however, despite their aggressive character, they are overshadowed by a much larger "modest" clan, Yaptik. Representatives of the Yaptik clan traditionally have had a legitimate access to the land in the surrounding Yaptik-Sale tundra, or at least to the largest part of that territory. They still make decisions about all of the questions concerning the timing and routes of the herding migration and the use and allocation of pastures. The Yaptiks could be characterized as the clan responsible for the reindeer herds' well-being in all of the Yaptik-Sale tundra. After all, the fetish representing the chief spirit-protector of the Yaptik-Sale tundra (and one of the central deities of the pan-Nenets pantheon), Yaptik-haesie, has always been cared for by one of the eldest men of the Yaptik clan.

Several esteemed male elders of the Yaptik clan have a major say in the decision-making process on the tundra. In communicating their decisions to the village, these men exercise extreme caution, as they know that these decisions might have negative consequences or bring no results. Instead of being communicated directly to the villages, the views of these elders are conveyed through their sons or younger relatives, who know Russian quite well and therefore freely communicate with the entire village, including its non-Nenets residents. Today most tundra dwellers agree that many important decisions affecting their lives, including those concerning the use of pasturelands for current industrial gas and oil development, are made without any significant participation of the reindeer herders. That these major decisions are the prerogative of the regional non-Nenets authorities and are then transmitted through the village authorities increases the communication gap between the tundra and village communities. Thus different forms of leadership exist on the tundra and in the village. In the latter, leadership is based on the native leaders' ties with the higher officials in charge of administration and industrial development, including transportation. From the natives' viewpoint, village leadership is exercised by women who mediate between the tundra dwellers and the outsiders—that is, the Russian and Nenets fishermen who arrive to work in the winter fishery. On the tundra, another version of leadership exists—this one based on traditional land use and social relationships.

The leadership situation in other areas of the Yamal Peninsula both resembles and differs from that of Yaptik-Sale. For example, in the northern Seyaha tundra, where traditional northern-Nenets values, lifestyle, and economic activities (reindeer hunting and herding and fishing) have been best preserved, the dominant clan, Ngokateta (in Nenets, "owners of many reindeer"), provides leadership for both the tundra and the village. For almost twenty years, one of the clan's male elders has served as the formal village leader in his capacity as head of the local state administration. Nevertheless, his relationship with the tundra dwellers has always been based on his frequent visits with them and, since 1990, through a new form of commercial activity conducted by him and his sons—the gathering of *panty* (reindeer antlers) for sale, trapping for furs, and the production of reindeer meat. In some respects his activity is greatly dependent for transportation and financing on the oil and gas enterprises in nearby Sabetta, a settlement run by the Russian gas industry.

In 1992 a new subdistrict for native self-governance was established in the Polar Urals by the regional administration in Aksarka, in cooperation with the local Nenets. The settlement of Laborovaia serves as this new subdistrict's administrative center. Its head administrator comes from the largest and the most influential tundra clan, Laptander. Yet in the village, he has been opposed by representatives of another clan, Nogo, headed by four highly educated middle-aged women. His youth (in 1993 he was twenty-nine) has clearly imposed limitations on his power, despite the support of his influential tundra kin. His situation exemplifies the aforementioned contradiction between the tundra and the village. Ultimately he has to choose between becoming a real reindeer herder based outside the village or continuing to manage the village affairs and thus remain outside of the reindeer herders' community. According to opinions expressed by both tundra and village inhabitants, he is both a good village administrator and fine leader of a nomadic camp. By 1992, however, his attempts to combine these two positions had not yet succeeded.

In recent years his closest relatives (his father and wife) have been urging him to return to the tundra. He is, after all, the most important figure in their private herding operation, while his efforts to accomplish something significant in the village often bring no results. Thus the clan structure, which helps to advance and maintain the authority of the tundra leaders, impedes their active participation in the modern village's social and political life. At the same time, the demands of successful village leadership interfere with effective leadership on the tundra. As we have seen in Laborovaia and Yaptik-Sale, a new pattern of "competition" is taking shape, one with men as leaders of the tundra and women as leaders of the villages.

It is true, of course, that the Soviet socialist state is at least partly responsible for the creation and rise of the current indigenous leaders. Almost all of them are, or at least used to be, residents of large villages or even towns. They are formally educated, incorporated into the governmental system, and fairly comfortable in the modern world. In the view of their own people, they are to a large extent the leaders-on-behalf-of-the-state. As the Russian authorities see it, however, they are the leaders-on-behalf-of-the-natives. It is hard to imagine today how these opposing views could be reconciled. One might conclude that their function is to be the intermediaries between the two opposite sides, to have "two faces."

Today's most fundamental obstacle in developing the native institutions of leadership is the adjustment of the traditional sociopolitical organization to the modern industrial, financial, and administrative institutions. For the Yamal Nenets, this is evident in the opposition between the clan leadership and that of the modern village.

A major challenge for native leaders is reconciling the interests of outsiders, with whom they partially identify, with those of their own, more traditional people. At the time of our research, two Nenets leaders, Nikolai Khariuchi and Miron Yamkin, headed district administrations. Two other Nenets, Nikolai Ngokateta and Alexander Anagurichi, headed local administrations in Seyaha and Siunai-Sale, in the Yamal District. All of them maintain close ties with the reindeer herders, especially their own relatives.

One Nenets ex-president of the association Yamal-Potomkam was seen by Golovnev wearing a tie underneath his Nenets *malitsa* while visiting a nomads' camp on the tundra. This combination looked strange—a tie in a Nenets tent and a *malitsa* in the office—but he wore both, because he needed to be constantly going back and forth between the two places. Sometimes similar types of combinations fail. According to the latest information available to us, the aforementioned young leader of the Laborovaia (Polar Urals) community left his official position and returned to his nomadic camp. Other Nenets examples show the existence of a similar opportunity for native leaders to return to their own traditional environment from the "outside," as, for example, did Yuri Vaella-Aivaseda, mentioned earlier, who eventually left the village of Variogan for his remote family-owned land, and writer Anna Nerkagi, who returned to her nomadic camp in the Polar Urals.

Today a visitor to a Nenets tents can meet many native people wearing a *malitsa* or its female equivalent (*yagushka*) who have specialized education (for example, doctors, technicians, and teachers). These people, as they themselves explain, return because "here on the tundra things are better for us, while there in the city everything is foreign." Well versed in the subjects taught at the state schools as well as in traditional knowledge, these people constitute a new layer of the tundra society. One might even argue that this group resembles the traditional "democratic leadership," described earlier, a system in which a number of chiefs might rise or fall at any moment.

The very capacity of Nenets leaders "to go back and forth between the city and the tundra" is an interesting manifestation of this ideal of "having two faces." This shuttling between the tundra and the city could be seen as a new style of the native leaders' "nomadism," comfortable for these well-educated natives. At the same time, this is also a way of preserving and reviving traditional leadership.

Some shamanic features of leadership still exist among Nenets. The works of Nenets novelist Anna Nerkagi and Nenets poet Yuri Vaella-Aivaseda attempt to create a new native mythology that echoes the old shamanic mythological worldview. And what about "military leadership"? While there is no longer any chance for native people to engage in military confrontation with the authorities, there is still a great deal of potential for other forms of confrontation. Thus in 1991 both Vaella-Aivaseda and Nerkagi headed protests against the industrial invasions of their areas, Variogan and the Polar Urals, respectively. Both Nenets had to decide whether the relationship between the protesters and the authorities was going to be more confrontational or more cooperative. Both eventually decided to avoid any actions that might have led to an eruption of violence and thus not to repeat the terrible consequences of the armed rebellions of the 1930s and 1940s.

Nenets representatives have recently, and not accidentally, become national and even international leaders of indigenous organizations, not only because of their own capabilities but also because of the high respect with which other people treat Nenets. In June 1997 Sergei Khariuchi, deputy chair of the Yamal-Nenets Okrug State Duma (Okrug Parliament), was elected president of the Russian Association of the Indigenous Peoples of the North (RAIPON). In this post he will represent all the so-called small numbered peoples of Russia not only in national forums but also in international bodies such as the Arctic Council and the World Council of Indigenous Peoples. Another Nenets, Dmitrii Khorolia, director of the Yarsalinskii *sovkhoz*, was elected president of the Russian Reindeer Peoples' Union in 1995 and is also a vice president of the World Reindeer Herder's Association. In the 1990s Nenets leadership is once more demonstrating its flexible and democratic nature as Nenets themselves move into important positions in regional, national, and even international arenas.

Raisa Yaptik performs a purification ritual (*nibtara*).

Women of the Ngokateta clan with patron spirits, northern Yamal.

A typical Nenets above-ground burial.

Gathering for migration at the Yaptik clan camp, northern Yamal.

Women preparing for migration, northern Yamal.

Woman driving sledge in the caravan, northern Yamal.

Men driving sledges, northern Yamal.

Migrating caravan, northern Yamal.

Esiko Laptander, a participant of two revolts on Yamal, at his camp in the Polar Urals. He is seated on a newly made sledge. (Photograph by Svetlana Lezova, 1993.)

Men of the Saby clan, northern Yamal.

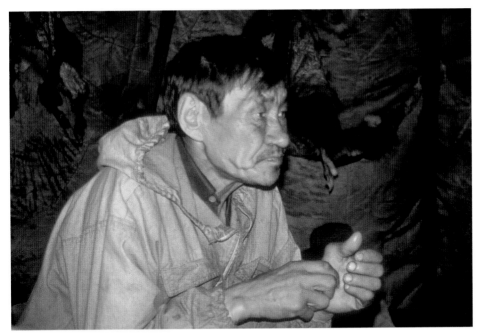

In the 1950s Ivan Khorolia was relocated from northern Yamal to Sunaisale, on the south coast of the peninsula, to work in the fishing collective.

Yuri Vaella-Aivaseda at his fish trap in Variogan.

Nenets women (right) prepare fishing nets for storage for the winter fishery. Their supervisor is a Ukrainian woman who has also organized the women in Yaptiksale to sew reindeer-skin boots to sell in Salekhard.

Influential Niarui women (mother and daughter) in Yaptiksale, 1992. The daughter, Nina, headed the village administration in 1996.

Yar-Sale, the administrative center of the Yamal District, with the Russian flag flying over the administrative office building, 1994.

Dmitrii Khorolia (left) and Mikhail Okotetto represent
Yamal Nenets at an international conference,
February 1999.

Viktor Tolstov, head of administration of the Yamal District, and Mikhail Ladukai, head of the
district land reform office, Yar-Sale, 1994.

Carrying soap powder, bread, and other supplies from the helicopter.

Yaptiksale village in the summer.

Reindeer herd corralled, Nadym tundra.

Yaptiksale village in the winter.

Yaptiksale family with seven children living in a small three-room apartment in the village.

The Labytnangi-Bovanenko railroad and road.

Gas-field construction workers' camp at Bovanenko in 1989.

Abandoned gas-exploration rig on the Yaptik-Sale tundra.

6

Tundra Crossroads:
Post-Soviet Reflections

Eldest Yaptik replied, "The matter is you are riding on my land. It would be better to kill you now."

The penalty for encroachment on the Yaptiks' hunting ground was swift and severe. The stranger's occupation of Nartsoolapta was a mortal threat to the Yaptik family's survival; thus the brothers reacted with force to protect their rights. They tried to kill the intruder. The four eldest brothers did not regard the stranger's "gift" of domesticated reindeer for transportation and food as acceptable compensation for unpermitted occupation of their hunting grounds. They untied and drove away the gift reindeer and returned to kill the "nomadic man" who occupied their hunting grounds.

A battle ensued, and the five brothers lost their lives. When the youngest brother awoke, he no longer knew where his land was and accepted the gift of a scrawny reindeer that became the basis of a new economic system. Under the new pastoral herding system, both ownership of reindeer and rights to pastureland became crucial. A set of rights to grazing lands, campsites, and fishing grounds developed as an extension of earlier rights. The bundle of property rights included not only use rights but also the right to exclude intruders, transfer reindeer and land, and dispose of the rights in accord with accepted custom. The herders assumed the risk of losses from harsh weather and conditions beyond human control but expected compensation should a neighbor or stranger cause the loss of reindeer or damage to grazing lands. The system of property rights was well established by the beginning of the twentieth century.

Soviet rules regarding property rights and decision making facilitated entry of newcomers with competing economic interest to the shared grazing lands of Yamal Nenets. Not surprisingly, when the intrusion of outsiders on the commons violated Nenets' well-understood rules and property rights in a manner that threatened their livelihood, the Nenets reacted as swiftly and harshly, as had the four eldest Yaptik brothers. They revolted.

Although the Nenets' transition from hunters to herders created a more elaborate system of property rights and governance to regulate relations among herders, it does not appear to have changed many basic cultural norms, values, and roles. Nor did the Soviets' institutional changes destroy the Nenets' nomadic culture. Although the state eventually claimed all the lands and waters as public property, the lands continued to be regulated as limited (restricted) common property with a well-understood (although altered) allocation of grazing territories and migratory routes.

The critical question for the future is whether current efforts to privatize land and transform the economic system in Russia will lead to more dramatic disintegration of Nenets culture, provoke rebellions, or trigger a tragedy of the commons. In his well-known essay, Garret Hardin asserted that a "tragedy of the commons" or destruction of shared lands occurs when individual herders attempt to maximize their own welfare on common pastures open to all.[1] The villagers in England who presumably provided the model for Hardin's theory, in reality, had well-developed rules limiting access to and use of the shared fields.[2] The tragedy Hardin posits did not occur in the English countryside on which the metaphor is based.[3] Nor is a "tragedy of the commons" likely to occur in closely knit communities in which individuals are sanctioned for violations of the behavioral code.[4] On the other hand, those whose use rights are threatened will and did riot or revolt when the actions of others undercut their livelihood. Riots broke out in the English countryside in the sixteenth and seventeenth centuries as individuals or groups attempted to "enclose" meadows, forests, and woodland pastures.[5] While many patterns of land use and ownership on Yamal in the early twentieth century differ from those of the English countryside a few centuries earlier, the response to attempts to radically change the system of rights to access and use was not so different.

The system of property rights that emerges on Yamal in the twenty-first century will have a powerful impact on the Nenets' culture and economy. It will determine, in large measure, whether the Nenets have a say in or even benefit from development of the super-giant gas fields on the peninsula. As potential Western investors know from experience elsewhere in the circumpolar North, the vast energy resources of Yamal could be developed in a more secure political environment with (rather than without) the support of indigenous residents. Experience in Alaska and the Canadian North demonstrates that according substantial property and even political rights to indigenous peoples does not create a barrier to larger national agendas for development of oil and gas resources.[6] Recognition and implementation of indigenous property rights would allow the indigenous population to participate meaningfully in decisions regarding the timing, manner, and conditions of development.

Crucial to the local reindeer herding economy predominant on the Yamal Peninsula are rights and rules regarding (1) reindeer, (2) land, and (3) the economic infrastructure or productive arrangements for processing, storing, marketing and transporting reindeer meat and other products. This chapter examines the shifts in rights and rules regarding each of these during and after the Soviet period and considers the environmental, social, and economic impacts that are likely to emerge from the combination of property rights that develops. We discuss the concept of property rights, the system of property rights that exists in the 1990s, and options for the future. Finally, we examine the indigenous rights movement in the Russian North and the role of international institutions.

Yamal in the 1990s

The Yamal District, with a population of 13,700 in 1993 and with its administrative center in Yar-Sale, covers most of the Yamal Peninsula. Three large state farms (the Yamalskii, Yarsalinskii, and Panaevskii *sovkhozy*) direct the main economic activity of indigenous people—reindeer herding, which in the 1970s was still considered one of the most productive branches of the economy.[7] The state farms also engaged in fur farming, hunting, dairy farming, and livestock breeding. Two fish factories—Puiko and Novyi Port—conduct commercial fishing. Of the 903 nomadic households (4,609 individuals) in the Yamal District in 1994, more than two-thirds (623 households including 3,408 individuals) worked within the *sovkhoz* system for the state department of agriculture, and only 25 families (148 individuals) operated privately, unconnected to any state agency.[8] The Priural District (population 6,800 in 1993), with headquarters in Aksarka, includes the base of the peninsula and contains only one *sovkhoz*, Baidaratskii. (See Map 3.)

Oil and gas production to the south and east fuels the economy of the okrug.[9] With the discovery of the huge Bovanenko and other natural gas fields, Nadymgazprom (the branch of the Russian State gas company, Gazprom, with a monopoly in this region)[10] plays a major role in shaping the future of Yamal. At the federal level, the Russian Ministry of Fuel and Energy exercises regulatory and policy authority for development of the gas and oil fields and related transportation network. The State Committee for Mineral Resources (Roskomnedra) is of equal importance federally, while the Russian Ministry of Ecology and Natural Resources is responsible for environmental protection. The major non-Russian player has been Amoco Corporation of Houston, Texas, the only foreign company to have established offices in Nadym.[11]

In the 1990s a new set of natural and human-induced changes have produced conditions of stress and crisis for Nenets herders. These include the threat of climate change, both natural and human-induced; the reduction of available pastureland owing to competing uses for gas and oil development (as well as the transportation infrastructure related to that development); the pressure to create new national parks (*zapovedniki*) and protected areas; and, most important, the changing systems of rights and rules governing access to and management of land and resources. The large state farms have suffered economic stresses of the transition to a market economy, including a breakdown of the distribution systems, inadequate storage and processing, and repercussions of the crisis of nonpayment. The *sovkhozy* were on the verge of financial breakdown by June 1994, with a debt of 12 billion rubles.

Overgrazing, long a problem on the peninsula, is exacerbated by the transfer of thousands of acres from the state farms to the oil and gas industry. Scientists and land managers from the okrug express concern about overgrazing in some areas, and regional newspaper articles report very large herds. Land use in Yarsalinskii *sovkhoz* (the largest of the four state farms on the Yamal Peninsula) is intensive—"a tight situation" in the words of Mikhail S. Ladukai, who headed the land reform/resources office in Yar-Sale (a branch of the Salekhard office) in 1994: "The herders move in very narrow corridors [during the spring migrations north]. The northern group stays only one day in Yar-Sale, and only the southern group [the last to cross Ob Bay from the mainland] may stay a week. The northern group only rests when it reaches its northern pastures." Ladukai described how the herders themselves feel they are "racing," pressured to move daily, quickly, to new pastureland as the herds have become larger while pastures have been reduced and the quality of vegetation has declined. Researchers of the Yamal agricultural station in Salekhard have called for drastic cuts in the herds, especially on the peninsula.[12] Using data from 1988 and earlier, biologists consider the total number of reindeer on the peninsula to be almost double the winter pasture capacity.[13]

Although in the 1930s Soviet authorities disrupted the system of ownership by a few large herders and divided pastures into numerous family units, the underlying system of pastureland control by kinship groups initially survived within the framework of the newly instituted collective farms. Individuals or families retained private ownership of herds and continued rights to use specific pasturelands in specific seasons.[14] One of the most disruptive elements in this reorganization was that boundaries between the *sovkhozy* became rigid, reducing the former flexibility that the Nenets had used to cope with natural fluctuations in climate, vegetation, and animal populations. The *sovkhoz* structure also concentrated control in the hands of a few managers at the top—people who were until recently nonnatives.

Despite the imposition of outside institutions described in the previous chapter, the Nenets managed to retain and, from the late 1980s, revive elements of their traditional organization. For example, the director of the Yarsalinskii *sovkhoz* reported that most of the numerous brigades therein are composed of family members, somehow related—father, sons, brothers. According to one *sovkhoz* director, brigade leaders are likely to be herders with the largest holdings of private reindeer.[15] Still, the modern brigade camps are considerably larger than were traditional camps, and migration routes have been radically altered.

Property Rights Dimensions

A growing body of scholarly literature suggests that small and stable societies have often worked out successful common-property systems to manage land, water, and other natural resources on which their economy and way of life depend. These systems of rights for dealing with shared resources such as fisheries, reindeer pasture, or forest lands provide better protection of natural resources and are more likely to ensure survival and health of diverse cultures than either systems of purely private or purely public property. Successful common-property arrangements are not those in which the common property is open to all with no or few rules but are, in fact, systems in which access is limited to a specific group of users, and rules for use are well-defined.[16] We divide property rights into four categories, none of which makes the property definitively public or private. Conceptually, property rights are really bundles of rights, and these bundles can be divided into proprietary, exclusionary, disposition, and use rights.[17]

1. *Proprietary* rights are possessory rights. The right of possession (of land, machinery, tools, livestock, or even stock in a corporation) entitles the owner (who might be an individual, a family, a group of investors, or even a government entity) to keep, reinvest, or apportion the value that accrues to the property and exposes the owner to the risk of loss if the property loses value. Proprietary rights may entitle the holder to collect for damages to the value of the property (that is, compensation for damage to a car or unlawful killing of a reindeer) and expose the owner to liability for damage caused by the property (a collision caused by a car, disease spread by an infected reindeer).

2. *Exclusionary* rights entitle the holder to exclude others from using the property (prevent trespassers from crossing a field, exclude those who don't hold a proper fishing license from fishing in state waters, set conditions or rent for others to use the property). Some property rights allow the holder to exclude certain groups of people from sharing in the rights. For example, only Alaska natives may hold shares of stock in Alaska Native corporations. The holder of exclusionary rights may grant others the privilege of using the property, set fees or rent for use by others, and determine other conditions of use.

3. *Disposition* rights entitle the holder to dispose of the property or, in legal terminology, to "alienate" the property. Full rights of disposition or alienation would allow the landowner to sell or give land to any legal person or entity. In the case of common property, however, rights of alienation might be restricted so that fishing rights or pastureland could only pass to other members of the local community or to clan members. Members of a farming cooperative might be required to sell only to the cooperative; we would say that their disposition rights are restricted. States frequently prohibit sale of certain lands or resources to foreigners.

4. *Use* (*usufructory*) rights entitle the holder to use a particular property for specific (usually limited) purposes (such as housing, commercial business, extraction of oil and gas, or grazing of livestock). Use rights may be limited to a particular time (a ninety-nine-year lease or a fixed season, as is the case with annual hunting and fishing licenses). With the state as the legal owner of title to land in Russia, until recently, virtually all real property rights held by individuals and enterprises in Russia have been usufructory rights, although not without elements of each of the other three categories of rights.

In the current move to privatize property, Russian citizens are receiving a somewhat larger bundle of rights, with elements from each of the preceding categories. It is important to notice that when individual land rights were limited to specific uses, as they were in the Soviet Union, fewer regulatory restrictions would have been needed than in a system in which private ownership encompasses a wider range of proprietary, exclusionary, disposition, and use rights. Where the state does not retain proprietary, exclusionary, and disposition rights, and allows those uses not specifically excluded, extensive laws and regulations have been adopted over time to protect the public interest in safety and environmental quality or to prevent one owner from using the property in a manner harmful to a neighbor's interests. And in the preexisting indigenous system of property rights, an unwritten (but orally communicated) set of rules governed and limited the time, place, and manner of use of land and resources. The implications of this are significant in a period of transition from state to private ownership as restrictions for health, safety, environmental quality, and equity built into the prior systems (both indigenous and Soviet) may be dropped in the initial privatization period, and it may be years before safeguards can be replaced by laws that are implemented and enforced. At present at least in the agricultural sector of Russia, laws regulating land relations and agrarian reform retain use restrictions. Members of state and collective farms who receive a share of land have the right to mortgage, lease, exchange, bequeath, and even sell their allotment, but the use of the land remains restricted to agricultural production except in special cases where local authorities permit a change in use.[18]

Two types of property—reindeer and land—together with the economic infrastructure or productive arrangements for herding are central to the future of the herding economy. Since the 1960s the *sovkhozy* have controlled the storage, processing, transportation, distribution, and marketing of reindeer. These large, government-owned enterprises, similar to public corporations, hold the capital assets such as reindeer, meat-processing plants, and storage facilities. They also arrange provision of supplies to *sovkhoz* herders. The *sovkhozy* hold limited but extensive proprietary, exclusionary, and use rights to the vast pasturelands of the peninsula and play a key role in determining disposal of these lands either to individual herders or to industrial enterprises. From the 1930s through the Soviet period, private herds on Yamal were diminished but not eliminated. Today reindeer ownership is shifting again from the *sovkhozy* to private individuals and families.

Reindeer

To ask the number of reindeer a Nenets owns is as impertinent as asking an American to tell you his net worth. And while a stranger might receive an answer to such a question, the answer could not be regarded as reliable. Whenever we recorded figures from the official statistical tables regarding the number of reindeer owned by individuals, we were cautioned that herders regularly underreported their wealth. Nevertheless, figures from a variety of sources are useful for a rough comparison of the total number of reindeer in different geographic areas of the okrug over time and for comparing the relative number of private versus *sovkhoz* herds. In the view of some officials, the problem of underreporting is declining as incentives change. Rights to land and compensation for damage to pastures may be calculated on the basis of the number of reindeer owned, making it advantageous under certain circumstances to report actual or, possibly, higher numbers.

In January 1941, before the drastic decline in herd populations during World War II, the total number of reindeer reported in the Yamal-Nenets Okrug was 358,000.[19] With shrinking area available for pastureland today, the official count of 357,000 is widely regarded as exceeding pasture capacity.[20] One specialist in agriculture calculated in 1994 that herds should be cut by 120,000 to 130,000 head okrug-wide, with half of that reduction necessary in the Yamal District (60,000) and up to a quarter in the Priural District (25,000 to 30,000 head).[21] Privately held reindeer pastured on Yamal for all or part of the year are located on lands to which the large *sovkhozy* hold use rights.[22]

In the 1980s the government abolished laws strictly limiting privately held herds. This policy change produced a dramatic increase in private stocks that was only partly offset by reductions in *sovkhoz* herds. Official statistics for the Yamal District in 1994 established herd numbers at 170,077,[23] with 59 percent held privately. Although overall herd numbers have grown by 23 percent since 1980, privately held deer doubled from 50,070 to 100,021, while state farm herds in the district declined from 1980 by only 11,062. (See Table 5.1 and Figure 5.1.) The trend is toward further reduction of *sovkhoz* herds as private ownership increases. The current ratio of private to public herds is reversing the situation in the 1970s, when only 35–37 percent of deer in the okrug were held privately.

Herders wish to own a sufficient number of reindeer to secure their families' well-being. Enough reindeer are needed to provide food, clothing, shelter, and transportation (pulling the sledges that carry the herders' family and belongings) plus the sale of at least ten head per year. Two letters that appeared in the journal *Severnye prostory* (Northern Scopes) in 1990 suggest that a herd of 200–250 reindeer is necessary to sustain a household on Yamal today.[24] Additionally, in the opinion of one *sovkhoz* director, "Nenets are as concerned about prestige as we are, and prestige is tied to the number of reindeer one owns."[25] Today, several hundred reindeer would be considered a large private herd.

The determination of appropriate herd size may also be influenced by Russian oil company officials, who have computed compensation for "temporary" use of land for industrial purposes and damages owing to oil and gas exploration and development at least partly by multiplying the number of reindeer owned by the estimated number of hectares needed to support one reindeer. This may have heightened incentives to enlarge herds. In addition, Western oil companies have talked about financial compensation to individuals or families. "For the first time, herders have a real opportunity to get money without working, and they are naturally interested," offered Vladimir Istomin by way of explanation.[26]

The size of private herds varies depending on location, quality of pasture, wealth, and know-how. In the Baidaratskii *sovkhoz* in the Priuralskii District, 153 households held an average of 126 reindeer per household at the beginning of 1994.[27] A large herd in that region, according to official statistics, would be about 200 head in the production herd and 90 additional animals used for transport. A wealthy herder in the Yarsalinskii or Yamalskii state farms might own privately 300 or more reindeer.

Women frequently own reindeer as their separate property, although the number of reindeer recorded as owned by them separately is usually small. A woman is given reindeer when she marries, and these become the breeding stock for a herd that belongs to her. A wife's reindeer are naturally mixed on the range with those of her husband and possibly her brothers and other kin. According to Nenets norms, a man would not make a decision regarding sale or disposal of his wife's reindeer without consulting her.[28]

Land

To understand the current division of authority over land, it is useful to examine relevant provisions of the Constitution of the Russian Federation (RF) as well as presidential edicts regarding indigenous rights. Under Article 72 of the constitution adopted December 12, 1993, the Yamal Nenets Autonomous Okrug (like other "subjects" of the RF) has joint jurisdiction with the RF over issues of (1) possession, use, and management of the land, mineral resources, water, and other natural resources; (2) delimitation of state property; (3) protection of the environment and of historical and cultural monuments; and (4) ecological safety and protection of the original environment and traditional way of life of small ethnic communities. Section 6 of Article 74 appears to give considerable deference to okrug law in the event of a conflict with federal laws. The RF has the authority (under Article 71c,f), however, to regulate and protect the rights of national minorities and to determine basic principles of federal policy and programs regarding the economy, the environment, and the social, cultural, and national development of the Russian Federation. The RF thus retains considerable authority to protect the environment and rights of indigenous peoples, but the component republics, provinces, territories, and okrugs now enjoy greatly expanded rights to adopt legislation particular to their regions.

Two presidential decrees issued prior to the constitution's adoption   are particularly relevant to Yamal. On April 22, 1992, President Yeltsin signed Edict 397, "On urgent measures for the protection of the place of residence and economic activities of the numerically small peoples of the North." It called for the Council of Ministers and organs of executive power, together with regional associations of northern indigenous peoples, to define areas in which people use traditional methods of harnessing nature, and declared that these areas cannot be alienated without consent of the indigenous minorities of the relevant area. The decree further called on the government of the Russian Federation to determine a precise list of areas, to draft regulations for land use in those areas, to develop proposals for game reserves, and to draft laws on the legal status of northern indigenous peoples and the legal status of ethnic districts, settlements, and tribal and communal councils. The decree anticipated that areas of traditional use for reindeer herding, fishing, hunting, and so forth would be permanently transferred to the indigenous users. Although officials in the Yamal-Nenets Okrug have argued that implementing legislation by the Russian Parliament is necessary to provide guidance regarding transfer of property rights to the indigenous peoples, other regions of the Russian Federation have adopted their own legislation that at least partially implemented Edict 397.[29] About a month later, on June 1, 1992, Yeltsin signed a decree calling for the "urgent development" of new, large natural gas deposits of the Yamal Peninsula, the Barents Sea, and the Sakhalin Island shelf. Central ministries as well as *oblast* and okrug authorities were to draw up and implement measures to commence extraction of deposits on Yamal no later than 1997. Although the June edict did not repudiate the April edict calling for protection of indigenous lands, in practice the latter edict dominated.

Drafts of the Law on the Legal Status of the Numerically Small Peoples of the North have circulated since the early 1990s. As Gail Fondahl noted, succeeding drafts show a shift away from protection of indigenous rights toward protection of "traditional" activities or occupations of northern peoples.[30] Although the law regarding indigenous rights to land today is underdeveloped and internally conflicting, it is possible to characterize the system of land ownership existing on Yamal.

The system of land ownership and use in the current period of transition has elements of public, common, and private property. Land on Yamal is legally "public," owned by the state, although management authority increasingly rests with the okrug as opposed to the central/federal government. The land resources or land reform committee of the okrug allocates land use rights and determines disposition or transfer of lands either from the *sovkhozy* to private herders or from use as pastureland to land for industrial purposes (oil and gas exploration or development). The land reform/resources committees have granted long-term rights to *sovkhozy* to use the land only for traditional activities—herding, hunting, fishing, and trapping.

Although the *sovkhozy* are to be consulted prior to transfer of land use rights to oil and gas enterprises, in practice they have had little power. The deputy head of the okrug Committee on Land Resources and Land Planning,

Evgeny Kuzyukov, explained, "If the *sovkhoz* doesn't sign, the land service will sign [authorize transfer even without *sovkhoz* approval]."[31] The okrug land resources committee has in fact (arguably illegally) transferred use rights from the *sovkhozy* to oil and gas enterprises for the Bovanenko-Kharasavei gas fields, the Novyi Port and Rostovtsevo oil fields, and the 530-kilometer corridor for the railway under construction from Ob Bay to Kharasavei. Only once, in the case of approval of transfers for the Bovanenko field, did the land service refuse to officially approve, and in that case the land office had the strength of the okrug behind it, opposing oil and gas development. Even in 1994, Kuzyukov explained, the oil and gas enterprise was carrying out pilot production in Bovanenko without legal right.[32] In recent years the state farms have been able to negotiate with oil interests to obtain a share in expected revenues of development on state farm lands. According to the director of the Yamal *sovkhoz* in 1994, the *sovkhoz* approved development of a pilot project to produce gas condensate in the Tambei field in exchange for 30 percent of the revenue.[33]

Proprietary rights are also shared by the okrug and the *sovkhoz* (public corporation). There is currently no system for permanent transfer of land title from the state either to individual herders or to industry, but enterprises are able to obtain the right to use the land for exploration and development of oil and gas for limited periods (usually three years for exploration and ten for development), with the expectation of extension for the life of the field. The rights to the subsurface are owned by the government but transferred to the oil and gas enterprise with a royalty payment apportioned among the central republic, *oblast*, okrug, and *raion* governments, respectively, according to the formula 20–20–30–30.[34] The former owners of use rights participate in a system of "compensation" for pasturelands transferred to or damaged by oil and gas enterprises. As of April 1993, according to a law passed by the council of the Yamal-Nenets Okrug, 50 percent of the compensation for damage should be paid to the land user (the *sovkhoz*) and 50 percent to the *raion* government. In practice both the okrug and the *sovkhoz* spend the compensation money for the same purposes—to provide housing, supplies, and other material support to the local (not just native) population.

In regions to the south and east of the Yamal Peninsula, extensive land use rights have been transferred from state farm use to the oil and gas industry. The Nadym District of the Yamal-Nenets Autonomous Okrug (encompassing 11.5 million hectares; larger in size than the whole Moscow Oblast) has a high density of gas and oil fields, including the Medvezhye, Yamburg, and Yubileinyi fields. Four more fields and a dozen gas pipelines will be added soon. While there are only five *sovkhozy* in the district, their territory covers five million hectares—almost half of the district. When land is transferred from *sovkhoz* use for pastureland to gas field development, the implications are significant. Development of a new structure in the Yamburg field (Khargutinski Dome) displaced 1,000 reindeer herded by only 3 families comprised of 17 people. Displaced families must either leave herding or relocate on land already intensively used by other herders. Thus each new oil and gas field increases grazing pressure on the remaining pastureland.

Rights to use the land for reindeer pasture (the dominant use) extend beyond the *sovkhoz* herds to members of the *sovkhoz* who use the pasture for herds belonging to the *sovkhoz* as well as for their own reindeer. The private herds may follow, lead, or even be mixed with *sovkhoz* herds, and only herders are able to identify which belong to them and which to the *sovkhoz*. Thus rights to use the pastures may be analyzed as a form of limited common property, open to entry by member of the *sovkhoz* brigades with time and manner of use conditioned by the *sovkhoz* and negotiated at biannual meetings of brigade members. Since the end of the 1980s, when the government lifted restrictions on private ownership of reindeer, neither policy nor law has limited the number of reindeer in private ownership on Yamal. Prevention of overgrazing appears to depend on the collective action of individual herder families and brigade members.

According to the law, every worker can leave the *sovkhoz* and obtain private use rights to land, but few have seriously contemplated this move. As of July 1994, the Land Resources office of the okrug, in Salekhard, had approved only one allotment of *sovkhoz* land to individual herders or their families, and that only for a period of one year. The few other requests to privatize plots for indigenous economic activities had not reached the okrug level. Approvals are required by both the *raion* and okrug offices dealing with land allocation. To understand the reluctance to divide the *sovkhoz* lands, one must understand the basic system of nomadic herding on the Yamal Peninsula.

In spring some herders travel as far as 550 kilometers from winter pastures south of the peninsula in the Nadym District to reach summer pastures along the Kara Sea. They cross the frozen Ob Bay and follow long, narrow migration routes that transect two-thirds of the peninsula. According to Dmitrii Khorolia, the Yarsalinskii Sovkhoz (the largest in terms of land) employs about 700 nomads, including women "tent workers" (usually wives). The yearly cycle is broken into six seasons, with specific pastures designated for each. Maps of the peninsula available in the land resources office in Salekhard demarcate the migration path and seasonal pastures of each brigade in a single *sovkhoz*. The Yarsalinskii *sovkhoz* had more than twenty brigades in the summer of 1994. The boundaries between state farms are fixed and quite strict, and the herds do not mix. But between brigades within a *sovkhoz* there may be some mixture. Given the complexities of pasture allocation, the economic difficulty of herding outside of the *sovkhoz* system of land allocation, supply, and payment of wages, herders are naturally reluctant to apply to separate their land from the common pool.

Evgeny Kuzyukov explained the reluctance on the part of okrug officials to approve privatization of pastureland: "First, no one would comply, and second, many veterinary matters would be complicated. There would be no way to insure that herds received inoculations on schedule."[35] The risk of diseases spreading and massive die-off of reindeer is made more real by the need to avoid certain well-known areas of the tundra, where reindeer died by the thousands during past epizootics.

Land distribution committees had another economic concern. As the law on farmland privatization entitles each newly privatized farm to obtain a one billion ruble loan (then valued at roughly 500,000 dollars), the committee expects the individual to show an economically viable plan that would enable repayment to the okrug. If an individual were to default on the loan, the okrug would be responsible for repayment to central authorities. Another concern expressed is that privatization of pastureland would create a few rich herders who would charge others for use of their land. Then there is the serious question of what period of history to return to in determining allocation of land to families or clans. New routes that developed over the past seventy years are now well established, and many herders argue that the law should protect this new "traditional" allocation. In addition to these complexities, officials are aware of conflicts and problems created in the Khanty-Mansiisk Okrug, where lands have been divided among families. The head of the administration for the Yamal District explained that herders are not anxious to separate clan or family lands from *sovkhoz* lands.[36]

Another frequent argument of officials against land privatization was that there is no legal basis for it yet. Authorizing legislation has not been worked out at the federal level, and okrug officials need guidelines before moving forward. That one proposal has been acted on and others are under consideration by the *raion* administration in Yar-Sale indicates, however, that federal authorizing legislation might not be a serious obstacle if practical problems could be resolved.

In the Yamal District the few individuals who had sought to privatize the lands they use engaged primarily in fishing or hunting. Their preliminary proposals were not regarded by the land resources committee as serious prospects for privatization in 1994. The process of privatization requires multiple approvals by the relevant *sovkhoz*, the district land resources or land reform committee, the district veterinary official, and, finally, the okrug land distribution committee.

The one case of privatization, portrayed by government officials as unique, may nevertheless set a precedent for others to follow. Notably, a Nenets woman, Anna Nerkagi, was the first person anywhere on the Yamal Peninsula to seek and succeed in obtaining agreement from administrative officials to privatize lands traditionally used for her herd. She received a one-year provisional grant for 11,507 hectares in the Priural District, an area composed of three nonadjacent plots that are the winter and summer pastures and breeding grounds used by her husband's and her own herds. Nerkagi had requested permanent privatization of a larger portion of land based on a formula of 100 hectares per deer. Scientific norms for the number of hectares needed for pasture are set at 80–100 hectares per reindeer in the Priural District.[37] Fewer hectares results in poor health of reindeer, the current state of affairs. Nerkagi's lands, nestled in the foothills of the Polar Urals, are not in the heart of *sovkhoz* pastures, where conflict with other herders would be a problem. More significantly, however, Nerkagi is not just an ordinary herder; she is a well-known novelist, an advocate for native rights, and a powerful Nenets figure.[38] The head of the land reform committee, not a deputy or lower official, handled negotiations for the okrug. From another source, we learned of Nerkagi's intention to permanently privatize these lands together with lands of her brothers (who are herders) and to capitalize the herding operation in part by developing a tourist camp where visitors could see and, in moderate comfort, experience the lifestyle of Nenets herders. Initial funds to develop this tourist camp were to come half from Nerkagi and half from the okrug office of culture and tourism.

The Baidaratskii *sovkhoz*, from which Nerkagi's land was allotted, owns use rights to almost 3.5 million hectares, 3 percent of which is to be set aside by the land resources committee for redistribution to private owners for operations that are restricted to use for such traditional activities as reindeer herding, hunting, and fishing.[39] Although the okrug administration also has made agreements with other *sovkhozy* for redistribution of part of the *sovkhoz* lands, these have not been on the Yamal Peninsula, where herders, at least in the summer of 1994, were skeptical of plans to divide the land into clan or family parcels.

Economic Infrastructure

Since their creation in the 1960s, the *sovkhozy* have been the organizing mechanism for reindeer herding. They are responsible for the allocation of migration routes and for the production, marketing, and distribution of meat, antler, and other products. The *sovkhozy* have contracted with other state-run enterprises for the provision of supplies—fuel, food, housing, tools, ammunition, and so on. Herding households are dependent on the *sovkhoz* in large measure to buy their reindeer (usually in trade for supplies), to pay wages, to market their product, and to deliver supplies.

Economic difficulties of the transition to market economy in the rest of Russia have combined to make the economic situation of reindeer-herding *sovkhozy* extremely difficult. These include:

1. The loss of old markets and the failure to develop new markets resulting in huge surpluses of reindeer meat.[40]

2. The crisis of nonpayment that has spread to affect the income of *sovkhozy*.

3. The lack of adequate processing facilities.

4. A dramatic decline from 1992 to 1994 in prices on the international market for "velvet" reindeer antler (*panty*), which is especially valued in Asia for medicinal purposes, coupled with a loss of profits owing to a multiplicity of brokers between herders and final markets.

5. A significant drop in prices for polar fox fur on both the domestic and international markets.

The crisis of nonpayment has *drastically* reduced the security of remote settlements and disrupted former economic links. The effects are felt on the tundra among the herders. In the past, the *sovkhozy* provided meat, skins, boots, and fur to other state enterprises and received commodities useful to them—bread, flour, sugar, tea, vodka or spirits, canvas for tents, wood for tent poles, fuel, and other necessities. In the first half of the 1990s, this system of exchange was breaking down.

At the same time, government subsidies from central, *oblast,* or okrug budgets for housing, shipment of fuel and supplies, health care, education, and other services have made life in this remote region possible, as do government subsidies in remote northern regions of Alaska, Canada, Greenland, and Scandinavia. The crisis of nonpayment, as it ricocheted through the economy, left regional government coffers without means to pay for essential services. Prior to July 1, 1994, 10 percent of oil produced in the okrug was set aside for the okrug to sell directly, ensuring some revenue to the okrug government. When this quota was abolished in mid-1994, the central government provided no financial substitute for the loss in revenue. Nonpayment of the okrug's 30 percent share of oil revenues or even late payment (which markedly devalued the payment) left the okrug with "almost nothing."[41]

Additionally, lack of funding from the Russian government has slowed and even prevented delivery of goods that are the "life support system" of the northern territories.[42] Federal funds are used for oil, oil products, sugar, meat, vegetables, canned foods, medicines, machinery, equipment, and other vital necessities for the population. While the federal fund finances central supplies and delivery, the territories are responsible for delivery. Funds are transferred in the form of a loan into regional accounts at one-third of the central bank's interest rate.

Under crisis conditions, Russian oil and gas enterprises have offered *sovkhozy* the option of becoming subsidiaries. While some, including the Baidaratskii *sovkhoz* and others in the southern part of the okrug, accepted this option and became subsidiary economic activities of regional gas and oil companies, others have been more cautious.[43] A similar arrangement was being debated by the Yamalskii *sovkhoz* in 1994. The farm's director rejected an offer by Nadymgazprom in July 1994, owing to his concern not to compromise *sovkhoz* land rights. *Sovkhozy* in timber areas such as Tarko-Sale[44] chose this option. Tarko-Sale is a forested area poorly adapted for large herds owing to its lack of fresh water, its great number of mosquitoes, and its dearth of wind in the summer. Families typically own only ten to twenty reindeer. Herding there plays a smaller role in the overall native economy, and oil and gas development has already spread throughout the district. According to Kuzyukov, the transferred *sovkhozy* are a burden for the oil and gas enterprises that now provide subsidies instead of the state.

In agreements between a *sovkhozy* and an oil company, the parent oil and gas enterprise does not obtain property rights greater than those possessed formerly by the *sovkhoz* and cannot dispose of land or transfer use rights to individual herders or to industrial purposes without permission of the okrug and *raion* land use committees. As explained previously, transfers of use rights remain subject to multiple approvals. Nevertheless, the independent bargaining power of a *sovkhoz* is diminished following its reorganization as a subsidiary of a large regional gas company.

Options for the Future

What mix of property rights to reindeer, land, and enterprises or infrastructure will lead to increased efficiency in the Russian economy while also protecting and enhancing the local herding economy? By exclusively focusing on privatization of state farms and enterprises without developing the underlying framework of property rights, reformers miss opportunities to strengthen both local and national economies. Similarly, the World Bank as well as the European Bank for Reconstruction and Development (EBRD) and other international lenders are trying to buttress the Russian oil and gas industry without requiring the restructuring of property rights in a manner that is likely to increase long-term economic efficiency. Experience elsewhere in the circumpolar North suggests that restructuring property and political rights to accord indigenous peoples greater control and self-government over lands they have occupied for centuries is not an obstacle to energy and mineral development and can lead to the design of industrial projects that provide more sustainable economic and social benefits to the localities in which they occur and to the larger society.[45]

Not unlike the situation in Alaska in the early 1970s following the discovery of huge oil deposits at Prudhoe Bay, the government of Russia is pressing for rapid development of nonrenewable resources and, at the same time, aims to protect the economy and culture of the indigenous peoples residing there. In the United States the conflict between rapid development and the protection of indigenous rights was resolved in 1971, with a sizable transfer of land (almost 44 million acres, 11.6 percent of Alaska lands) and money ($962.5 million) from the federal government into newly created regional and local corporations owned by Alaska Natives. The shares of these corporations are held by indigenous people originally from the locality of the corporation, although not necessarily still living there.

In Canada, when the desire for rapid development of a gas pipeline from the Beaufort Sea through the Mackenzie Delta south conflicted with aboriginal claims to the land, a massive study resulted in a ten-year moratorium on pipeline construction. The conflict eventually led to lengthy negotiations among federal and provincial authorities and native organizations. This resulted in the acknowledgment of native title to vast areas of the Canadian North, sizable financial payments, and, most significantly, to the recognition of new political rights of indigenous self-government.[46]

With regard to the question of the future existence and structure of the *sovkhozy* on Yamal, there are three basic options:

1. Reconfiguration as cooperatives with herder families as members succeeding to rights and responsibilities of the *sovkhoz*.

2. Elimination of *sovkhozy* and transfer of their property rights, including rights to use the land for traditional activities, to private individuals or families.

3. Restructuring *sovkhozy* as subsidiaries of the existing Russian oil and gas enterprises.

The first option offers the greatest opportunity to continue traditional use, regulate herd size, and protect traditional land and culture. This option would eliminate the state as a dominant figure. Members of the cooperatives would have increased ownership rights rather than status as workers only. Membership might be limited to tundra families, with restrictions on disposition rights designed to retain pastureland to support continued herding, hunting, fishing, and gathering. This approach would further self-determination by the Nenets and the Khanty of the peninsula.

Enormous problems of financial solvency and the ability of the successor entities to survive in times of the shift to a market economy make a transition to herder cooperatives precarious. For this reason the option of protection under the umbrella of a wealthy gas company has been seductive. Insolvency problems of cooperatives, however, could be addressed through small-scale loans by international and multilateral lending institutions and donor nations. Cooperative entities, once formed, could become successors not only to the land use rights of the *sovkhoz* but also to proprietary, exclusionary, and limited-disposition rights as well. How extensive the rights might be would depend in large measure on the authorizing legislation of the Russian Federation or the resolution of land rights by the courts. With an increased bundle of rights over land, members of a cooperative would be in a strong position to negotiate with oil and gas companies over the conditions of industrial use and to collect rents and royalties from the industrial use of the land. Such rents or royalties could be used by indigenous cooperatives to finance improved meat storage and processing, to develop broader national and international markets, and to provide for the needs of their members. A favorable arrangement regarding disposition of rights to land would be critical to the success of herder cooperatives.

One of the most difficult issues to resolve is the relative rights of indigenous peoples who have settled (both forcibly and voluntarily) in the villages in contrast to those who continue to derive their livelihood from herding and hunting. Arguably, all indigenous residents should share in increased rights to historic homelands and to the economic rent derived from lands transferred to industry. In the villages, commercial fishing enterprises, meat processing, fur farming, and other state-owned or -operated businesses might similarly be converted to cooperatives and financed by a share of "rents" paid by industrial interests for access to oil, gas, and mineral reserves.

Space does not permit a full evaluation of the pros and cons of cooperative versus corporate structures of ownership. Some form of corporation with shareholders limited to members of the indigenous minorities who live on the relevant lands may be as successful a structure as the cooperative model. The agreements negotiated between the Canadian government and the Inuit (the Inuvialuit Final Agreement resulting from First Nation land claims in the western Canadian Arctic or the Mackenzie Delta region and the more recent Nunavut Agreement covering claims in the eastern Canadian Arctic)[47] provide more relevant and useful models than the legislated Alaska Native Claims Settlement Act that created for-profit, native-owned corporations.

Creation of for-profit (as opposed to nonprofit) corporations would mark a drastic change in the incentive structure and value system of Nenets tundra society. In its pre-Soviet form, Nenets society was highly stratified. Igor Krupnik describes a society with people of high, middle, and low wealth, with wealth enumerated in herd size. Nevertheless, the purpose of that accumulation of capital on the hoof was and is quite different from accumulation of capital in a for-profit corporation. In the former, the goal is to sustain the family and community and to reproduce and continue the reindeer-herding culture. Even production for commercial sale outside native communities is linked to sustaining the family and community. Among some indigenous cultures of Alaska, it used to be that individuals accumulated wealth simply for distribution, to show rank and power within the community. Under the corporate system now in place in Alaska, incentives of many Alaska Natives have changed to fit the new institutions created by the Alaska Native Claims Settlement Act. Accumulated wealth is no longer spread or redistributed widely within the community. In the case of a for-profit corporation, the purpose of capital accumulation is the growth and continuation of the corporation, and profits (in the form of dividends) pass to individuals rather than to the group. Leaders in these new corporate structures assume new roles that reshape their goals and tend to create intracommunity conflicts.

Unquestionably, the structure of increased indigenous rights to land and resources will affect the ability of indigenous people to continue their traditional occupations and move to a more diversified economy. While these are crucial issues to be resolved in restructuring property rights, they are issues best resolved by the indigenous population.

The second option is the least likely and most impractical of the three. Some marginal areas may be separated from the *sovkhoz* and become financially stable private farms, tourist bases, or other enterprises, but the central migratory routes and core pastures cannot be divided into individual or family plots while still maintaining the large-scale herding practiced by the Nenets today. Dividing all lands among households would be extremely difficult because of the complexity of pasture allocation and overlapping migration routes. This option is also historically unlikely. Traditional activities of the small numbered nationalities (herding, hunting, and trapping) have been accorded special protections in the law prior to and throughout the Soviet period. Although implementation and enforcement of such laws has been weak, abandoning these protections is not popular, nor is allocation of individual as opposed to communal rights.

The third option would in the short run allow the farms to survive financially and enhance prospects for processing and marketing of reindeer products. For these reasons, this option is fast becoming a reality in the okrug. Under it, however, the voice of the *sovkhoz* will be dominated by the parent oil/gas company's interests rather than herders' interests. Long-term protection of grazing land and the reindeer-herding lifestyle would be uncertain. Following privatization of the gas companies, the herders' interests may be further diminished as private individuals and entities would control almost half the shares, diluting the voice of the central government, which, though not benign, at least has a history of policies protective of the interests of numerically small nationalities. If the subsidiary reindeer farms are not independently productive (or even profitable by capitalist standards), will oil and gas enterprises continue to subsidize them from profits of other business activities? As Russia's monopolistic regional gas enterprises are forced to become more efficient in order to compete in the international market, will their incentives and policies change to the detriment of the reindeer-herding subsidiaries? Do the written agreements commit the parent company to continue support for the herding economy?

Natives in Defense of Their Land

Indigenous leaders in Russia, beginning in 1989, created a national organization as well as regional associations to lobby for self-determination, protection of traditional activities, and rights to land, water, and resources. In March 1990, at the First Congress of the Association of Small Numbered Peoples of the North, indigenous leaders called for a return to tribal councils and councils of elders as well as formation of ethnic districts and village councils, priority for traditional use of natural resources in areas settled by indigenous peoples, and ratification of the International Labor Organization Convention concerning Indigenous and Tribal Peoples in Independent Countries (ILO Convention No. 169, adopted in June 1989). Following the creation of the national association and affiliated regional associations of indigenous minorities, the federal and regional governments have turned to the regional associations as a legitimate voice on behalf of indigenous minorities. Approval by the relevant regional association, Yamal Potomkam (Yamal for Our Descendants), for example, is legally required to privatize facilities or enterprises that are part of the traditional economic complex of the peoples of the North.[48]

At the time of Yamal Potomkam's creation in 1989, Yeremei Aipin, a Khanty writer from Northwestern Siberia, urged creation of "sanctuaries, reservations, and autonomous territories" where the homelands of Khanty, Mansi, and Nenets would be protected from intrusions and pollution from oil and gas development.[49] By 1995 proposals by representatives of regional indigenous groups had expanded to include the following:

1. Guarantees of indigenous peoples' rights to ownership of land, resources, water, plants, and animals found on traditional-resource-use territories.

2. A law on compensation to indigenous peoples that would require payment of 12 percent of the hard currency generated by industrial development in the northern territories as restitution for "decades of predatory plundering" of the environment.

3. The creation of a Ministry of Northern Territories and Affairs for Indigenous Peoples to be headed and predominantly staffed by representatives of the indigenous peoples of the North.

4. Tax exemptions for traditional indigenous economic activities.[50]

Article 69 of the Constitution of the Russian Federation "guarantees the rights of numerically small indigenous peoples in accordance with the generally accepted principles and standards of international law and international treaties of the Russian Federation." The next step in clarifying and elaborating these rights would be for the state Duma to adopt a law on the legal status of northern indigenous peoples in accord with international norms and with ILO Convention 169. Another positive step would be for the Russian Federation to reaffirm the Yeltsin edict of April 22, 1992, by adopting and implementing regulations that would prevent the sale or transfer of traditional territories without the consent of the relevant native user groups.

Control of their land and increased political rights have not been secured by other indigenous peoples without long and hard struggles, a political revival, active leadership of indigenous peoples themselves, and a complex of other conditions favorable to recognition of indigenous rights. In the case of Alaska, indigenous peoples had the advantage of strong legal precedents, treaties, and interpretations of the U.S. Constitution. These provided a sound legal basis for aboriginal claims to a large part of the real estate of Alaska. Additionally, a combination of favorable external factors aided achievement of the Alaska Native agenda in the 1970s: the Prudhoe Bay oil strike, the rise of the environmental movement in the United States, and the presidency of Richard Nixon, who was sympathetic to indigenous peoples. In contrast, the weak economy of Russia, the absence of clear procedures for establishing title to lands traditionally used by indigenous minorities, and the lack of unified indigenous leadership have been obstacles to recognition of indigenous rights to land in Russia. Nevertheless, in some regions of Russia, indigenous minorities have been able to use existing laws to secure partial rights to their lands by establishing "territories of traditional nature use" and increased rights of self-government within family or clan communes (*semennye-rodovye obsh-*

chiny).[51] When regional governments are willing, progress can be made in increasing self-government by indigenous communities and increased protection for traditional land and resources.

International Actors

In large part, the failure to reform Russia's huge state oil and gas enterprises plays a central role in both the cause of the current economic crisis and the options to restructure the state reindeer farms and system of property rights. As Arild Moe and Valeriy Kryukov (Norwegian and Russian economists) explain,

> A very considerable portion of crude oil deliveries takes place without payment. As a result, more than one-half of the volume of mutual arrears of Russian enterprises is comprised by debts owed to the fuels and energy complex.
>
> These problems were compounded through 1993. In the course of the first nine months, debt to the whole fuel and energy sector increased 3.5 times. . . . Indeed, it has been calculated that 30 percent of the non-payments in the fuel and energy sector are between enterprises within the sector. . . . The government has postponed repayment of bridging loans to oil producers (to support energy purchases by enterprises) and continues to waive payment of a share of hard currency revenues from the oil and gas industries in the treasury.[52]

Moe and Kryukov blame not only the failure of Russian oil and gas enterprises to institute financial reform but also these enterprises' disregard for savings and rational use of materials, energy, and labor resources. That the oil and gas industries continue to operate as monopolistic enterprises works against increased efficiency. Moe and Kryukov conclude that the oil industry is engaging in "crisis maximization"—using crisis to extract more from government—in tax reductions and export credits.[53]

These unruly industry giants are also using the self-created crisis to "save the *sovkhozy*," but their disregard for the environment and the protection of the herding culture belies any altruistic intention. By manipulating the crisis, the oil and gas industry that caused forced relocation of indigenous camps and people throughout Northwestern Siberia is now moving to place the traditional economy even more securely under its control. As Moe and Kryukov conclude, "Posed in the bluntest terms, one must question whether real improvement of industry performance can be expected until the government has nothing more to give."[54] What these critics failed to discuss was the willingness of international lenders to step in to assist the as-yet-unreformed industry and thus to further delay essential reforms.

The World Bank and the European Bank for Reconstruction and Development (EBRD) have approached improving the economy of Russia by focusing primarily on revitalization of the Russian oil and gas industry. Initial World Bank loans targeted reconfiguration of old fields to enhance recovery of oil and gas. By the spring and summer of 1995, the World Bank was considering a loan to Yuganskneftegaz for a joint-venture project to develop a new oil field (Priobsk) in the Khanty-Mansiisk Okrug. While this loan did not go forward,[55] the EBRD, the International Finance Corporation (one of the group of banks composing the World Bank), and the Overseas Private Investment Corporation (OPIC, a U.S. agency) are financing frontier development of the Timan-Pechora oil and gas fields located on traditional territory of Nenets reindeer herders in the Nenets Autonomous Okrug. No effort has been made to approach the problem of revitalization of the Russian economy from a more local or even regional perspective. The health of small-scale economies dependent on renewable resources has been considered only insofar as World Bank policies require studies of the social, cultural, and environmental impacts of proposed projects on local, and especially indigenous, peoples. Protection of the reindeer-herding, fishing, and hunting economy of Siberia's indigenous population is mistakenly viewed as a nuisance to move forward with revitalization of the dominant industry—oil and gas.

The World Bank aims to enable the Russian oil and gas industry to improve oil recovery, reduce spills, repair broken pipelines, and reduce waste through improved environmental technology. Without restructuring property rights, however, the population with the greatest interest in protection of the environment remains powerless to protect its interests against monopolistic and unreformed oil and gas enterprises. If the World Bank took seriously its obligation to advise and assist borrowers in establishing legal recognition of indigenous land rights,[56] native peoples could become partners in the economic revitalization of their regions. With an increased bundle of property rights and legal mechanisms to enforce them, indigenous peoples would be empowered to influence oil and gas company behavior and thus enhance environmental protection. Indigenous peoples of Northwestern Siberia would then have a stake in the development of oil and gas, as well as an interest in assuring environmental safeguards that would increase efficient recovery of oil and gas reserves. In all probability, this would pressure monopolistic enterprises to use more efficient extraction and delivery technologies. Assisting in and insisting on the restructuring of property rights would be a more effective tool for revitalizing the Russian oil and gas industry than simply lending billions of dollars to monopolistic actors.

The World Bank's Operational Directive on Indigenous Peoples (OD 4.20) requires preparation of an indigenous peoples development plan in conjunction with any investment project that affects indigenous peoples.[57] Such plans are to give "particular attention . . . to the rights of indigenous peoples to use and develop the lands that they occupy, to be protected against illegal intruders, and to have access to natural resources . . . vital to their subsistence and reproduction."[58] "When local legislation needs strengthening," the World Bank is instructed "to advise and assist the borrower in establishing legal recognition of the customary or traditional land tenure systems of indigenous peoples."[59] Additionally, any displacement of indigenous peoples by development projects funded by the World Bank requires resettlement plans to ensure that the displaced population (including pastoralists with use rights or customary rights) benefits from the project.[60] As restructuring of property rights will entail considerable time and study, international lenders should initiate this process well in advance of specific loan proposals for development of Yamal and other regions of the Russian North.

International investors and lending agencies could advance reform of the Russian economy by insisting on adherence to international principles of indigenous rights, local self-government, and sustainable development. Observation of foreign oil companies suggests that while corporations are not altruistic, they need not be an obstacle to enhancing the rights of indigenous peoples. Foreign industries need a secure political climate in which to operate and are often as willing to pay private individuals, cooperatives, or corporations owned by natives for using land and extracting resources as they are to pay government entities or nonnative owners. Their experience elsewhere in the world has led the larger companies to adjust to, and even anticipate, the interests of the native population. Foreign oil companies cannot be expected to fight the battle for either land rights or political power for indigenous people, but they will not want to be exposed in the international or national press as being obstacles to the development of such rights.

Economic reform in Russia needs to be supported by a clear elaboration of rights to property. It is not in keeping with principles of indigenous self-governance to make more specific recommendations for the design of property rights systems appropriate to conditions such as those on the Yamal Peninsula. Decision makers must learn to govern the commons to avoid rebellions. To do so, they should expand the range of property rights—proprietary, exclusionary, disposition, and use rights—held by indigenous peoples. Restructuring property rights to strengthen the local economies and cultures of indigenous peoples of the Russian North is likely to facilitate both Russian and international interests in sound economic development of energy resources. Those involved in the delivery of aid to and the reform of the Russian economy should focus on the design of equitable political and legal institutions that will sustain the indigenous economies that have evolved and persisted over centuries. These economies could survive well beyond the life of the oil and gas fields, which is reason enough to assist rather than undermine them.

Cultural Survival in the Twenty-first Century

Will the transition occurring at the end of the twentieth century to democratic institutions and an open market system foster another "rebirth" of Nenets culture as successful as the transition recorded in "Five Yaptiks"? From the seventeenth to the nineteenth centuries, the Nenets culture evolved from hunting and foraging to active management and production of domesticated reindeer. The dynamic herding culture we see today developed as an economic necessity impelled in large part by forces external to the culture—the need for more reindeer for transportation to escape intruders as well as the scarcity of wild reindeer owing to a combination of natural and social factors (climate change and hunting pressure). The pace of gas and oil development, however, may not allow such an extended time period for adaptation. During the twentieth century, outsiders have asserted control and authority over indigenous land and resources as well as over the education of native children—thus striking at the heart of the herding economy and the transmission of knowledge necessary to that economy and culture. Nevertheless, the Nenets' culture has endured.

Sources of Resilience

We began by asking why some indigenous peoples resist cultural disintegration and assimilation when faced with intruders from outside while others do not. We have sought to identify the internal characteristics of a culture that make it resistant to external pressures and to determine the external influences that undermine cultural stability. These questions are especially important in the Russian North and around the circumpolar region, where large-scale development of natural resources threatens the values and the sustainable economies of native societies.

The Nenets, to a remarkable degree, have retained their reliance on the herding culture as well as their native language, traditional beliefs, community values, and behavioral norms. In contrast, those settled in villages drastically reduced hunting and herding activities. Gender roles determine the rhythm of activity in nomadic life. In the villages this rhythm is broken; both men and women lose their previous roles, although women retain a more active position than men. In villages, women continue to keep some of their "home" traditions, but men cannot fulfill their former roles as "masters of open space." The loss of control over land and resources reduces men's social status. The difference in the two patterns of life—tundra dwellers and villagers—is most obvious in the tundra region, where reindeer herding is an everyday practice. In the northern forest or taiga zone, hunting and fishing places might be reached from the village, seasonally or temporarily, by riverboat or snowmobile. Reindeer herders, in contrast, need to watch their herds constantly. This difference between occasional and constant activity determines the frequency of use of traditional culture, and therefore influences cultural stability.

Outside cultural influence touched first and much more deeply those who lived in villages rather than nomad camps, providing a variety of opportunities to use imported goods, tools, transport, and so on. Additionally, the proximity to villages determined the level of impact by outside institutions and the level of dependence on outsiders. Those who live apart from close contacts with outsiders preserve their autonomy in consumption and production and their ethic of minimum consumption. Villagers eventually lose all of these; they form new patterns of life based on purchase and consumption of imported goods. Because the largest part of domestic (home) consumption is under the control of women, they have attained an advanced social position (compared to men) in village society.

The nomadic lifestyle might be estimated as one of the basic conditions of cultural survival in Northwestern Siberia. Not accidentally, the strongest traditions are still alive among those northern groups of Khanty, Mansi, and Sel'kup who practice reindeer herding. Historically, nomadic groups were most resistant to outside impact. All the centers of twentieth-century rebellions coincided with reindeer-herding territory.

In rebellions we see the ultimate expression of a culture—what it does when backed against a wall—when people feel that their livelihood and culture is mortally threatened. Certainly nation-states consider their ability to wage war in order to prevent the loss of their livelihood, values, and culture as a strength, a sign of viability. So, too, might we count it a strength among indigenous nations if they have the organization and means to prevent destruction of their people and culture. Violent resistance and the ability to present a credible threat today cannot ensure protection of distinct cultures and traditional livelihoods. Ultimately, indigenous peoples must rely on other sources of strength to prevent being overrun by outsiders' rules. They cannot hope to win military battles against well-armed states, and few have the option to hide in remote regions. The Yamal tundra no longer offers an escape from outside authorities. Helicopters transport personnel and supplies to the remotest spots on the peninsula. The ability to organize, to draw the attention of international media to their plight, and the presence of able leaders who have the backing of their people are the bulwarks of a strong defense.

Several significant distinctions help to explain the resilience of the Nenets culture:

1. A nomadic lifestyle that requires daily use of a fund of traditional knowledge.

2. An economic autonomy that guarantees survival in times of catastrophe—that is able to provide essential human needs for transport, food, shelter, clothing, and tools.

3. A minimalist ethic that limits the need for material goods and intercultural interaction.

Probably all of these factors generate flexibility rather than rigidity—the most important feature of the Nenets' character. Flexibility has enabled the Nenets to survive as a strong culture closely linked to the land and the economic activities pursued by their ancestors.

By its nature, the Nenets' nomadic culture is flexible. By the seventeenth century the Nenets had found a remedy against invasion and starvation; when their hunting culture was on the verge of collapse, they became herders. In the twentieth century the Nenets used their flexibility to survive equally trying tests, as outsiders pushed into their remote regions and pressed neighboring populations northward. In response to the demands of Soviet powers, some forest Nenets even changed their traditional manner of burials, conforming to commands to provide underground rather than above-ground tombs. In the Soviet period, the Nenets' culture became more resilient despite, and even owing to, the pressure of the Communist power. For the Nenets, the capacity and readiness for change is tradition.

Leadership in Nenets society reflects this flexibility. Military leadership among the Nenets historically had a democratic character and might pass quite easily according to the nature of the activity (war or revolt). Likewise, leadership in economic activities might rotate among those skilled in a particular field. Nenets leaders are not confined to a particular gender; they shift with the economic fortunes of herders and flex in the face of obstacles. Nenets leaders' capacity today to go back and forth between the tundra and the city is a new expression of flexible "nomadism." Likewise, gender roles, though clear, are not inflexible. Women have assumed leadership roles in some villages and have become the conduit for communication between tundra dwellers and outside authorities. Furthermore, Nenets leaders both historically and today avoid rigid positions; sometimes they may confront authorities and other times they may avoid confrontation. Anna Nerkagi at first opposed construction of the supply road that transects Yamal from Labytnangi to the gas fields of the North. More recently, however, as she saw trucks regularly using the road instead of crossing the tundra, she has come to regard the road favorably.

Flexible adaptation may appear to be acceptance of and assimilation into the larger society, but it also might be a unique strategy for the culture's preservation. Historically, the Nenets produced as many leaders as were necessary to fit different circumstances. Today their leaders appear in new forums and at many levels, from the local to the international.

Conditions for Sustainability

The Nenets' remoteness and their vast territory enabled them to retreat from the most devastating impacts of Russian and early Soviet influence. The size of the territory made it impossible for outsiders to manage and control without the cooperation of the indigenous population. Nevertheless, remote and large territories alone would not have ensured the survival of the Nenets' culture. Rather, it was the Nenets' mobility that enabled them to avoid outside intrusion and control in a way that peoples more dependent on localized and stationary resources within a smaller territory could not. The geography influenced the internal character and culture of the people, so it is not geographic remoteness and size alone that is crucial for cultural survival, but geography in combination with the way that it shapes values and behavior and allows for a particular economic complex to emerge. Even protected by this natural refuge, the Nenets endured perpetual impact from outside.

We do not dismiss the role of geography, ecology, or the intrusion of outside cultural values and practices in explaining the rate and extent of cultural change, but we find the social (institutional) changes to be the primary drivers in the causal chain. The movement of other peoples, colonization, ecological change, and even climate change are intervening variables, in large part induced by institutional factors.

To determine the specific policies or intrusions of outside institutions most destructive to indigenous cultures, we may look to the rebellions of the 1930s and 1940s, during which the Nenets themselves identified the specific actions by Soviet authorities that threatened their existence. The Nenets tolerated some contact with outsiders and traders and, in certain cases, even benefited from the arrangement. At some point, however, the impact of outside policies may threaten even the strongest and most flexible indigenous culture. Nenets' grievances throughout the period of Russian and Soviet rule and particularly those preceding each outbreak of violence can be condensed to a list of violations of the indigenous code that have threatened to undermine and destroy the Nenets' culture:

1. The taking of property and reindeer or even the forced sale of reindeer.

2. The occupation of traditional lands (by forts, villages, cultural stations, trade posts, and so on).

3. The persecution of shamans and the desecration of sacred places.

4. The institution of forced labor (most evident in collectivization and sedentary-occupation policies, when herders became "workers").

5. The denial of voting rights (especially to wealthy and honored leaders) and any role in decision making.

6. The forced removal of children to boarding schools, which both undermined the traditional system of transmission of knowledge and skills and presented a threat to a family's economic viability.

By responding to (reversing) the preceding list of grievances, we can delineate the conditions necessary both to avoid conflict and to ensure the sustainability of the Nenets' culture. These are as follows:

1. Secure property rights to reindeer.

2. Secure property rights to pastureland and priority rights to hunt and fish on traditional territories and to harvest waterfowl and marine and terrestrial animals and to fish on a sustainable basis.

3. Protect sacred places and burial grounds and guarantee the right to practice religious beliefs, rituals, and ceremonies.

4. Restore self-determination and community control over economic affairs and activities.

5. Institute self-government (the right of the native community to chose its own leaders in its own ways and to exercise autonomy over decision making regarding indigenous lands, waters, and resources).

6. Institute self-determination in the transmission of knowledge and the system of educating younger generations.

These might be further distilled into two essential conditions for indigenous cultural survival: (a) secure property rights and (b) institute self-determination. Remembering that institutions are "social practices consisting of easily recognized roles coupled with clusters of rules or conventions governing relations among the occupants of these roles," we have seen how the institutions imposed by Russian and later Soviet authorities attempted to alter the gender roles and relations of indigenous cultures of Northwestern Siberia; to undermine indigenous leadership patterns and governance systems; to disrupt the transmission of knowledge, values, and beliefs; and to erode indigenous property rights. Among the Nenets and the nomadic Khanty of Yamal, none of the changes to date has destroyed the herding complex and culture.

Loss of control over land and resources, however, cuts at the heart of the distinctive characteristics of the Nenets' society. Loss of land and resources narrows the space available for a nomadic lifestyle, undermines economic autonomy, and alters the minimalist ethic. Reversals in the institutional intrusions should enable the Nenets as a distinct people to survive in the twenty-first century.

Loss of control over land and resources makes it difficult for the Nenets to address the two biggest threats to their livelihood today: (1) overgrazing of pastureland and (2) gas and oil development. Guaranteeing indigenous property rights to land in Northwestern Siberia would not be likely to result in termination of extractive resource development. Native ownership and control more likely would lead to creation of a mixed economy in which some of the revenue generated by development could be used to finance the herding economy and secure the future of both the nomadic and settled population. At the same time, herders would be likely to seek environmental precautions sufficient to preserve the herding-hunting complex.

Overgrazing of pastures presents the most imminent threat to the herding culture. Still, herders try to increase their private herds as the perceived need to maximize individual or family herds persists. Government land management agents, environmentalists, and scientists anxiously fearing a crisis are tempted to follow the usual course of outsiders and call for imposition of rules and regulations to reduce the herds. Our own inclination is to adopt a policy position that allows the herders to use their own systems of management and decision making to address the issue of overgrazing. By 1994 herders perceived the disequilibrium between herd size and herd health in a more hurried migration. In the summer of 1996 Golovnev witnessed the initiation by knowledgeable herders with some administrative experience in the northern *sovkhoz* of an ambitious plan to collect several thousand reindeer from private herds in northern Yamal and drive them to Yarano, in southern Yamal, near the newly constructed railroad, where a new slaughtering station was being arranged. The project was carried out by a newly formed enterprise called the Association of Reindeer Herding Enterprises of Yamal (SOKh, Soyuz Olenevodcheskikh Khoziaistv) and supported financially by the Yamal-Nenets Okrug Administration and Nadymgazprom. The Nenets themselves regard this as a new and necessary form of economic development. Certainly assistance in thinking of new ways to avoid a crash in the herds would be welcome. Acute overgrazing in areas close to slaughterhouses and processing facilities might be reduced. Increased small trade or supply posts would lead to redistribution of herds on Yamal and could facilitate reduction in herd size. Allowing the herders to actually participate in developing a solution is more likely to succeed than are rules imposed from outside.

Considerable grazing land already has been damaged by or converted to industrial use, although delays in full-scale development of gas reserves on the peninsula have spared the core pastureland. Some scenarios for full-scale development would drastically diminish and degrade the core areas and leave the herders precariously dependent on the peripheral hunting and fishing zones with no reserve for times of hardship. Development options that minimize overland pipelines and rely on transport via the Kara Sea and Ob Bay would be less destructive of the herding complex on Yamal. In any case, decisions regarding oil and gas development should not be made prior to putting in place the conditions essential for the culture's survival—the securing of property rights and the institution of self-determination.

In 1996 the prospects for gas development on Yamal dimmed. Amoco closed its office in Nadym, and Nadymgazprom considerably reduced its operations. The number of gas and oil workers on Yamal dropped from thousands to hundreds. For herders, this marked a return to survival in conditions of extreme autonomy—few helicopters, reduced supply lines, closure of trading points, and limited contact with outsiders. The loss of transport, communication, and supply lines creates hardship for the whole population of Yamal. For the Nenets' culture, however, the withdrawal of oil and gas enterprises provides a reprieve. Development of Yamal gas is likely to be postponed by a decade, or perhaps several decades. The difficult current conditions may well strengthen the internal characteristics of the herding culture. The Nenets, government officials, and researchers now have time to consider options for revitalizing indigenous institutions and securing indigenous property rights and self-determination—for sharing power with indigenous peoples.

Arctic Choices

Other regions of the circumpolar North provide various models for restoring rights and decision-making authority to the native peoples of Northwestern Siberia. For simplicity, we group these into three broad categories: tribal governments, public governments in regions where the indigenous population constitutes a majority, and co-management.

Indigenous peoples today are calling for self-government and tribal sovereignty, a new nation-to-nation relationship between indigenous or "First Nations" as they are called in Canada and the dominant state governments of the nations in which they live. Law in the United States has used the term "domestic dependent nations" to describe the relationship of indigenous tribes to the state. Understandably, states are frightened by application of the term "sovereignty" to indigenous nations or peoples as it implies recognition of their freedom from outside interference in internal affairs. Nevertheless, indigenous peoples of North America have forged agreements with the larger federal governments that define the set of social, cultural, educational, and even economic affairs over which the native "nation" has primary jurisdiction. While the federal governments of Canada and the United States have always retained sovereignty in the field of foreign policy and military affairs, the scope for governance by exclusively native authorities is growing.

A second model for sharing power with indigenous peoples is the creation of a regional "public" government in areas within which the indigenous population is concentrated and composes a large majority. The relationship between the Greenland Home Rule Government and Denmark exemplifies this model. The Home Rule government has more extensive powers of self-government over native homelands than anywhere else in the circumpolar North. It is a "public" rather than a native or ethnic government, as all permanent residents have voting rights regardless of ethnicity. The fact that the permanent population is 80 percent Greenlandic (*Kalaallit,* Inuit) ensures the dominant position of the native group in running the government. The Home Rule government, like other public governments in remote arctic regions, continues to depend heavily on the central government (Denmark) for support.

The government of Nunavut in the eastern Canadian Arctic, now being formed, will similarly operate as a public government subordinate to the Canadian federal government with powers similar to that of a province but with a predominately native (Inuit) population. In Alaska, two regional public governments covering territories roughly equivalent to a Russian *raion* but with powers approximating that of an *okrug* are similar to the Greenland model, although, as municipal governments, they have fewer powers than the Home Rule government. The North Slope Borough, covering a huge territory along the arctic coast of Alaska, is a public government incorporated under, and therefore subordinate to, the state of Alaska, but its voting population is roughly 70 percent Alaska Natives (Inupiat). Its jurisdiction includes the Prudhoe Bay oil fields, providing the borough with a strong tax base that has enabled it to set its own economic and social priorities and to impose environmental and social stipulations on industrial development. Seeing the success of its neighbors to the north in achieving increased self-government, the Inupiat of northwest Alaska formed a similar borough (the Northwest Arctic Borough).

A similar form of public government might provide a useful model for reconfiguration of the Yamal District, with increased autonomy from the *okrug.* With a more secure source of revenue tied to the land, the district would be able to provide schools, housing, and infrastructure in accord with voter wishes. It would be difficult to ensure the dominant voice of indigenous residents, however, given the presence of enclaves of nonnatives who are economically dependent on long-term extractive industries. Additionally, the financial dependence of the North Slope on the oil and gas industry has pitted indigenous populations in Alaska against one another. Interior Athabaskan communities dependent on caribou hunting oppose the borough's position favoring opening of the Arctic Wildlife Refuge (which contains the caribou calving grounds) to oil development.

A third model for sharing power with indigenous peoples, co-management has spread rapidly in North America in the last two decades.[1] States are more comfortable with the concept of cooperative management or co-management, as it does not require the state government to relinquish legal authority to manage resources but brings the native community into a partnership with administrative agencies. The Canadian comprehensive land claims settlements have spawned numerous co-management arrangements for use and conservation of fish, wildlife, and park lands. These are generally governed by boards composed of an equal number of native and government agency representatives. The U.S. government has entered into co-management or joint management agreements that delegate considerable decision-making power to native organizations in Alaska. Through these agreements, native organizations such as the Alaska Eskimo Whaling Commission, Alaska Eskimo Walrus Commission, and the Association of [Native] Village Council Presidents develop regulations for hunting and allocate harvest quotas for whales, walrus, and migratory waterfowl among native villages. Co-management falls far short of the self-government sought by native peoples, but it has provided a politically acceptable way for governments to reduce conflict with native populations and to provide a modest degree of "ownership" and participation in decisions regarding the management of national parks as well as fish and game species in native territory. Canadian co-management boards have become part of a package of rights to settle native claims to land, and thus are coupled with transfer to native peoples of title to large tracts of land including subsurface rights as well as exclusive rights to harvest some wildlife species and priority rights to use other species. The comprehensive claims in northern Canada have restored to native populations considerable control over land, resources, education, and local communities.

None of the preceding three models provides perfect solutions to restoration and protection of indigenous systems of governance. We need only remember the perils inherent in Speranskii's reforms to see that formation of new "native" governmental structures risk undermining indigenous leadership and destroying existing indigenous modes of decision making. We should exercise caution before devising new organizational structures so that native leadership may emerge from within the indigenous society rather than as a creation of outside authorities. It is one thing to delegate authority to an indigenous community and quite another to appoint an indigenous delegate to participate in outside governmental structures.

Co-management regimes can provide effective communication between government officials and local native populations, but they are more likely to succeed in this task when local hunter and trapper organizations within the native communities are empowered to make decisions than when a single representative of a community, or even several communities, is appointed to serve on a co-management board that meets in a distant, regional center. When a chosen few possess information from government sources, they may easily abuse their power by withholding or selectively transmitting information to some groups in the community and not others. When outside authorities create or empower leaders, they risk undermining the indigenous systems of governance, splitting the native community into factions, and undermining communal norms.

Nenets nomads who travel lightly across the tundra have the internal quality of flexibility to adapt to new conditions. They used their own means to endure the Ermak, Leshchinskii, and Speranskii epochs of Russian colonization and then the harsher periods of creeping, galloping, and retiring Soviet power. We, as outsiders, must allow them the space for adaptation and the opportunity to retain control over their lives.

Notes

Introduction

1. Titov 1890, 4–5.

2. Dolgikh 1952, 6; Khomich 1966, 26–27.

3. Kan (1995) translates *inorodtsy* as "alien" or "peoples of a different birth," in contrast to Slezkine, whose translation designates them as "foreigners."

4. See Fenge 1992.

5. Finkler 1995. See also Bogoyavlinsky 1996, 36, 37; Pika 1993.

6. Some of these we published. See Golovnev 1995 and 1997, 149–66; Osherenko 1995a and 1995b.

7. In the early twentieth century the Yamal tundra was relatively isolated from direct contact with Russians. Russian was spoken in only 8 of the 612 households (3,233 individuals) that were counted on the Yamal tundra in the census of 1926–27.

8. The Yamal-Nenets Autonomous Okrug and the Tiumen Oblast have recently been locked in a power struggle, in no small part driven by the fact that most of Russia's natural gas is produced within the okrug. Yuri Neelov, elected "governor" or administrative head of the Yamal-Nenets Okrug in October 1996, declared that signing a power-sharing agreement with the *oblast* is a precondition for the *okrug* to allow a gubernatorial election for the Tiumen Oblast to be held on *okrug* territory. Orttung 1996.

9. Zapadnaya Sibir 1963, Yamalo-Nenetskii 1965, Priroda Yamala 1995.

10. Zapadnaya Sibir 1963, Priroda Tiumenskogo Severa 1991, Priroda Yamala 1995.

11. Priroda Yamala 1995.

12. *Carex chordorrhiza.*

13. Fox are important ecologically because they are so closely tied to the lemming population cycles. Normally fox populations will peak (along with raptors) one year after a lemming peak. Bruce Forbes memo to Osherenko, 12 March 1996.

14. Vilchek 1992, 75. Additionally, the INSROP GIS data base (produced and maintained by the Intenational Northern Sea Route Programme, Fridtjof Nansen Institute, Lysaker, Norway) contains information on important marine resources throughout the Northern Sea Route, including waters surrounding the Yamal Peninsula.

15. Golovnev 1995, 62, 63.

16. Data for this and the preceding three paragraphs on the ecology of Yamal are from Chernov 1985, Danilov 1966, Kalyakin 1985, and Zapadnaya Sibir 1963. Data and maps

showing species distribution can be found in Vilchek 1992, especially figures 3.4.2 and 3.4.3 at pp. 75 and 76.

17. A little more than one-fifth of proven gas reserves in Russia are located on the Yamal Peninsula. Reserves of the huge Bovanenko and twenty-four other fields on the peninsula are reported to hold about 10.2 trillion cubic meters of gas (Estrada, Moe, and Martinsen 1995). Investment costs, especially for construction of pipelines under conditions "that have no analogue in the world," are high and uncertain (Dienes et al. 1994, 61 and note 18 at p. 223). Gazprom hoped to raise a good part of the projected $50 billion cost to develop Yamal by sale of 9 percent of its stock in the West ("Russia: Gazprom Stock Offer" 1994, 3, 4). For recent estimates of recoverable reserves of oil and gas condensate in the Tiumen Oblast, including the Yamal-Nenets Autonomous Okrug (see Kryukov et al. 1995, 219–35).

18. Forbes, 1995.

19. Possible scenarios for pipeline and ports and shipping routes for oil and gas condensate are discussed and evaluated in Kryukov et al. 1995.

20. Backlund 1995, 19.

21. Matthew J. Sagers, a consultant to the World Bank and noted American specialist on the Russian oil industry, has estimated that Yamal gas will not be needed until at least 2005 and perhaps not until 2030. Personal communication to Osherenko, 1996.

Chapter 1

1. Moshinskaia 1953, 81, table 4.

2. Krupnik 1993, 163–64.

3. Krupnik 1993, 160–84.

4. See Kolycheva 1956, 76–88; Khomich 1966, 50–51.

5. Khlobystin and Gracheva 1974, 83–85.

6. Dolgikh 1970, 98–99. See also Gurvich 1983, 115.

7. Krupnik 1993, 168, 169.

8. Krupnik 1993, 165–66.

9. Golovnev 1993, 92–93; 1995, 195.

10. See Krupnik 1993, 167.

11. Golovnev 1995, 488–92.

12. Golovnev 1995, 412–13.

13. A Nenets legend (*lahnako*) told by Ngoet (Vladimir Stepanovich) Tadibe of Yaptik-sale on the Yamal Peninsula, July 1992; translated from Nenets into Russian by Lidia V. Kiripova and Andrei V. Golovnev and from Russian into English by the authors.

14. "Rested" in the sense that they have become fat; they haven't been hunted or disturbed by people.

15. *Yagushka* is the name for the woman's garment. Unlike a man's garment, *malitsa*, it is open in the front and is used as a blanket for men while sleeping.

16. The sea, *yaw* in Nenets, refers here to Ob Bay.

17. The side of the tent where sacred objects are kept is called *si* in Nenets.

18. The literal translation is "Now we are people who ask from the street."

19. When Nenets die, their relatives place their sledges upside down and pointed to the

northwest, toward the sunset. So the overturned sledges are a sign of their death, the standing sledge a sign of life, or here, a symbol of rebirth.

20. All the destiny of a character in folklore may be recognized by the condition, color, or behavior of his reindeer.

21. The tired reindeer fell to the ground.

22. Sihirtia (or alternate spellings *sirte, siirte, siirtya*) is the name of mysterious people living underground. Among Nenets clans, the Yaptik clan is supposed to be closest to Sihirtia, and legends such as this one tell of marriages between Yaptik and Sihirtia.

23. The border of the camp beyond the corral area is called *ngevalanse yahanda* (literally "the place for the way").

24. Nenets called mammoths "earthen reindeer" (*yan-khora*).

25. The Nenets call a subterranean dwelling or pit house *yan-mya*.

26. The *sovik* is a winter garment with the reindeer fur on the outside; it is worn over the *malitsa* (reindeer fur on the inside).

27. This is a sign of a hospitable reception.

28. This is equivalent to "Dear Junior Yaptik." Using the possessive "my" indicates a close relationship has emerged between them.

29. The daughter of Sihirtia Old Man and Old Woman.

30. Whistling is a frequent sign in folktales of contact with the spirits of the netherworld. Here it is a sign of next-to-eldest brother's previous death.

31. Junior Yaptik, sitting on the sacred *si* place, pronounced the key phrase "*Vaesako baertm Ilebts*" ("Old Man gave me life"), which is derived from the name of the god Ilibem-Baertia Vaesako, who is the giver of life and reindeer. The words "life" and "wild reindeer" have the same root in Nenets. *Ile* means "to live"; *ilebts* means "wild reindeer."

32. Here it becomes clear that Nomadic Man, the old man, and the god Ilibem-Baertia are the same.

33. Seven is a sacred number for measuring time and space in the world of the gods.

34. "Word" (*lahnako*) is used here to indicate that the narrator has moved from one scene to another.

35. Golovnev 1996, field notes.

Chapter 2

1. The data that follows is more widely represented in Golovnev 1995, 198–230; 298–328, 380–493.

2. Vasil'ev 1978, 436. P. Bolina is Enets, but the Enets' culture is close to and mixed with that of the Nenets; thus Vasil'ev describes the spiritual traditions of Nenets and Enets jointly.

3. Evladov 1992, 166.

4. Lepekhin 1805, 117, 257.

5. Tereshchenko 1965, 479, 480.

6. Golovnev 1992, field notes, Variogan.

7. Gemuev 1980, 125.

8. Donner 1926, 107.

9. Castrén 1860, 229.

10. Kupryanova 1965, 35, 36.

11. N. Laptander, personal communication, Polar Urals; Golovnev 1993, field notes.

12. V. Lapsuy, personal communication, Gydan; Golovnev 1979, field notes.

13. Evladov 1992, 161.

Chapter 3

1. See Forsyth 1992.

2. Zibarev 1990, 35–38.

3. Golovnev 1992, 7–8.

4. Skrynnikov 1986, 104–11. The S. Berro referred to here is actually Stephen Borough (see Hakluyt 1589, 318).

5. Soloviev 1988, 622–23.

6. Dolgikh 1960, 133.

7. Bakhrushin 1955a, 6–12.

8. Bakhrushin 1955a, 5–6.

9. Bakhrushin 1955a, 5–6.

10. Castrén 1860, 252.

11. Bakrushin 1955b.

12. Stepanov 1936.

13. See Patkanov 1891, Golovnev 1995, 96–154.

14. Miller 1937, 204–205.

15. See Bakhrushin 1955b, 133–35.

16. Sulotskii 1915.

17. Abramov 1846, 3; Gerasimov 1909, 30.

18. Sulotskii 1915, 30.

19. Pamiatniki 1882, 413–14.

20. Sulotskii 1915, 32–33.

21. Abramov 1851, 15; TF GATO 144, 1, 48: 23.

22. Pamiatniki 1885, 179–80; TF GATO 144, 1, 45a: 1–2.

23. Pamiatniki 1885, 181–82; Golovnev 1995, 104–105.

24. Abramov 1946, 16; 1851, 20: TF GATO 144,1, 48: 37.

25. Abramov 1946, 16; 1851, 20; TF GATO 144, 1, 48: 37.

26. Gerasimov 1909, 32–33.

27. TF GATO 144, 1, 43: 28–29.

28. Irinarkh 1910, N3: 117–18, N4: 183–84; TF GATO 144, 1, 45a: 208.

29. TF GATO 144, 1, 45a: 2–3.

30. Bakhrushin 1955b, 134–35.

31. Zibarev 1990, 35–36.

32. See Kulemzin 1976, 47–64; Khomich 1981; Prokofieva 1981; Chernetsov 1987.

33. Ustav 1822, 34–35.

34. Islavin 1847, 117–19.

35. Irinarkh 1916, 7–8, 242.

36. TF GATO 152, 41, 8: 3, 28–29.

37. Speranskii's reforms did include four relatively "enlightened" principles designed, at least in part, to protect native societies and their institutions. As summarized by Marc

Raeff, these were (1) "the administration of the nomads and vagrants [wanderers, *brodi-achie*] should be based on their old customs, but these had to be better defined and organized; . . . [2] local authorities should have only general supervisory police functions, and the internal autonomy of the tribes should be left untouched; . . .[3] the freedom of trade and industry should be protected; . . .[4] taxes and tribute should be proportional to the abilities of each tribe and assessed at regular intervals" (Raeff 1957, 271–72, citing *Obozrenie glavnykh osnovanii*, 60–61).

38. See Fondahl 1998, 4.

39. GAOO 3, 1, 300: 25–26.

40. TF GATO 152, 37, 495: 42.

41. Beliavskii 1833, 84, 128, 170–72.

42. TF GATO 154, 41, 8: 28–34.

43. GAOO, F. 3, op. 2, d. 1960, ll. 35–36. See a more detailed account in Golovnev 1995, 155–63.

44. GAOO, F. 3, op. 2, d. 1960, ll. 35–36.

45. GAOO, F. 3, op. 2, d. 1960, ll. 35–46.

46. Abramov 1857, 357.

47. Budarin 1968, 88.

48. Slavin 1911, 6, 7.

49. TF GATO 152, 39, 5: 335.

50. Irinarkh 1916, 30–33; TF GATO 144, 1, 45-a: 34–36.

51. Kushelevskii 1868.

52. TF GATO 152, 39, 116: 1–23.

53. Golovnev and Zaitsev 1992, 49–50.

54. Golovnev 1993, 31–35, 139–51.

55. Dunin-Gorkavich 1904, 243–48.

56. Golovnev 1993, 31, 34.

Chapter 4

1. The derogatory label *kulak*, a Soviet ideological classification for "class enemies" or "capitalists," was applied to the richest people; in the case of natives of Siberia, those who owned many reindeer and used the labor of others to herd them.

2. SR refers to the Socialist Revolutionary party.

3. *Sud'by narodov* 1994, 199.

4. *Natsional'naia Politika* 1992, 6.

5. Slezkine 1994, 138. Slezkine also recounts the difficulties and eventual demise of the Siberian branch office of *Narkomnats* in 1923 (1994, 140, 141).

6. Slezkine provides a rich intellectual history of the immediate post-Revolutionary period that places the ideas that emerged in context (1994, 131–50).

7. Proponents of the three alternatives, as explained by Zibarev (1968, 119–21) were (a) V. K. Arsenyev and V. G. Bogoraz, (b) S. V. Kertselli, and (c) D. E. Lappo.

8. Kiselev 1974, 75–78, 103; Slezkine 1994, 136.

9. Slezkine 1994, 136.

10. Forsyth 1992, 242–43.

11. At the beginning of the century, the territory of the Khanty, the Mansi, the Sel'kup, and the Nenets had been incorporated into three provinces (*guberniia*)—Tobol'sk, Enisei, and Tomsk—and these in turn had been divided into districts or counties (Russian singular: *uezd*), and further into small administrative townships (*volosti*). In 1912, the two northern counties of Tobol'sk province, Surgut and Berezovo, contained 452 settlements grouped into 12 townships. Each township encompassed the nomadic camps within its boundaries. The total population of Surgut and Berezovo counties was 19, 871 in 1912; the majority of both counties were native (63 percent and 77 percent, respectively, in 1914). *Obzor Tobolskoi Gubernii* 1916, appendix, table 5; the counties are listed with the number of settlements and population of each in *Spisok naselennykh mest* (list of inhabited places) 1912, 562–603.

12. Mazurenko 1975, 174–75.

13. Vakhtin 1992. See also Forsyth 1992, 244, 245, and Slezkine 1994, 150–52.

14. "Temporary regulations about the rule of native peoples and tribes of the northern regions" affirmed by VTsIK and SNK (*Sovnarkom*) on 25 October 1926, *Natsional'naia Politika* 1992, 20–23.

15. Abramov 1857, 426.

16. *Komseveroput* (*Komitet Severnogo morskogo puti* or the Committee of the Northern Sea Route). Slavin (1939) refers to this organization as the *komissiya* or commission, not Committee of the Northern Sea Route.

17. *Izvestiya VtsIK* 1920, 28.10.

18. Slezkine 1994, 202.

19. TF GATO, f.690, op. 1, d.6, ll: 7–11.

20. Tobol'sk Okrug, founded in the 1920s as a subdivision of the Ural Oblast, encompassed approximately the area of the modern Tiumen Oblast. TobOkrug refers to all the area formerly called Tobol'sk North or Tobol'sk krai ("area") by the name of its prerevolutionary "capital"—Tobol'sk.

21. TF GATO, f.690, op. 1, d.6, ll: 7–11, as quoted in Golovnev 1995, 166.

22. TF GATO, f.690, op. 1, d.6, ll: 7–11.

23. TF GATO, f. 690, op. 1, d. 6, ll: 115–20.

24. Vanchitskaya 1993, 12.

25. Afanasieva authored a Khanty alphabet book; G. N. Prokofiev, a Sel'kup, and E. D. Prokofieva, a Nenets. But several years passed before these were published: the first Khanty reader appeared in 1930, and a Khanty alphabet book was published in 1931. Alphabet books for the Nenets, Sel'kup, and Mansi appeared in 1932 and 1933. All the books were printed using the Latin alphabet and only in 1937 were transferred to the Cyrillic alphabet used for Russian, a change that accelerated the process of teaching Russian to native students.

26. Vanchitskaya 1993, 13.

27. Evladov 1992, 13–14.

28. Evladov 1992, 23–24.

29. *Nationalnaia Politika* 1992, 83–86. These national okrugs (which became national "autonomous" okrugs in 1977) were subordinated to three higher authorities: the *oblast*, the Russian Federation, and the central government of the Soviet Union. Despite the urging of the Committee of the North for direct funding of the national okrugs from the central

government, the new okrugs and nomadic councils came to depend on the provinces for their budgets. It is no surprise, therefore, that the national districts were poorly funded and poorly staffed.

30. Kiselev 1974, 138–42.

31. *Organizatsiia Glavnogo upravleniia Severnogo morskogo puti* (GUSMP).

32. *Resheniya partii* 1967, 408.

33. Decree of August 10, 1935, *Sbornik uzakonenii RSFSR* 1936, 27.

34. Luzhnikov et al. 1967, 10.

35. About one-third of the indigenous people in the Yamal-Nenets and Khanty-Mansi-isk okrugs lived within the territories of *kultbaza* activity. The Kazym cultural station, located on the Amnya River, was active among the Khanty, forest Nenets, and Komi of the Kazym area; the Sos'va station, in areas inhabited by the Mansi and Komi. The Yamal station in Yar-Sale worked with Nenets herders. The Taz station, placed in the village of Khal'mer-Sede, was active on the territory of the Tazovsk *raion*, among the Nenets and Sel'kup.

36. Brodnev 1967, 87.

37. Brodnev 1967, 87–102.

38. GAYaNAO, f. 12, op. 1, d 142.

39. Khomich 1980, 68.

40. Bol'shakov 1936, 19.

41. *Tridtsat let* 1960, 26–37.

42. A fuller account of the three uprisings can be found in Golovnev 1995, 165–89.

43. *Sud'by narodov*, 1994.

44. *OGPU, Otdel Glavnogo Politicheskogo Upravleniya* (Department of the Supreme Polit-ical Management); NKVD, *Narodnyi Komissariat Vnutrennikh Del* (Peoples' Commissariat of Internal Affairs); KGB, *Komitet Gosudarstvennoy Bezopasnosti* (Committee of State Security).

45. This description and interpretation of the events is pieced together from three main sources of information about rebellions: (1) oral histories told to Golovnev by old men of the Nenets, Khanty, and Sel'kup; (2) detailed evidence of the rebellion on the Kazym River con-tained in court Case No. 2/49, one copy of which has been preserved by chance in the Bere-zovo local museum; and (3) the publications of KGB and Communist party archival docu-ments previously not uncovered *(Sud'by narodov* 1994). To present a coherent story from these disparate sources, all the facts are presented in chronological order and linked with a logical thread. (Many direct quotations appear in the text.)

46. *Sud'by narodov* 1994, 238.

47. *Seredniak* was a Sovietic category for "average" person, in between a rich one *(kulak)* and a poor one *(bedniak)*.

48. *Sud'by narodov* 1994, 238.

49. *Sud'by narodov* 1994, 238–39.

50. *Sud'by narodov* 1994, 240–41.

51. *Sud'by narodov* 1994, 241–43.

52. Esiko Laptander, communication to Golovnev, Polar Urals, 1993.

53. *Sud'by narodov* 1994, 265.

54. *Udarnik Arktiki,* 23 February 1936.

55. *Udarnik Arktiki,* 30 May 1935.

56. *Tridtsat let* 1960, 26–37.

57. *Udarnik Arktiki*, 30 May 1935.

58. Petrushin 1991, 35, 36.

59. See Petrushin 1991; Golovnev and Zaitsev 1992, 75–76.

60. Petrushin 1991; Golovnev and Zaitsev 1992, 75–76.

61. Petrushin 1991, 35, 36.

62. Case No. 2/49, BKM, N767: 2, 32.

63. RGAE, 9570, 2, 343, 28.

Chapter 5

1. Golovnev 1996, field notes.

2. Vostriakov and Brodnev 1964, 25.

3. Khomich 1980, 72.

4. Ivan V. Khorolia, from Osherenko 1994, field notes, Siunai-Sale.

5. Pribyl'skii and Petkevich 1967, 31.

6. In addition to these Yamal District herds, the Baidaratskii *sovkhoz* in the Priural District recorded an average of 126 reindeer per household held privately by 153 households at the beginning of 1994, or 19,308 reindeer in private ownership.

7. Lagunov 1993, 100.

8. Lagunov 1992, 85.

9. Research into educational history is hampered by inaccurate records. For example, the Nizhnetavdinsk regional department of public education reported only 18 children of school age not attending school on 15 October 1947. But closer examination of the records indicates that 344 children were not in school, and 75 of them were expelled during the first quarter. In 1952 the regional department of public education recorded 438 children of school age in the region, while the regional statistics board counted 359 and the Party Committee cited 410. Lagunov 1992, 86.

10. *Narody Severa* 1992, 368.

11. *Narody Severa* 1992, 368.

12. Aipin 1989, 140. This frequently cited figure includes destruction of pastures on the Taz Peninsula from the development of the Yamburg fields. By 1988, 594,000 hectares (2,293 square miles), and 24,000 reindeer, had been lost by five *sovkhozy* of the Yamal-Nenets Okrug following the beginning the construction of the Labytnangi-Bovanenko railroad (Vahktin 1992, 24, citing *Severnye Prostory*, no. 6 [1988]: 11).

13. *Nuclear Wastes in the Arctic* 1995, 8, 30.

14. *Nuclear Wastes in the Arctic* 1995, 28, 29.

15. *Nuclear Wastes in the Arctic* 1995, 34. The tests at Novaya Zemlya constituted about 94 percent of the total yield of all Soviet nuclear tests.

16. *Nuclear Wastes in the Arctic* 1995, 34.

17. Pika 1990.

18. *Pravda*, 1 June 1989, 5; Aipin 1989, 136–43.

19. See Vitebsky 1990; Chance and Andreeva 1995, 226–29.

20. Compare Vitebsky 1990 with Andreeva et al. 1995.

21. Minutes of *sel'sovet* (village council) meeting in Yaptiksale, April 1990.

22. Svarovskii 1991, 18–22; photo reprinted in Slezkine 1994, 336.

23. In the end of the 1980s and the beginning of the 1990s, the Yaptiksale *sel'sovet* had 370 inhabitants, with about 350 of them indigenous. The information about leadership that follows consists mostly of A.V. Golovnev's observations made during field research conducted from 1987 to 1993. Information for the Yaptiksale case was collected by the co-authors during 1993.

Chapter 6

1. Hardin 1968.

2. Campbell and Godoy (1992) present a nuanced picture of common-field agriculture in medieval England and contrast it with common-field agriculture still practiced in the Andes.

3. Cox 1985, 53–55.

4. See Ostrom 1990, 58–102.

5. Manning 1988.

6. See Osherenko 1995a.

7. Khomich 1980, 72, 73.

8. Nonworking pensioners headed the remaining 255 households (1,053 individuals).

9. Oil and gas accounted for 98 percent of industrial output of the *okrug*, and agriculture only 0.7 percent, according to N. A. Lukiyanova, first deputy of head of administration of the Yamal-Nenets Okrug. *Krasniy Sever*, June 1994, 9.

10. Nadymgazprom is one of twenty-five natural gas production and transportation associations that constitute RAO Gazprom, the Russian joint stock company that controls the industry. Smaller geological exploration firms also operate on the peninsula.

11. Amoco and the Russian joint stock company, RAO Gazprom, signed a cooperation agreement on July 30, 1992, that established Amoco's right to participate in the development of oil fields at Novyi Port and Rostovtsev and, more significantly, in the gas-condensate (found at deeper zones) parts of the Bovanenko gas field. Nadymgazprom is to be accorded exclusive development rights.

12. Podkorytov 1994, 8.

13. Vilchek 1992, 52.

14. The degree to which kin ties continued to form the basic organizing units of *kolkhozy* and later of brigades within *sovkhozy* on the Yamal Peninsula requires further research.

15. Dmitrii Khorolia, director of Yarsalinskii *sovkhoz*, interview in Osherenko 1994, field notes, Yar-Sale.

16. McKean and Ostrom 1995, 3–15, list the conditions, synthesized from case studies, that are associated with successful common property regimes. See also Ostrom 1990 and McKean 1992.

17. Oran R. Young, undated manuscript.

18. Russian Federation, October 27, 1993, decree "On the Regulation of Land Relations and the Development of Agrarian Reform in Russia." See description of this decree in Wegren 1994a, 168–171. See also Wegren 1994b, 218 and note 12.

19. Khomich 1980, 72.

20. Posaeva 1993, 5.

21. Podkorytov 1994, 8.

22. The railroad corridor from Labytnangi to the north has already destroyed many hectares of pastureland through this *sovkhoz*.

23. In addition to these Yamal District herds, the Baidaratskii *sovkhoz* in the Priural District recorded 19,308 reindeer in private ownership in 1994. Land reform office, Aksarka, 1994.

24. "Two letters," in Pika et al. 1996, 217, 220.

25. Vladimir B. Istomin (director of Yamalskii *sovkhoz*), interview, in Osherenko 1994, field notes, Salekhard.

26. Istomin interview, Osherenko 1994.

27. Official figures obtained from the land reform office in Aksarka.

28. Lidia V. Kiripova and Elena G. Susoi, interview, in Osherenko 1994, field notes, Salekhard.

29. Fondahl 1995a, 1995b, 1998. See also Olga Murashko, "Introduction" to *Anxious North*, in Pika et al. 1996, 9–13.

30. Fondahl 1995a, 220.

31. Evgenii G. Kuzyukov (deputy head of the Yamal-Nenets Okrug Committee on Land Resources and Land Planning), interview, in Osherenko 1994, field notes, Salekhard.

32. Kuzyukov interview, Osherenko 1994.

33. Istomin interview, Osherenko 1994.

34. The formula for revenue sharing is determined by the Russian Federation Law on the Subsurface (N. A. Lukiyanova [first deputy head of administration of the Yamal-Nenets Autonomous Okrug], interview, in Osherenko 1994, field notes, Salekhard).

35. Kuzyukov interview, Osherenko 1994.

36. Viktor G. Tolstov, interview in Osherenko 1994, field notes, Yar-Sale. Nevertheless, one group from the Panaevskii *sovkhoz* sought to have an area designated as their clan lands for fur hunting and fishing, but the administration had not granted their request.

37. G. K. Arkhipova, in Osherenko 1994, field notes, Aksarka.

38. The video film *Khadampae* by Golovnev featured her. Slezkine (1994, 369–71) discussed one of her short stories, "Aniko from the Nogo Clan." *Krasnyi Sever* published parts of her novels and stories, and a documentary about her life and work aired on national television in Russia, viewed by the authors in the summer of 1993 in Tobol'sk. One of her short stories appeared recently in English (Nerkagi 1996, 273–89).

39. Under the agreement between the *sovkhoz* and the administration, signed by Yamkin, head of the administration of Priuralskii Raion, on May 16, 1994, Number 125, the committee will set aside 107,032 hectares for future privatization.

40. Although reindeer meat is high in protein, the high cost of transportation and processing in remote regions makes it noncompetitive in today's Russian market. Nonnative consumers appear to prefer other meat over reindeer sausage available in food stores in Salekhard (Osherenko 1994, field notes, Salekhard).

41. Lukiyanova interview, Osherenko 1994.

42. Ob Bay usually becomes passable about mid-July; supply ships must leave southern ports before then to reach northern territories, but delays in payments from the central gov-

ernment have impeded shipments and produced severe shortages of food and fuel in northern communities.

43. Kuzyukov interview, Osherenko 1994.

44. Kuzyukov interview, Osherenko 1994.

45. See Chance and Andreeva 1995, a comparative study showing how sharing of wealth from oil and gas development has brought substantial benefits to northern native people.

46. For a discussion of the effects of transferring large areas of land (including some subsurface rights) and government-owned businesses to native entities in the Canadian Arctic and Alaska, see "Private Initiatives: Arctic Problem Solving," in Osherenko and Young 1989, 186–95.

47. Canada 1985 and 1993.

48. Russian Federation 1994, 7 (Annex 2, Section 3.4). See also Section 10.1, which requires consultation with these regional associations in development of local privatization programs.

49. Aipin 1989, 136–43. Aipin served as a people's deputy in the Russian Parliament and, in November 1993, was elected president of the Association of Small Numbered Peoples of the North.

50. These proposals were put forward at a Conference on Problems of the Indigenous Peoples of the North that took place at Komsomol'sk-na-Amure, reported by Sergei Akulich, 1995. See also V. Lebedev, "Who Owns the Land?" and Anastasia Lapsuy, "Where Is My Share?" both in Pika et al. 1996, 207–15, 223–26.

51. Fondahl 1995a, 219 and 1995b; Boyakova et al.

52. Moe and Kryukov 1994, 99.

53. Moe and Kryukov 1994, 99, 100.

54. Moe and Kryukov 1994, 100.

55. The Western partner in this joint venture, Amoco, pulled out for economic reasons.

56. World Bank, OD 4.20, para. 15(c).

57. World Bank, OD 4.20, para. 13.

58. World Bank, OD 4.20, para. 15(a).

59. World Bank, OD 4.20, para. 15(c).

60. World Bank, OD 4.30, para. 3.

Conclusion

1. Osherenko 1988; Circumpolar Aboriginal People, 1996.

Bibliography

Abbreviations for Russian Archival Material

BKM   Berezovskii Kraevedcheskii Muzei (Archives of the Berezovo Museum)

GAOO   Gosudarstvennyi Arkhiv Omskoi Oblasti (State Archive of the Omsk Oblast)

GAYaNAO Gosudarstvennyi Arkhiv Yamalo-Nenetskogo Avtonomnogo Okruga (State Archive of the Yamal-Nenets Autonomous Okrug)

RGAE   Rossiskii Gosudarstvennyi Arkhiv Ekonomiki (Russian State Archive on Economics) Moscow.

TF GATO   Tobol'skii Filial Gosudarstvennogo Arkhiva Tiumenskoi Oblasti (Tobol'sk Branch of the State Archive of the Tiumen Oblast)

TsGAOR   Tsentral'nyi Gosudarstvennyi Arkhiv Oktyabr'skoi Revolutsii (Central State Archive of the October Revolution)

Abramov, Nikolai A. 1846. "Filofei Leshchinskii, mitropolit tobol'skii i sibirskii" (Filofei Leshchinskii, the Metropolitan of Tobol'sk and Siberia). In *Zhurnal ministerstva narodnogo prosveshcheniia* 12: 1–18.

_____. 1851. "O vvedenii khristianstva u berezovskikh ostiakov" (About the Introduction of the Christianity among Berezovo Ostiaks). In *Zhurnal ministerstva narodnogo prosveshcheniia*, part 72, nos. 10–12: 1–22.

_____. 1857. "Opisanie Berezovskogo kraia." (Description of Berezovsky territory). In *Zapiski IRGO*, no. 12: 329–448.

Aipin, Yeremei D. 1989. "Not by Oil Alone." *Moscow News* 2, 9,10. Reprinted in *IWGIA [International Work Group for Indigenous Affairs] Newsletter* (Copenhagen) 57: 136–43.

Andreyeva, Ye.; O. I. Larichev; N. E. Flanders; and R. V. Brown. 1995. "Complexity and Uncertainty in Arctic Resource Decisions: The Example of the Yamal Pipeline." *Polar Geography and Geology* 19, no 1: 22–35.

Backlund, Anders. 1995. "Development of Oil and Gas Exports from Northern Russia." *INSROP Working Paper No. 22*, III.01.3. Lysaker, Norway: Nansen Institute.

Bakhrushin, Sergei V. 1955a. "Samoyedy v XVII v" (Samoyeds in Seventeenth Century). In Bakhrushin, *Nauchnye Trudy*. Vol. 3, Part . 2, pp. 5–12 . Moscow: Academy of Sciences.

_____. 1955b. "Ostyatzkie i vogul'skie kniazhestva v XVI–XVII vv" (Ostyak and Vogul Princedoms in Sixteenth–Seventeenth Centuries). In Bakhrushin, *Nauchnye Trudy*. Vol. 3, Part 2, pp. 86–152. Moscow: Academy of Sciences.

Beliavskii, Franz. 1833. *Poezdka k Ledovitomu moriu* (Trip toward the Polar Sea). Moscow.

Bogoyavlinsky, D. D. 1996. "Peoples of Russia's North: Demographic Information." In *Anxious North: Indigenous Peoples in Soviet and Post Soviet Russia,* ed. Alexander Pika, Jens Dahl, and Inge Larsen, no. 82, pp. 35–43. Copenhagen: IWGIA.

Bol'shakov, M. A. 1936. "Problema osedaniia kochevogo naceleniia (Na Yamale)" (The Problem of Sedentarization of Nomadic Population on Yamal). Sovetskaia Arktika 5: 14–24.

Boyakova, S. I., et al. 1996. "Influence of the Northern Sea Route on Social and Cultural Development of Indigenous Peoples of the Arctic Zone of the Sakha Republic (Yakutia)." *INSROP Working Paper No. 49,* IV.4.1. Lysaker, Norway: Fridtjof Nansen Institute.

Brodnev, Mikhail M., 1967. "Yamal Rukopis" (Yamal Manuscript). Personal archive of Yuri P. Pribyl'skii, Tobol'sk.

Budarin, M. E. 1968. *Put'malykh narodov Krainego Severa k kommunizmu* (The Way of the Small Peoples of the Far North to Communism). Omsk: West-Siberian Books IZD-VO.

Buhl, Cindy M. 1994. *Citizens' Guide to the Multilateral Development Banks and Indigenous Peoples.* Washington, D.C.: The Bank Information Center.

Campbell, Bruce M. S., and Ricardo A. Godoy. 1992. "Commonfield Agriculture: The Andes and Medieval England Compared." In *Making the Commons Work: Theory, Practice, and Policy,* ed. Daniel W. Bromley. San Francisco: Institute for Contemporary Studies.

Canada. 1985. *The Western Arctic Claim: The Inuvialuit Final Agreement.* Ottawa: Department of Indian Affairs and Northern Development.

———. 1993. *Agreement between the Inuit of the Nunavut Settlement Area and Her Majesty the Queen in Right of Canada May 25, 1993.* Ottawa: Deptartment of Indian and Northern Affairs. Summarized in "The Nunavut Agreement." *Northern Perspectives* 21, no. 3 (Fall 1993): 2. Ottawa: Canadian Arctic Resources Committee.

Castrén [Kastren], M. A. 1860. "Puteshestvie po Laplandii, Severnoi Rossii i Sibiri (1838–1844, 1845–1849 gg)" (Traveling through Lapland, Northern Russia, and Siberia). *Magazin zemlevedeniia i puteshestvii* (Moscow) 6, no. 2.

Chance, Norman A., and Elena N. Andreeva. 1995. "Sustainability, Equity, and Natural Resource Development in Northwest Siberia and Arctic Alaska." *Human Ecology* 23, no. 2: 217–40.

Chernetsov, V. N. 1987. [Diaries of Expeditions.] In *Istochniki po Etnografii Zapadnoi Sibiri.* Tomsk: University Press.

Chernov, Y. I. 1985. "Sreda i soobshchestva tundrovoi zony" (Environment and Association of Tundra Zones). Soobshchestva Krainego Severa MS, 25–30.

Circumpolar Aboriginal People and Co-management Practice. 1996. *Current Issues in Comanagment and Environmental Assessment.* Calgary, Alberta: Arctic Institute of North America.

Constitution of the Russian Federation. 1993. As approved by the National Referendum on December 12, 1993. English Translation by Federal News Service. In Albert P. Blaustein and Gisbert H. Flanz, eds., *Constitutions of the Countries of the World: The Russian Federation.* Dobbs Ferry, N.Y.: Oceana Publications, 1994.

Cox, Susan Jane Buck. 1985. "No Tragedy on the Commons." *Environmental Ethics* 7, no 1: 49–62.

Danilov, N. N. 1966. *Puti prisposobleniya nazemnykh pozvonochnykh k usloviyam sushchestvo-vaniya v Subarktike* (The Adaptation of Terrestrial Vertebrates to Life in the Subarctic). Vol. 2 of *Ptitsy* (Birds). Sverdlovsk: Sredne-Ural'skoie Knizhnoe Izdatel'stvo.

Dienes, Leslie; Istvan Dobozi; and Marian Radetski. 1994. *Energy and Economic Reform in the Former Soviet Union.* New York, St. Martin's Press.

Dolgikh, Boris O. 1952. "O nekotorykh etnogeneticheskikh protsessakh (pereseleniiakh narodov i rasprostranenii iazykov) v Severnoi Sibiri" (On Some Ethnogenetic Processes [Migrations of Peoples and Diffusion of languages] in Northern Siberia). *Sovetskaia etnografia* 1: 51–59.

_____. 1960. *Rodovoi i plemennoi sosnav narodov Sibiri v XVII veke* (Clan and Tribal Composition of the Siberian Indigenous Peoples in the Seventeenth Century). Moscow: Trudy Instituta Etnografii.

_____. 1970. "Osnovnye cherty ottsovsko-rodovykh otnoshenii u narodov Severa" (The Main Features of Patriarchal-Tribal Relations among Northern Peoples). In *Obshchestvennyi stroi u narodov Severnoi Sibiri, pp. 88–102.* Moscow: Nauka..

Donner, Kai. 1926. *Bei den Samojeden in Sibirien.* Stuttgart: Strecker und Schroeder. *Among the Samoyed in Siberia,* translated by Rinehart Kyler. New Haven, Conn.: Human Relations Area Files, 1954.

Dunin-Gorkavich, A. A. 1904. 1910. 1911. *Tobol'skii Sever,* T. 1, 2, 3 (Tobol'sk North, Vols. 1, 2, 3). Tobol'sk, St. Petersburg.

Estrada, Javier; Arild Moe; and Kare Dahl Martinsen. 1995. *The Development of European Gas Markets: Environmental, Economic, and Political Perspectives.* London: John Wiley & Sons.

Evladov, V. P. 1992. *Po tundram Yamala k Belomu ostrovu: Ekspeditsiya na Krainyi Sever poluostrova Yamal v 1928–1929 gg* (Across the Tundra of Yamal toward White Island: Expedition on the Far North of Yamal Peninsula in 1928–29). Edited by Alexander Pika. Tiumen: Institut problem osvoeniya Severa (Institute for Problems of Northern Development, Siberian branch of the Academy of Sciences).

Fenge, Terry 1992. "Political Development and Environmental Management in Northern Canada: The Case of the Nunavut Agreement." *Etudes/Inuit/Studies* 16, nos. 1–2: 115–41.

Finkler, Harald W. 1995. "Health Care in the Russian and Canadian North: A Comparative Perspective." *Post-Soviet Geography* 36, no, 4: 238–45.

Forbes, Bruce C. 1995. "Tundra Disturbance Studies, III: Short-term Effects of Aeolian Sand and Dust, Yamal Region, Northwest Siberia." *Environmental Conservation* 22, no 4:335–44.

Fondahl, Gail 1995a. "The Status of Indigenous Peoples in the Rusian North." *Post-Soviet Geography* 36, no 4: 215–24.

_____. 1995b. "Legacies of Territorial Reorganization for Indigenous Land Claims in Northern Russia." *Polar Geography* 19, no. 1: 1–21.

_____. 1998. *Gaining Ground? Evenkis, Land, and Reform in Southeastern Siberia.* Needham Heights, Mass: Allyn & Bacon.

Forsyth, James. 1992. *A History of the Peoples of Siberia: Russia's North Asian Colony 1581–1990.* Cambridge University: Cambridge University Press.

Gemuyev, I. N. 1980. *K istorii sem'i i semeinoi obriadnosti sel'kupov, Etnografiia Severnoi Azii.* (Toward a History of Sel'kup Family and Family Rituals). Novosibirsk: Nauka.

Gerasimov, V. N. 1909. *Obdorsk: istoricheskii ocherk* (Obdorsk: A Historical Essay). Tiumen: A. A. Krylov.

Golovnev, Andrei V. 1992. "Russkoe vliianie na kul'turu narodov Severo-Zapadnoi Sibiri" (Russian Impact on Culture of the Northwestern Siberian Peoples). In *Kul'turnyi potentsial Sibiri v dosovetskii period.* Novosibirsk: Pedagogical Institute Press.

———. 1993. "Istoricheskaia tipologiia khoziaistva narodov Severo-Zapadnoi Sibiri" (Historical Typology of the Economy of the Peoples of Northwestern Siberia). Novosibirsk: University Press.

———. 1995. *Govoriashchie kul'tury: traditsii samodiitsev i ugrov* (Talking Cultures: Samoyed and Ugrian Traditions). Ekaterinburg: Academy of Sciences (Ural branch).

———. 1997. "Indigenous Leadership in Northwestern Siberia: Traditional Patterns and their Contemporary Manifestations." *Arctic Anthropology* 34, no. 1: 149–66.

Golovnev, Andrei V., and G. S. Zaitsev. 1992. *Istoria Yamala* (A History of Yamal). Tobol'sk and Yar-Sale: Ethnographic Bureau.

Gurvich, Il'ia S. 1983. "Problema etnogeneza olennykh grupp chukchei i koriakov v svete etnograficheskikh dannykh" (Questions of Ethnogenesis of the Reindeer Divisions of the Chukchi and Koriak in Light of Ethnographic Data). In *Na styke Chukotki i Aliaski,* pp. 143–67. Moscow: Nauka.

Hakluyt, Richard. 1589. *The Principall Navigations, Voiages, and Discoveries of the English Nation.* London.

Hardin, Garrett. 1968. "The Tragedy of the Commons." *Science* 162: 1243–48.

Irinark. 1910. "V debriakh severo-zapada Sibiri" (In the Wilderness of Northwest Siberia). *Pravoslavnyi blagovestnik,* 2, 3, 4.

———. 1916. "Khronologicheskii obzor" (Chronological Survey). *Pravoslavnyi blagovestnik,* 7–8.

Islavin, Vladimir. 1847. *Samoedy v domashnem i obshchestvennom bytu* (Samoyeds in Their Home and Daily Social Life). St. Petersburg.

Istoriya Sibiri. 1968. *Sibir' v period stroitel'stva sotsial'izma* (The History of Siberia: Siberia in the Period of the Building of Socialism). Vol. 4. Leningrad: Nauka.

Izvestiya VtsIK, 25 December 1921, 28 October 1920.

Kalyakin, V. N. 1985. "Mlekopitayushchie v nazemnykh ekosistemakh" (Mammals in Terrestrial Ecosystems). MS.

Kan, Sergei. 1995. Book Review of *Arctic Mirrors* by Slezkine. *Arctic Anthropology* 32, no. 2: 127–31.

Khlobystin, Leonid P., and Galina N. Gracheva. 1974. "Poiavlenie olenevodstva v tundrovoi zone Evropy, Zapadnoi i Srednei Sibiri" (The Appearance of Reindeer Breeding in the Tundra Zone of Europe, Western and Central Siberia). In *Formy perekhoda ot prisvaivaiushchego khoziaistva k proizvodiashchemu* (Proceedings of a Conference), pp. 81–86. Leningrad.

Khomich, Liudmila V. 1966. *Nentsy: Istoriko-etnograficheskie ocherki* (The Nenets: Historical and Ethnographic Essays). Moscow and Leningrad: Nauka.

———. 1980. "Yamalo-Nenetskii avtonomnyi okrug (K 50-letiiu obrazovaniia)" (The

Yamal-Nenets Autonomous Area [to the 50th Anniversary of Its Creation]). *Sovetskaia Etnografiia* 6: 67–77.

_____. 1981. "Shamany u Nentsev" (Nenets Shamans). In *Problemy Istorii Obschestvennogo Soznaniya Aborigenov Sibiri*, pp. 5–41. Leningrad: Nauka..

Kiselev, L. E. 1974. *Ot patriarkhalshchiny k sotsializmu* (From Patriarchy to socialism). Sverdlovsk: Sredne-Uralskoe Izdatelstvo.

Kolycheva, Elena I. 1956. "Nentsy Evropeiskoi Rossii v kontse XVII—nachale XVIII veka" (The Nenets of European Russia during the late 1600s and early 1700s). In *Sovetskaia Etnografiia* 2: 76–88.

Krupnik, Igor. 1993. *Arctic Adaptations: Native Whalers and Reindeer Herders of Northern Eurasia*. Hanover, N.H.: Dartmouth College, University Press of New England.

Kryukov, Valery; Vladimir Shmat; and Arild Moe. 1995. "West Siberian Oil and the Northern Sea Route: Current Situation and Future Potential." *Polar Geography* 19, no 3: 219–35.

Kulemzin, V. M. 1976. "Shamanstvo Vasyugansko-Vakhovskikh Khantov" (Shamanism of Vakh-Vasyugan Khanty). In *Iz Istorii Shamanstva*. Tomsk: University Press.

Kupryanova, Z. N. 1965. *Epicheskie pesni nentsev* (Epic Songs of Nenets). Moscow: Nauka.

Kushelevskii, Yuri I. 1868. *Severnyi polius i zemlya Yamal* (The Northern Pole and the Land Yamal). St. Petersburg.

Lagunov, V. I. 1992. *Nekotorye osobennosti razvitiia narodnogo obrazovaniia v oblasti (1944–1964 gg.) Istoricheskii opyt narodnogo obrazovaniia* (Historical Experience of People's Education). Tobol'sk: Tiumenskogo kraia.

_____. 1993. "Otrazhenie istorii razvitiia narodnogo obrazovaniia ovlasti na stranitsakh 'Tiumenskoy Pravdy' (1944–1964 gg)." In *Narodnoe obrazovanie Tiumenskogo kraia: istoriografiia, istochnikovedenie*. Public Education in Tiumen Province: Historiography, Sources. Tiumen: Tiumen University Press.

Lepekhin, I. 1805. *Dnevnye zapiski puteshestviia po raznym provintsiiam Rossiiskogo gosudarstva* (Diary of Travel along Different Provinces of Russia). Chap. 4. St. Petersburg.

Lukiyanova, N. A. 1994. Speech before a meeting of the Yamal-Nenets Autonomous Okrug State Duma. Reported in *Krasniy Sever*, nos. 49 and 50, June 1994, 9.

Manning, Roger B. 1988. *Village Revolts: Social Protest and Popular Disturbances in England, 1509–1640*. Oxford: Clarendon Press.

McKean, Margaret A. 1992. "Success on the Commons: A Comparative Examination of Institutions for Common Property Resource Management." *Journal of Theoretical Politics* 4, no. 3: 247–82.

McKean, Margaret, and Elinor Ostrom. 1995. "Common-Property Regimes in the Forest: Just a Relic from the Past?" *Unasylva* 46: 3–15.

Miller, Gerard P. 1937. *Istoriia Sibiri* (The History of Siberia). Vol. 1. Moscow and Leningrad: Academy of Sciences.

Moe, Arild, and Valeriy Kryukov. 1994. "Observations on the Reorganization of the Russian Oil Industry." *Post-Soviet Geography* 35, no 2: 89–101.

Moshinskaya, Vanda I. 1953. "Material'naia kul'tura i khoziaistvo Ust'-Poluia" (Material Culture and Economy of Ust'-Polui). In *Materialy i issledovaniia po arkheologii SSSR*. No. 35, pp. 72–106 . Moscow: Academy of Sciences.

Narody Severa Rossii. 1992. Vol. 18, chap. 2.M.

Natsional'naia politika v Rossii. 1992.

Nerkagi, Anna. 1996. "About That for Which There Is No Name." In *Anxious North: Indigenous Peoples in Soviet and Post-Soviet Russia,* ed. Alexander Pika, Jens Dahl, and Inge Larsen, pp. 273–89. Copenhagen: IWGIA.

Nuclear Wastes in the Arctic: An Analysis of Arctic and Other Regional Impacts from Soviet Nuclear Contamination. 1995. OTA-ENV-623. Washington, D.C.: U.S. Government Printing Office.

Obzor Tobol'skoy. 1916. *Obzor Tobol'skoy gubernii 1914 goda* (Survey of Tobol'sk Province for 1914). Tobol'sk.

Orttung, Robert. 1996. *OMRI Daily Digest* 1, no. 199, 14 October. "Khanty-Mansi Withdraws from Tyumen Oblast," *OMRI Daily Digest,* no. 188, part 1, 27 September.

Osherenko, Gail. 1988. "Can Comanagement Save Arctic wildlife?" *Environment* 30, no. 6: 6–13, 29–33.

———. 1995a. "Indigenous Political and Property Rights and Economic/Environmental Reform in Northwest Siberia." *Post-Soviet Geography* 36, no. 4: 225–37.

———. 1995b. "Property Rights and the Transformation in Russia: Institutional Change in the Far North." *Europe-Asia Studies* 47, no. 7: 1077–1108.

Osherenko, Gail, and Oran R. Young. 1989. *The Age of the Arctic: Hot Conflicts and Cold Realities.* Cambridge: Cambridge University Press.

Ostrom, Elinor. 1990. *Governing the Commons: The Evolution of Institutions for Collective Action.* Cambridge: Cambridge University Press.

Patkanov, Serafim K. 1891. *Tip Ostyatskogo bogatyrya po ostiatskim bylinam i geroicheskim skazaniyam* (The Ostyak bogatyr in Ostyak Legends and Heroic Tales). St. Petersburg.

Petrushin, A. 1991. *Mandala* (Rebellion), pp. 35, 36. St. Petersburg.

Pika, A. I. 1990. "'SOS' Iz Surguto-bermudskogo treugol'nika" ("SOS" from Surgut's Bermuda Triangle). *Severnye Prostory,* no. 3: 27.

———. 1993. "The Spatial-Temporal Dynamic of Violent Death among the Native Peoples of Northern Russia." *Arctic Anthropology* 30, no. 2: 61–76.

Pika, A. I.; Jens Dahl; and Inge Larsen, eds. 1996. *Anxious North: Indigenous Peoples in Soviet and Post-Soviet Russia: Selected Documents, Letters, and Articles.* International Working Group on Indigenous Affairs, Document No. 82. Copenhagen: IWGIA.

Podkorytov, F. 1994. "Olenevodstvo: real'nost i perspektivy'" (Reindeer Herding: Reality and Perspectives). *Krasnyi Sever,* nos. 41, 42, May 1994, 8.

Posaeva, Natalia. 1993. "Interview with Vladimir Kalyakin, Director of Institute of Nature Protection and Security of Nature Using Fund." *Zelenyi Mir* 5: 5.

Pribyl'skii, Yu P. and A.N. Petkevich. 1967. Rybnaia promyshlennost Tiumenskoi oblasti za 50 let sovetskoi vlasti (Fish Industry of Tiumen Province in 50 Years of Soviet Power). Tiumen: Knizhnoie izdatel'stvo.

Priroda Tiumenskogo. 1991. *Priroda Tiumenskogo Severa* (Nature in the Tiumen North). Edited by B. K. Ryabitsev. Sverdlovsk: Sredne-Ural'skoe Knizhnoie izdatel'stvo.

Priroda Yamala. 1995. *Priroda Yamala* (Nature of Yamal). Edited by L. N. Dobrinskii. Ekaterinburg: Nauka.

Prokofieva, Ekaterina D. 1981. "Materialy po Shamanstvu Sel'kupov" (Data on Sel'kup

Shamanism). In *Problemy Istorii Obschestvennogo Soznaniya Aborigenov Sibiri*, pp. 42–68. Leningrad: Nauka.

Raeff, Marc. 1957. *Michael Speransky: Statesman of Imperial Russia, 1772–1839*. The Hague: Martinus Nijoff.

Resheniya partii. 1967. *Resheniya partii i pravitel'stva po khozyaistvennym voprosam* (Decisions of the Party and Government on Economic Questions). Vol. 2. Moscow: Politizdat.

Russia: Gazprom Stock Offer. 1994. *East West Business & Trade* 22, no. 24 (December 21), 3, 4.

Russian Federation. 1992. "O neotlozhnykh merakh po zaschite mest prozhivaniia i khoziaystvennoy deyatel'nosti malochislennykh narodov Severa" (On Urgent Measures for the Protection of the Place of Residence and Economic Activities of the Numerically Small Peoples of the North). Ukaz Prezidenta Rossiyskoy Federatsii, No. 397 (Edict of the President of the Russian Federation No. 397), 22 April 1992.

––––––. 1993. October 27, 1993, Decree "On the Regulation of Land Relations and the Development of Agrarian Reform in Russia." Published in *Krest'yanskiye vedomosti*, no. 43: 8–9.

––––––. 1994. "Gosudarstvennaia programma privatizatsii gosudarstvennykh i munitsipal'nykh predpriiatiy v Rossiyskoiy Federatsii" (State Program of Privatization of State-Owned and Municipal Enterprises in the Russian Federation). Published in *Rossiiskaya Gazeta*, 4 January, 2–8.

Sbornik uzakonenii. 1936. *Sbornik uzakonenii RSFSR* (Collection of Edicts of the RSFSR). No. 6. Moscow.

Skrynnikov, Ruslan G. 1986. *Sibirskaia expeditsiia Ermaka* (Siberian Expedition of Ermak). Novosibirsk: Nauka.

Slavin, S. V. 1939. "Severnyi Morskoi Put v Tret'ei Stalinskoi Piatiletke" (The Northern Sea Route in the Third Stalinist Five-Year Plan). *Sovetskaia Arktika* 5: 24–37.

Slavnin, P. 1911. *Samoyedy-grabiteli v Obdorskom krae* (Samoed Robbers in Obdorsk Territory). Tobol'sk: Tobol'sk Provincial Museum.

Slezkine, Yuri 1994. *Arctic Mirrors: Russia and the Small Peoples of the North*. Ithaca, N.Y.: Cornell University Press.

Soloviev, Sergei M. 1988. *Sochineniia* (Works). Vol. 1. Moscow: Mysl.

Spisok naselennykh mest (List of Inhabited Places). 1912. In *Obzor Tobol'skoi Gubernii* (Survey of Tobol'sk Province). Tobol'sk.

Stepanov, Nikolai N. 1936. "K voprosu ob ostyako-vogul'skom feodalizme" (To the Problem of Ostyak-Vogul Feudalism). In *Sovetskaya Etnografiya.*, no. 3: 19–34.

Sudby narodov. 1994. *Sudby narodov Ob'-Irtyshskogo Severa: Iz istorii natsional'nogo gosudarstvennogo stroitel'stva. 1822–1941 gg"* (Destinies of the Peoples of the Ob-Irtysh North). Edited by D. I. Kolylov. Tiumen: Archival Dept.

Sulotskii, A. 1915. *Zhizn sviatitelia Filofei, mitropolita Sibirskogo i Tobol'skogo, prosvetitelia sibirskikh inorodtsev* (The Life of Preacher Filofei, Metropolitan of Siberia and Tobol'sk, Enlightener of Siberian Non-Russians). Shamardino, Russia: M. D. Usov.

Svarovskii, Nikolai. 1991. "Piket: Segodnya v fokuse" (Picket: Today in Focus). *Severnye Prostory* 39 (March): 18–22.

Tereshchenko, N. M. 1965. *Nenetsko-russkiy slovar* (Nenets-Russian Dictionary). Moscow: Sovetskaia Entsiklopediia.

Tridtsat' let. 1960. *Tridtsat' let Yamalo-Nenetskogo okruga: Istoriko-ekonomicheskii ocherk* (Thirty Years of the Yamal-Nenets Okrug: Historical-Economic Essay.) Edited by D. I. Kopylov. Tiumen: Archival Dept.

"Two Letters." 1996. "Two Letters to the Journal *Severnye Prostory"* (The Yamal-Nenets Autonomous Area). In Pika et al. *Anxious North,* 217–21.

Udarnik Arktiki. 1935, 1936, 1938. *Udarnik Arktiki. Organ Obdorskogo politotdela GUSMP* (Arctic Shockworker: Organ of the Obdorsk Political Department of the Main Administration of the Northern Sea Route.) Salekhard

Ustav. 1822. *Ustav ob upravlenii inorodtsev Sibiri* (Statute on Administration of Non-Russians in Siberia). In *Polnoe sobranie zakanov Russiiskoi imperii (Full Collection of Laws of the Russian Empire) 38, no. 29, 126.* Tobol'sk.

Vakhtin, Nikolai. 1992. *Native Peoples of the Russian Far North.* Report No. 5. London: Minority Rights Group International.

Vanchitskaya, L. N. 1993. "Stanovlenie i razvitie natsional'noy shkoly v usloviyakh Obskogo Severa" (Formation and Development of National Schools in Existing Conditions of the Ob North). Ph.D. dissertation. Avtoref.

Vasil'ev V. I. 1978. "Animistic Notions of the Enets and the Enisei Nenets." In *Shamanism in Siberia,* ed. V. Dioszegi and M. Hoppal, pp. 429–34. Budapest: Akademiai Kiado

Vilchek, Gregory E. 1992. *West Siberian North: Environmental Disturbance and Management.* Moscow: Orbis Independent Research Center.

Vitebsky, Piers. 1990. "Gas, Environmentalism, and Native Anxieties in the Soviet Arctic: The Case of Yamal Peninsula." *Polar Record* 26, no. 156: 19–26.

Wegren, Stephen K. 1994a. "Yeltsin's Decree on Land Relations: Implications for Agrarian Reform." *Post-Soviet Geography* 35, no. 3: 168–71.

———. 1994b. "Rural Reform and Political Culture in Russia." *Europe-Asia Studies* 46, no. 2: 215–41.

World Bank. 1991, 1990. Operational Directive 4.20, "Indigenous Peoples," September, and Operational Directive 4.30, "Involuntary Resettlement," June. In *The World Bank Operational Manual.* Washington, D.C.: World Bank. Reprinted in Buhl.

Yamalo-Nenetskii natsional'nyi okrug. 1965. *Yamalo-Nenetskii natsional'nyi okrug (Ekonomiko-geograficheskaya kharakteristika)* (The Yamalo-Nenets National District: Economic-Geographical Characteristics). Moscow: Nauka.

Young, Oran R. 1980s (n.d.). "Theories of Property: Structures of Property Rights as Social Institutions" (unpublished manuscript). Chap. 1.

Zapadnaya Sibir. 1963. *Zapadnaya Sibir* (Western Siberia). Edited by G. D. Rikhter. Moscow: Academy of Sciences.

Zibarev, Viktor A. 1968. *Sovetskoe stroitel'stvo u malykh narodnostei Severa (1917–1932)* (Soviet Construction among the Small Nationalities of the North, 1917–1932). Tomsk: Tomsk State University.

———. 1990. *Yustitsiya u malykh narodov Severa (17–19 vv)* (The Justice System among Small Peoples of the North from the Seventeenth through the Nineteenth Centuries). Tomsk: Tomsk State University.

Index

Numbers in *italic* refer to maps.